Diving Bali

THE UNDERWATER
JEWEL OF
SOUTHEAST ASIA

David Pickell and Wally Siagian

PERIPLUS

Published by Periplus Editions (HK) Ltd

Copyright © 2000 Periplus Editions (HK) Ltd

ALL RIGHTS RESERVED

ISBN 962-593-323-9
Printed in Singapore

Publisher: Eric Oey
Series editor: David Pickell
Text editor: Leigh Anne Jones
Photo editor: David Pickell
Cartography: David Pickell
Interior design: David Pickell with Peter Ivey

DISTRIBUTORS

ASIA-PACIFIC   Berkeley Books Pte Ltd
5 Little Road #08-01
Singapore 536983
Tel: (65) 280-3320
Fax: (65) 280-6290

INDONESIA   PT Wira Mandala Pustaka
(Java Books–Indonesia)
Jl. Kelapa Gading Kirana
Blok A-14 No. 17, Jakarta 14240
Tel: (62-21) 451-5351
Fax: (62-21) 453-4987

JAPAN   Tuttle Publishing
RK Building, 2nd Floor
2-13-10 Shimo-Meguro
Meguro-ku
Tokyo 153 0064
Tel: (81-3) 5437-0171
Fax: (81-3) 5437-0755

USA   Tuttle Publishing
Distribution Center
Airport Industrial Park
364 Innovation Drive
North Clarendon, VT 05759-9436
Tel: (802) 773-8930, (800) 526-2778

COVER   The famous wreck of the *Liberty*, Tulamben. Mike Severns.
PAGES 4–5   Bali is in the world's richest biogeographic region. Mike Severns.
FRONTISPIECE   The crab *Lauriea siagiani* was discovered in Bali in 1984. Mike Severns.

Contents

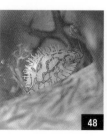

Part IV Nusa Penida

Part V The South

Part VI Practicalities

Preface
and Acknowledgments

Wally Siagian

David Pickell

IN A WAY, THIS BOOK BEGAN THE DAY WALLY and I met, almost eight years ago now. I had just finished putting *Underwater Indonesia* (now *Diving Indonesia*) on press, and flew to Bali to meet Kal Muller, my friend and the author of that volume, for some diving and general R&R. Kal wanted me to meet a dive guide living in Bali whose knowledge had been essential to the Bali, Komodo, and Banda Islands sections of that book. He thought I might get along with this guy.

That turned out to be something of an understatement, and for whatever reason—we were both born in the Year of the Rat, we both love fixing things, we both drink beer with immoderate relish, we'd both be happy picking up a snake or a spider or a whip-scorpion but very unhappy sitting on the back of a horse, we'd both make lousy accountants, who knows?—on the day we met it was as if we had been friends since childhood.

As soon as we started diving together, we realized that our philosophy and approach to diving was another thing we shared. Diving, to us, is not a sport. It is a means to explore the diverse community of plants and animals that constitutes the coral reef. More than anything, we like the riddles: Why does this fish look like a leaf? Why does that sponge grow sideways? The idea of collaborating on a book to share our philosophy and experience arose almost immediately.

Wally is from Java, but he and his family have lived in Bali now for more than a decade and a half. He is without a doubt the most experienced and knowledgeable diver working on the island. The long free-diving fins he favors, their cracked blades repaired with dental floss, are recognized by every operator, porter, and skipper on the island. You could say he is famous, but "infamous" would be more accurate. His personality combines irresistible charm and stubborn prickliness, a fierce intellect and a sometimes fierce temper,

and this mix is reflected in a reputation that has a few grease stains on it. To me this seems appropriate. In his field Wally is an artist, and an artist's job is insight, not consistency.

I have a twenty-year-old C-card that isn't in much better shape than Wally's fins, and have dived more or less regularly, particularly over the last ten years. But as a diver, I am an amateur. My professional work takes place over a keyboard.

Wally has a favorite phrase: "Trust me, I'm a dive instructor." My experience has been that he is only being sarcastic by half, and I have always found trusting him in these cases to be at least interesting. By the time we had finished the fieldwork for this book, I had my own corollary to this phrase: "I'm a *writer*, not a dive instructor." I would invoke this complaint after, say, a deep mapping dive that required more than an hour of decompression, or after an exploration dive that required swimming upcurrent across a kilometer-wide wasteland of coral rubble using a borrowed regulator with a flow adjustment set by Scrooge himself.

The voice of this book, unavoidably, belongs to me. But the information in it, just as unavoidably, belongs to Wally, coming from his deep knowledge and long experience of these reefs. I have maybe two hundred dives in Bali; Wally has *five thousand*. The philosophy behind the book—its heart—is ours together, as was the three years, on and off, of fieldwork. This book, for better or worse, is a true collaboration.

We have tried to arm our readers with the proper tools to decide for themselves where and how to dive Bali's reefs. The most important of these are the maps. Cartography is (and should be) a conservative trade, and I have rendered these using the metaphor provided by the British Admiralty and the rest of the world's navy cartography offices. If you are not used to looking at sailing charts the maps may be unfamiliar at first (my girlfriend tormented me by calling the reef areas "shrubbery"), but I think as you get used to them you will find they present the information clearly. In the text I have tried to communicate some of the enjoyment that Wally and I feel when we are diving these reefs.

Success, for us, does not mean that you agree with our opinions—and I think you'll find a few in these pages—but that we have helped you, in your own way, come to love these reefs as much as we do.

THE ANGELS

Any project like this has to have angels, and we had ours. Kal Muller supported us like an ancient, immovable ironwood root. He gave us slides, provided us with a collection of underwater camera equipment worth as much as a down payment on a house, and even loaned us cash when the car rental agencies were chasing us. But most important, he offered the kind of advice, judgment, and emotional support that can only come from a close friend.

Several other photographers, all friends, rose to the occasion on our behalf. Mike Severns made two special trips to Bali to shoot especially for this book, and in just a couple of weeks produced some stunning work. Burt Jones and Maurine Shimlock happily dug into their extensive archives and found some beautiful and unique images from Bali. Scientist and photographer John E. Randall provided both slides and interesting back-ground information. Ichthyologist Gerald R. Allen also happily came to our assistance, but due to a misfortune that was no fault of his own, his pictures did not make this edition.

My old friend and editor Leigh Anne Jones was tolerant where she needed to be, intolerant everywhere else, and always supportive. Peter Ivey, also an old friend and co-conspirator, stepped in with crucial design advice. Michael Wijaya and Agnes Indrasari Winarno took on the important—but tedious—task of collecting data on Bali's dive operators, and did an admirable job.

A slightly reluctant angel, but an angel all the same, was Eric Oey, who agreed to publish this title after only one bottle of wine (although even after the second, he still drove a hard bargain). The commercial rewards of a book like this are modest, and it was his friendship, along with a persistent, atavistic belief that publishing is foremost about enthusiasm and quality, not money, that put this book on the shelves.

Many helped with the fieldwork for this book. Yos W. K. Amerta of Yos Diving Centre and Marine Sports provided boats, fills, and once, with exquisite grace and timing, a case of cold beer; Danny Hermawan was, at times, simply indispensable; Mahin Ickna took us on the beautiful *Ana' Ruyung* to Nusa Penida in the rain; Bob and Sue Jarvis of Geko Diving provided boats, fills, information, some peculiar entertainments, and a friendship both fast-blooming and rare; Ibu Kadek and the members of the Tulamben Diving Club faithfully tended our gear, and even provided a proper, spicy breakfast on occasion; Rolf Lohmann of the Pondok Sari offered the hospitality of his beautiful resort; Nengah Putu of the Sunrise kept us in fills and gear at Tulamben; and Pak Wirya Santosa of Mimpi Resorts provided hospitality at two of his elegant resorts, and most important to us, a wise and receptive ear to our ideas about diving and conservation.

And there were still others whose contribution is harder to specify. For advice, aid, indulgences, and comforts of various kinds, we thank Bob Bruman, Nyoman and Reno Kirtya of Grand Komodo Tours & Travel, Colleen Lye, and Uli Siagian.

— David Pickel
Berkeley, 1999

NASA   East Java, Bali, Lombok, and western Sumbawa from the space shuttle.
Photograph taken October 8, 1994, from an altitude of 207 kilometers.

FOR MATHEUS AND REBEKKA

MIKE SEVERNS   Stonefish: Synanceia verrucosa; Jacks: Caranx sexfasciatus   Tulamben, just in front of the wreck

Having wandered a few meters from its normal haunt, this stonefish is unusually visible. At Tulamben these fish rest with the
tails perpetually curled, to match the round cobbles of the shallows. This one seemed quite curious about the school of jacks

"YOU KNOW, I CAN FOLLOW YOU UNDER-water," challenged the old man, as he watched a group of young sport divers struggle into their bright yellow and green wetsuits on the deck of his boat. "But *bapak*," said the dive leader, using the polite form of address for an elder, "we have scuba gear—how long will you be able to stay with us?" Mischief sparkled in the old pearl diver's eyes. "As long as you remain down." The dive leader looked up from the backpack harness he had been tightening. He saw that the old man had a face mask, but knew there was no other equipment aboard, not even a pair of fins. "*Bapak*, how is this possible?" The old man extended an arm, brown and corrugated from a lifetime on the tropical sea. In his hand was a soda straw. "With this."

The technique the old man described was remarkable. Swimming along with the divers underwater, always staying a few meters above them, he would periodically take his straw, pierce the bell of their rising exhalations, and breathe.

It is tempting to say that such a thing is impossible, but as far as I can

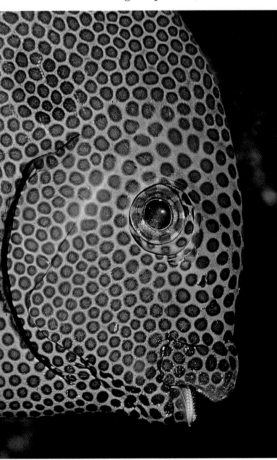

©BURT JONES/MAURINE SHIMLOCK *Siganus punctatus*

A gold-spotted rabbit-fish. The siganids carry venomous spines on their dorsal, pectoral, and anal fins that can inflict a wound victims testify is far worse than that caused by a scorpionfish. They are beautiful, though, and make very good eating, too.

tell, the old man's method breaks none of the laws of physics. Unorthodox, yes. Requiring supreme confidence in the water and profound thrift with one's air, yes. But not impossible. I don't think you'll learn it in a certification agency course, however, no matter how many times you put a dollar in.

The old man with the soda straw was just one of many stories traded in the course of pleasant, winding coversation Wally and I had one afternoon with a group of pearl shell divers in far west Bali.

We had hired Pak Haji's crew and boat to take us diving, and after a cold morning dive, Wally and I lay back in the blazing sun, trying to get some heat into our bodies. The hard *ulin* wood planks of the vessel, polished by twenty years of bare feet, were warm and smooth against our backs, and our beers, which had been incubating with a chunk of ice in the hold for the past hour and a half, were almost too cold to drink. The smells of saltwater, raw diesel, and old grease were reassuring. The stories were fascinating. We never did get in a second dive that day.

DUCKS AND GRASSHOPPERS

Lain ladang, lain belalang—"Different fields, different grasshoppers." This expression, which has some of the resonance of our "When in Rome...," is a common one in Indonesia, and is frequently invoked as a polite way to counter a visitor's surprise or disgruntlement at the way things are done in Bali. Wally first used it on me several years ago.

It was after dark, and we were in Ubud, searching for what Wally claimed was the very best *bebek betutu*—a spicy and uniquely Balinese type of slow-cooked duck—on the island. After considerable effort we found the shop, deep in the bowels of a closed market. We knocked on the door, waking the proprietor, and he happily fished through a pile of warm ashes and pulled out our dinner, wrapped tightly in foil. With no facilities for eating in sight, Wally stowed the duck in his backpack, and we rode our motorcycles straight to the fanciest restaurant in Ubud.

"Wally," I said as we walked into the swank establishment, "are you sure they aren't going to mind this?

I mean, bringing your own bottle of wine is one thing, but what is the corkage fee for bringing your own main course?" That's when he told me about the grasshoppers.

Our waiter was happy to take the dusty, foil-wrapped package back to the kichen, returning with a beautifully displayed *bebek betutu* on a porcelain plate. We lingered over a fine, relaxed dinner, in beautiful surroundings, and the bill we eventually received included only a couple of drinks and a plate of white rice. I am quite sure that if Wally and I showed up with our own food at Chez Panisse, one of the more well-known restaurants in my city, we would be firmly, and probably not even politely, shown the door.

In Bali, and in Indonesia in general, the prevailing rhythms of life are human and social, and the almighty dollar and its tireless enforcer, the clock, have not yet established their dictatorship. For most visitors, this truly makes Bali a different field, and the difference can be wonderful. But you also have to learn to be a different grasshopper. With the right attitude, the archipelago's famous *jam karet*—"rubber time"—can produce serendipity and pleasure: "The boat crew won't mind waiting, do you want to stop here for a glass of young coconut water?" With the wrong attitude it produces only frustration: "But you said we'd be diving at nine thirty, and it is *almost ten!*"

Bali is a place that rewards curiosity and whim. Maybe you really, really want to see a mola, or a shark, or a manta. These are fine things to see, and there are sites in Bali where your chances of encountering them are good. But if the season is wrong, or the tides, or simply your luck, don't keep banging your head against the same rock. Try another site. Or look for something different at the same site. A mola is nice, but so is a ghost pipefish.

Diving in Bali is still an intimate, small-scale activity. You do not have to climb on a boat with eleven other divers at 0700 hours and drop off in formation like you were training to be a Navy Seal. Find an operator you like and work out a custom program for yourself and a group of friends. Be flexible and

WALLY SIAGIAN Ovulid: Phenacovolva sp.; Gorgonian: Ctenocella (Ellisella); Tulamben 28m

open to changes brought on by the weather, water conditions, and even your own mood. If you take away only one piece of advice from this book, let it be: When diving in Bali, *allow yourself to be surprised.*

THE MAGIC TRIANGLE

The tropical Indo-Pacific, a vast swath of ocean from the Red Sea to

The spindle ovulids have evolved a slender shape to better blend in with their gorgonian hosts. Bali is rich in small treasures like these, and new species are still being discovered.

Map 0.2 Bali 1:600K physical, political

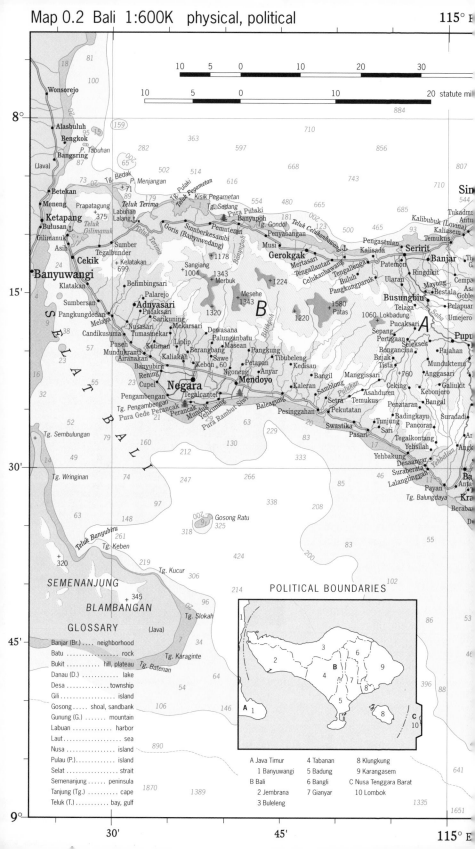

the west coast of South America, is the world's richest marine biogeographical region. Smack in the middle of this area, where the Indian Ocean meets the Pacific, is Indonesia, with its 17,508 islands, and estimated 85,707 square kilometers of living coral reef—a bit bigger than Maine, or about the size of Ireland, were it united. This single island na-

Porters from Tulamben's Diving Helper Club carry tanks, for a modest fee, from the resorts along the rocky shore to the entry points for the dive sites. Income from this well-run operation has bought the village a gamelan (metallophone set) and helped with other collective projects.

tion contains, by conservative estimate, fourteen percent of the world's coral reefs. And this is the very richest fourteen percent.

Biologists studying species distributions in the Indo-Pacific have rendered the pattern of decreasing diversity as concentric lines on a map, radiating out from the area of greatest richness. Whether the animals studied are fishes or corals, this

center stays the same: Indonesia. The very heart of this biologically rich area is a kind of triangle, with the southern Philippines, Bali, and western New Guinea forming the corners. This triangle encloses the richest (and most poorly studied) tropical marine fauna in the world, with eighty genera of coral and perhaps twenty-five hundred species of reef fishes. The Caribbean, by contrast, has twenty genera of coral and maybe eight hundred reef fishes.

What this richness implies for diving has not been lost on the world's sport diving community. To say that the reefs of this five-thousand-kilometer-long archipelago provide the best diving in the world is no longer even controversial. Photographer Roger Steene, in the introduction to his latest book, offers one of the more categorical formulations of this sentiment: "Any serious-minded underwater photographer not currently working in Indonesia is going backwards."

Indonesia's best reefs are starting to become familiar names: The Banda Sea, North Sulawesi, Komodo, Alor, and even Tukang Besi. Rarely, however, does one see Bali in this list. As the nation's most famous tourist island, perhaps Bali is just too familiar to be considered a great diving area. If so, this is a mistake. Most of the Banda Sea, an area frequently held up as the Holy Grail of world dive sites, does not fall within the "magic triangle." Bali does.

It is often assumed that the best diving areas are isolated, faraway islands, surrounded by nothing but open sea. Hawai'i is a classic example, but Hawai'i, for all its charms, has what a scientist would dryly term an "impoverished fauna." Not only does Hawai'i not have eighty genera of reef-building corals, it doesn't even have eighty *species*. (It has forty.)

Bali's great strength is that it is *not* isolated. The island's reefs are ideally positioned to receive a cosmopolitan assortment of plankton and juvenile animals from the Indonesian Throughflow, a massive flow of water that passes from the Pacific to the Indian Ocean. (See "The Indonesian Throughflow," pg. 130.) And Bali, which ten thousand years ago was the peninsular tip of mainland Southeast Asia, also benefits from the rich set of coastal fishes and corals from the Indian Ocean. Because of this combination, if a team of scientists took the time to survey the diversity of Bali's reefs, from the western tip around the island to Nusa Penida, their species counts would almost certainly be among the highest in the world for an area of equivalent size.

MIKE SEVERNS Tulamben

RICH, VARIED, AND INTERESTING

If you wanted to be able to identify all of the animals you can see on a diving trip to Bali, you would have to pack at least half a dozen field guides, and even then you would probably find some puzzles. But species richness is not the only measure of a good diving area.

Bali's greatest charm, perhaps, is its wide range and variety of sites. You can dive in Bali on a steel shipwreck. Or on a wooden shipwreck. Off vertical drop-offs. Over sand slopes. Off black, volcanic outcrops. Off limestone shores. Among huge bommies. In roaring currents. In quiet bays. Along deep, coral-covered ridges. Over seagrass beds in three meters. In short, all tastes are accommodated here, from snorkeling among mangrove roots to exploring a black coral forest at seventy meters.

Above water, the physical and cultural beauty of the island are legendary, which means that unlike so many other great diving areas, there is always something to do or see during your surface intervals. This is not the type of dive holiday where your time underwater is wonderful, but your time on land is an anesthetizing blur of bland hotel rooms with dripping air conditioners, indifferent food, packaged "attractions," and overpriced drinks full of canned pineapple chunks and decorated with little pink umbrellas.

Bali's hotels range from cheap and pleasant to an opulence approaching sin (a swimming pool for each room, for example), and the food ranges from rich, spicy hawker fare to French haute cuisine. The "attractions" are a unique Hindic culture fascinating enough to have made the careers of some of the world's most famous anthropologists. We've never seen a pineapple here come out of a can, and if you order a Bintang lager, a fine representative of its genus, we guarantee nobody will stick one of those little umbrellas in your glass.

The combination of beautiful, varied diving and plenty to do onshore makes Bali one of the world's best destinations for a long dive holiday. Even after three weeks—and make it a month, if you can afford the time—you will not get bored here.

NO REPORT CARDS

When we began work on this book, Wally and I sat down and tried to work out a system for ranking the various dive sites around the island, on a scale of one to ten. The system we came up with gave the

The jukung is Bali's traditional small craft. The hull is brightly painted wood (although fiberglass jukungs are now beginning to appear) and the outriggers are bamboo. The vessels seat no more than three, inline. Although many jukungs still run sails, those at Tulamben use small generator motors that drive a prop at the end of a long shaft. The paint jobs have evolved as well, with those in Tulamben now favoring imported American brand logos, and particularly, the PDI Perjuangan bull. All the boats must have eyes—a fisherman would no sooner go out on the water in a blind jukung than he would if he were blind himself.

KAL MULLER Mola mola Entai Point, Lembongan Island

The strange mola is an occasional pelagic visitor to Bali's reefs. This wanderer, in both temperate and tropical waters, is a true open-water fish, which feeds on the larger plankton, such as jellyfish, comb jellys, and salps. It is calm, and usually easily approached. Although most molas seen in Bali have a body size of about a meter or so in diameter, specimens of more than three meters—and 1,300 kilograms—have been recorded.

Kapal Budak off Menjangan, in Northwest Bali, would each get very high marks, and we highly recommend both of these dives. But you could hardly find two places that are more different. One is a calm, sand slope with a old wooden boat wreck, and the other is a wild, rocky chasm with huge schools of fish. So what good is it to give them both, say, an "8.5"? Take a random group of your friends (and to us these sites *are* friends). One is short, garrulous, and sweet. Another is tall, quiet, and drolly hilarious. Another is fat, sour, and very loyal. Whom do you love the most?

We have taken what we believe to be the best sites, and mapped and described them to the best of our ability. You will have to find your favorites from this. There are no numbers, no stars, and no little rows of scuba men. The way we figure it, maybe you like apples, maybe you like oranges—it's your choice. (Personally, we'll take durian.)

ADEQUATE, OLD CHAP

One of the most important qualities of a dive site is also one of the most paradoxical: water clarity. Some published guides confidently list numbers for horizontal visibility at every site. We haven't done this. We offer typical distances, but have avoided making categorical statements. The reason for this is that visibility changes.

Wally and I have been in the water at Tulamben when the vis was not even three meters (granted, only once). We've also been in the water there when it has been more than forty. Fifteen meters is probably typical, but you never really know. Even on the same dive, the visibility at the surface, and that at thirty meters, can be dramatically different. And it is not always the surface with the poorer visibility. On the East Coast, where a cold upwelling appears during the southeast monsoon, you can

most weight to the inherent interest of the bottom formation (Are there lots of bommies? A steep wall?) then biological richness (Is there good coral cover? Lots of fish?) and then conditions (What is the current like? Is the vis good?). Finally, we added a wild card—"special"—to give extra points to sites where you could, say, see big pelagics, or where there was a small wreck, or where conditions allowed the site to be dived in both seasons.

But you won't see any of these rankings in this book. After we worked through a number of them, we decided that they were, at best, distracting. For example, Tepekong's canyon, in East Bali, and be diving in crystal clear water and then at twenty meters, where the cold and warm water mix, not be able to see further than your hand.

Rolls-Royce used to describe the horsepower of the huge V-8 engines powering their cars with one word: "adequate." I don't possess the necessary upper-class British reserve to make a statement like this, but if forced to describe the overall underwater visibility in Bali, I would say something similar: "quite good enough, actually." And, perverse as this might sound, I wouldn't want it to get any better.

From a diver's point of view, the relationship between water clarity and the presence of animals is downright cruel: the better you can see, the less there is *to* see. Perhaps the single best place in the world to see manta rays, although this is not yet well-known, is a site off North Flores. But judging from the film footage I have seen, the visibility there is about eight meters. Maybe less. But the poor visibility and the huge number of mantas have the same cause—the great concentration of plankton in the water.

None of the good diving areas in Bali has a serious run-off problem, and when the visibility is down it is almost always the result of plankton in the water. And here is the rub: this is often the best time to go diving. When the plankton is there, and the current is up, the reefs come alive. This is when you will see big pelagics, and when the smaller reef animals are out of hiding and lively. With a manta soaring overhead, or when you are in the middle of a great, swirling ball of jacks, I'm sure you'll agree that fifteen meters of visibility is "adequate."

WEATHER, TIDES, AND SEASONS

When I was back in the United States writing up this manuscript, and just three weeks from my deadline (or was that after?—sorry, Eric)

I noticed several serious discrepancies in my notes concerning diving conditions at different times of year. The research for this book was carried out over a three-year period, and when I gathered my notebooks together at the end, I found that 1999 sometimes contradicted 1998, and it, in turn, sometimes contradicted 1997. So I sent a message to my partner, and asked him to rescue me from this mess.

In its raw state, Wally's language is far too colorful for a family publication, so I have made some judicious deletions in his response:

"The […] weather is the most frustrating thing to predict. It's because the globe has been […] with too many times, I guess. Things just don't work according to the months and seasons anymore […!] My base is to look at the visible direction of the wind, check the current angle and strength, and try to find the eddies."

There are patterns to Bali's weather, but you really can't count on them. The key, as Wally says, is to check conditions at a particular site, around the time you want to dive. Bali is small enough that you can chase the conditions, diving the Northwest, Northeast, or East, as wind and weather allow, and you might have to. "The job here for the future," Wally added, "is to build a communications system between the operators at the different sites."

At some sites local tide conditions, not the season, have the greatest effect on underwater conditions. Tides in Bali are diurnal, and average 2.6 meters. Slack tide produces the calmest conditions, particularly slack high, therefore a dive that begins at the very end of the flood tide is often your best dive. And tides at new moon and full moon—the springs—are stronger than at first and third quarters—the neaps. Thus, in places where the prevailing currents are strong and

Ranzania laevis
to 90 centimeters

Masturus oxyuropterus
to 2 meters

Mola mola
to 3 meters

All after Weber and De Beaufort

All of the molas I have heard of in Bali seem to be Mola mola. But this is not the only member of the family Molidae that ranges into Indonesia's, and perhaps Bali's, seas. At least one slender mola (genus Ranzania) is known from here, and two species of sharp-tailed molas (genus Masturus).

tidally generated, such as East Bali, a dive at slack water during a first-quarter neap might be calm and easy, while the same dive on rising water during a new moon spring tide might be nearly suicidal.

Bali lies between eight and nine degrees south latitude. The temperature is thus warm and constant, with a barely perceptible antip-

© BURT JONES/MAURINE SHIMLOCK Hypselodoris obscura on Nardoa sp.

odean summer and winter pattern, June through September being slightly cooler than November through April. Daily high air temperatures vary from 30°C to 32°C, and nightly lows from 24°C to 26°C. The water temperature is also quite constant year-round, varying from 26°C to 28°C at the surface. April and May bring the warmest water; September the coldest.

The climate is influenced by two marked seasons. The southeast monsoon, which runs from approximately June to September, is the drier season, as prevailing southeast winds bring dry air from over the Australian continent. The northwest monsoon, from approximately December to March, is the wet season, as northwest winds bring moist air from over the South China Sea. The winds during the heart of either of these monsoons can be steady and brisk, which can raise seas and make diving difficult, particularly on the side of the island

they hit most directly.

Strong northwesterlies can spoil diving at the more exposed sites of the Northwest, as well as at Tulamben. Conversely, steady southeasterlies can raise seas off the East Coast, making diving at the Amuk Bay sites and Nusa Penida difficult. From a diver's point of view, the wet northwest monsoon hurts conditions the most. The best times for diving are during the transition periods between monsoons: either April through May, or October through November. During these periods, winds are generally weak and unsteady, yielding calm seas.

The southeast monsoon also brings the influence of an upwelling to East Bali and Nusa Penida. This cold, rich water, liberated from a deep basin south of Bali, attracts molas and other pelagics. The fishermen out of Padangbai love this season, and when the upwelling is in force, their boats come home full of billfish and thresher sharks.

Bali is a world organized around auspicious and inauspicious days, weeks, and months, with at least three calendars to divine them from. The relevant one for diving is the Saka. The Saka is a true lunar calendar—each *sasih*, or month, begins the day after new moon, peaks at full moon, and ends on new moon—and thus does not precisely follow the Gregorian calendar. The best time for diving in Bali, according to the Saka, is Sasih Kapat, Gregorian September–October, and the worst time is Sasih Kesanga, Gregorian February–March.

If you add the monsoon patterns, the upwelling, and the advice from the Saka, the result is that September–November is the best diving season, April–June is very good, July–August and December are okay, and January–March is the worst. Remember, this is just a general guideline. Even in the worst season you should be able to find some good conditions, and even in the best season you should expect to encounter some bad ones.

THE BALINESE AND THE SEA

In Bali, traditionally, there is no north and south. There is east (*kangin*) and west (*kauh*). But the other axis is *kaja*, toward sacred Mount Agung, and *kelod*, toward the sea. It is as if one had a compass that always wished to point toward Agung (and when Wally and I were doing our mapping around the iron-rich lava runs of Tulamben, it seemed my little Swedish compass wanted to do just this).

This unique directional system has led to a misunderstanding about the Balinese and the sea. In Balinese cosmology, *kaja*, toward Holy Agung, is a "pure" direction; its counterpart *kelod*, toward the sea, is thus by the Hindu rule of balance "impure." This has led commentators to suggest that in Bali, the sea is considered impure, or evil, or in some other unspecified way malevolent, which is not true.

What is true is that Bali does not have much of a seafaring tradition. Bali was connected to the other islands by trade, but the Balinese themselves were rarely the traders. A lack of natural deepwater ports might be one reason Bali has been for the most part a civilization of land-lubbers, but the simplest explanation is the rich volcanic ash produced by Agung. With some of the most productive rice paddies in the world to farm, the Balinese had no need to climb on a boat and wander the archipelago to make a living.

This does not mean that the Balinese do not have a long tradition on the water. The Balinese outriggered canoe, the *jukung*, is small, but it makes an effective and stable fishing vessel. Every day pilots steer them, with only sails and small motors for power, across some of the world's most unpredictable water.

These skippers are the best source of information about water conditions in Bali. In the course of our research Wally and I have ridden with many, and there was not one who failed to impress me with his instincts and knowledge. Over the years, much of what Wally has learned about these waters has come out of his friendship with

MIKE SEVERNS Wrasse: Thalassoma lunare; Jacks: Caranx sexfasciatus

some of the more experienced Balinese *jukung* pilots. Speaking for myself, even the least among them has, as the saying goes, forgotten more than I will ever know.

A friend of ours named Bob Jarvis, an eighty-seven-year-old Yorkshireman who runs a dive operation in Padangbai, considers his Balinese captain's knowledge of the sea to be almost uncanny. Bob

The Tulamben wreck is exceptionally rich, and the fish are generally oblivious of, or downright interested in divers. The moon wrasse, here eyeing the photographer, is a particularly crafty species that is ever on the lookout for a situation it can exploit.

WALLY SIAGIAN Synanceia verrucosa; Tulamben, near the shipwreck, 6m

The stonefish is often a figure of loathing, but it is in reality a very inoffensive creature. These fish are so confident in their combination of camouflage and venomous spines that they possess a Buddha-like calm, and if a diver, say, carefully tickles one under the chin, their reaction tends to puzzlement rather than alarm. I don't necessarily recommend this, by the way, as the poison from the dorsal, pelvic, and anal spines is truly horrible. Victims have contemplated cutting off the afflicted limb, and the wounds often lead to necrosis. Still, it is the profound passivity of this animal that fascinates me: imagine, this fish is so integrated with its environment that the algae-like tufts on its skin are actually living algae.

was once on shore at Lembongan Island during a surface interval with his clients and a dive instructor. They were happily having a cold drink when the captain ran up to the little café and insisted that they board the boat and leave—immediately. Otherwise, he said, the boat will be swamped. It was a perfectly clear day, and calm. The sun was out. Bob looked out at the boat, at anchor in the little bay, and it seemed perfectly secure.

To his credit, and despite the protestations of the expatriate guide, Bob obeyed his captain and they hurried aboard. The motor caught, and the boat roared out of the bay. As they looked backward toward Lembongan, they saw a rogue wave rise up and crash into the bay, scattering beach umbrellas and reaching even past the high tide line to the café. If the boat had remained there, it would surely have been swamped. "Now how could he have known that?" Bob said.

The Polynesians could sense the approach of an island before they could see it, by reading faint reflections in the pattern of the swell. Balinese skippers, having studied the Badung Strait for a lifetime, must have acquired their own subtle way of reading these often rough and always inscrutable waters. There is a lot to be learned from them.

BOB-ON-THE-HILL

Not everyone does, however. One of the more interesting cases is a onetime charter client that Bob Jarvis, for the sake of clarity, calls "Bob-on-the-Hill." This Bob-on-the-Hill, said Sea-Level Bob, fancied himself the next Thor Heyerdahl, only in his case he wanted to recreate humankind's first crossing of the Lombok Strait.

Bob-on-the-Hill pulled out his map and ruler, and determined that the shortest distance across the strait was from Gili Selang, Bali to Gili Trawangan, Lombok. Then he built an appropriately prehistoric vessel on which to sail across.

Just the sight of Bob-on-the-Hill's craft, a bodged-together rafty

MIKE SEVERNS Hoplophrys oatesii, on Dendronephthya sp.

thing, came close to giving Sea-Level Bob's skipper an ulcer, but despite these misgivings, Sea-Level Bob accepted the charter to carry the crew who would record this historic (re-historic?) crossing on film.

On the appointed day, under a black and inauspicious sky, a peculiar flotilla crept east from Gili Selang: a twin-outboard fiberglass boat, barely afloat under the weight of cinematographers and gaffers and Arriflexes and film magazines, and an ugly snarl of wood, like something coughed out by a river after a storm, with a sail attached.

The result was unsurprising. Low on fuel, less than halfway across, and with high seas, a ripping current, and pouring rain threatening to drown them all, Sea-Level Bob's skipper decided to call the whole farce off. Bob-on-the-Hill put up a fight, but when Sea-Level Bob's crew threatened to abandon his raft and let it drift free like the flotsam it resembled, he relented. The pile of sticks was lashed to the boat, and the expedition limped back to Padangbai. Bob-on-the-Hill and what was left of his vessel disappeared soon after, said Sea-Level Bob, and he never heard anything more about the project.

The weak-minded often presume that "old"—at least sixty thousand years, in the case of the Lombok crossing—means "primitive," which is why Bob-on-the-Hill, in the name of "historical accuracy," cobbled together an object of the quality a boy playing out by a woodpile might accomplish in the course of an afternoon. But the fact that you didn't have access to a metal lathe doesn't mean that your craftsmanship was poor. Nor, more to the point, does it mean that your *thinking* was poor.

Considering the time and location he picked, it is clear that Bob-on-the-Hill knows nothing about sailing or how to read the behavior of water. This, not his silly raft, represents the primary inaccuracy of his re-enactment, and is what led to its failure. Crossing the Lombok Strait, whether today or sixty thou-

Many of the crabs in the family Majidae are decorators, and this Dendronephthya crab, a prickly little character the size of a bean, is no exception. Its camouflage is very good— the polyps, for example, are real, snipped from its host. The charade is let down only by the fact that the crab often seems to pull the coral over itself a bit too hard, creating a wilted knot in the billowing tentacles of its host that is visible to a practiced eye. This animal is not rare, but not everybody bothers to look out for it. If you see what appears to be a small shrunken area on an otherwise extended Dendronephthya, look closely—our friend might be there.

sand years ago, is not a *technological* problem. It is a matter of observation and knowledge. The first people to cross could have done so clinging to a log, if they first studied the water and waited for conditions to be right. And I'm very sure that, unlike Bob-on-the-Hill, the early Balinese would have done this.

BALI'S DIVING COMMUNITY

The Indonesian Navy sponsored a gathering of diving clubs at Menjangan Island, in Northwest Bali, in 1978, and organized diving began on the island soon after. The first operator was Baruna, which is still extant, and within a few years there were a handful of businesses for visiting divers to choose from. Since then, as Wally puts it, dive operators here "have sprouted like mushrooms in the rainy season." Most of them have about the lifespan of a mushroom as well.

There are currently about forty dive businesses in Bali. Some are good, some are okay, and some are frightening. Their quality fits no clear pattern. Length of time in business, size, whether the outfit is locally or expatriate-run—none of these seems to be an indicator of quality. There are good ones and stinkers (more stinkers, alas) in each category. In the appendix we have listed some operators with good reputations, including as much data as we had space for. We hope this is useful, but it is worth sniffing around a bit yourself. Before signing on, always try to have a look at the tanks and equipment and talk to the people who will be your guides.

The actual number of divers visiting Bali is unknown. Total tourist arrivals in Indonesia for 1998, the most recent data available as I write this, were 4.34 million, down sixteen percent from the year before, no doubt because of worries surrounding the downfall of President Suharto in the spring of that year.

Most of these visitors passed through Bali. Despite this large number, the diving-oriented hotels do not feel particularly crowded, and at most dive sites here it is rare to see any other divers underwater.

The exception is Tulamben, which can draw crowds, particularly in June, July, and August. Underwater the only site affected by this is the popular wreck of the *Liberty*, which can get a bit claustrophobic during high season. But, given the relative quiet and isolation of some of the other resorts, the boisterous atmosphere at Tulamben—the unofficial capital of Bali's diving community, both expatriate and local—can be enjoyable in its own right.

On an average night in Tulamben at the height of the tourist season, the restaurants at the resorts will be full of divers asking where they can see mantas, lying about how deep they've gone, complaining about the conditions, and doing what divers do when they are not underwater—basically, drinking beer and making noise. And since this is a multinational group, insulting other divers tends to be one of the bigger topics.

For reasons I still do not fully understand, the Japanese usually get the brunt of this punishment. I'll admit that concepts like "Hello Kitty" and "Tamagochi Pet" strike me as both ludicrous and bizarre, but you certainly can't argue with their financial success. When they are diving, I have found that the Japanese pay a lot more attention than the average European or American, and in most cases have more to say about what they have seen underwater. "They have eyes," is how Wally puts it, and that is a high compliment from him.

I once asked a young Japanese diver at Tulamben to name the most interesting animal she had seen underwater. After an elaborate session

The resident school of big-eyed jacks at the Tulamben wreck are normally quite cooperative, and very tolerant of divers. But if you know how to call them—the photographer says he learned the trick when he was a kid diving with his Hawai'ian spear-fishing buddies—they can be downright friendly.

The observations below will help you identify the sub-species of Homo nauticus most often sighted at Tulamben.

AUSTRALIANS are noisy, favor beer that will fit in a stubby holder but will accept any beer that is wet, are equally enthusiastic about everything they see underwater, bellow out foul jokes that make the quiet couple in the far corner of the restaurant twitch, and are obsessed with two species of birds: the kiwi and something called a "pom."

GERMANS are noisy, favor skunky beers like Carlsberg and tend to spill them, can't see anything underwater unless it is bigger than they are, don't feel like they've had a good dive unless a piece of equipment implodes from depth, and look silly wearing sarongs.

JAPANESE are not so noisy, drink beer discreetly but not always moderately, can see a bumblebee shrimp the size of a pea underwater but still bump into each other, dress in gear made from strange polymers and metals like beryllium, and kick funny when they're snorkeling.

AMERICANS are noisy, favor beer with a name they can pronounce, expect whale sharks on every dive ("Well how come there's one in the brochure, then?"), will tell you much more than you want to know about Bloomington, Minnesota, and find it inconceivable that the woman at the warung doesn't know what to do with their Visa card.

of charades and some picture-drawing in my notebook (alas, the Japanese I know is barely good enough to get me what I want in a sushi restaurant) I realized she was talking about a tarpon. This huge, silvery fish is beloved of game fishermen in the Caribbean and enjoys the odd distinction of being, in essence, the world's largest herring. I have never seen a tarpon underwater, but I would certainly love to, and it is a spectacular and very unusual animal to pick. I am very sure that ninety-nine percent of American divers would say "whale shark" or "manta ray" or some other common beast they can see every night on the Discovery Channel.

SAFETY AND RESPONSIBILITY

Bali is generally a safe place to dive, chiefly because at most sites the dive profile is not square. As divers move upslope they off-gas steadily without even thinking about it—like anti-lock brakes, perhaps—and since there is so much to see in the shallows, divers tend to linger there toward the end of their dive. In other words, the reef itself organizes a safety stop.

Menjangan, with its steep walls, is one of the few sites in Bali where this is not true, and more cases of decompression sickness originate there than anywhere else on the island. Also bad for DCS are the Gili Islands, across the strait in Lombok. Their combination of strong current, a steep profile, and a dull reef makes a dangerous cocktail.

The Sanglah hospital's hyperbaric chamber has been operational for three years now, and it is run by a very competent team of doctors. And oxygen, usually a DAN kit, is now common on boats run by the more reputable diving outfits. These are big improvements over what was available even just five years ago. But most of the dive sites are hours away by car from the

chamber, and although there might be an oxygen kit onboard, you cannot be sure that there will be someone around who really knows how to use it. Use caution when diving in Bali, and be conservative.

In this book we have decided to treat our readers as adults, and on occasion we mention things to see at fifty meters or more. You must decide for yourself if these kinds of depths are appropriate to your level of experience, and even to your mood on a particular day. The same goes for some of the reefs with tricky conditions. We have tried to be as accurate as possible about currents and swell. When we say a current is three knots, we are not exaggerating. You decide whether or not that is something you can handle, or something you *want* to handle. Bali has no legislated depth limits or other legal constraints, and your safety is your own responsibility.

The health of Bali's reefs is also in your hands. Only the Menjangan area, which is part of the national park system, is protected by law, and enforcement there is lax. It is up to the operators and divers to look after the environment. This means watch your anchoring, and no collecting or pestering the animals. If you are a photographer, try not to use your camera as a weapon, and please try to watch where you put your fins and knees.

We don't talk about spearfishing in this book, for the simple reason that it does not belong on any of the reefs we discuss. A very large grouper that had lived at Tepekong for a decade is no longer there, and our intelligence suggests it was a spearfisherman who took it. If we had caught the culprit red-handed, we would have held him—and I'm very sure it was a him—at his own spearpoint until he ate the entire fifty kilos of our friend on the spot. If you are a spearfisherman, do everybody a favor and practice

WALLY SIAGIAN Pterois volitans; Tulamben, sand ridge at rivermouth, 25m

our sport while free-diving off South Nusa Penida or at a similarly isolated, non-reef site. Spear a single pelagic fish of reasonable size, and take it home and eat it.

USING THIS BOOK

We have grouped Bali's dive sites into five regions, starting in the northwest and moving clockwise round the island—The Northwest, the Tulamben Area, The East Coast, Nusa Penida, and The South. Each of these areas has its own character, and the seasons—to the extent they can be predicted—are similar for all sites in each region.

The sites we have listed are the most popular, or the most interesting, or favorites of ours—sometimes all three. We have been as comprehensive as the limitations of space have allowed, but of course these are not the only places on the island to dive. We heartily recommend that you explore further whenever you have the opportunity, even if it means just making a quick run

around the point from a known site.

The maps and information here are meant to be a starting point for your investigations. Armed with these tools, we hope that you will be able to make your own decisions about where to dive.

Also, bear in mind that dive sites change. Reefs are much more dynamic than most divers realize, at least in an explosively rich setting like Bali. I have seen reefs that have sprouted so much new growth in just two years that I could hardly recognize them. I have seen others that I once loved turn somehow barren in just as little time. Some of Bali's reefs sprang back from the 1998 El Niño–prompted bleaching in a matter of months; others turned to sand. These reefs are not the stable, slow-growing aquatic deserts I was taught about in high school. Wally has witnessed this cycle for more than fifteen years, and it is one of the things that makes diving in Bali so fascinating. You really never know what you'll see.

To me, 'lionfish' always seemed a worse name for this fish than the rarely used (but more physically descriptive) 'turkeyfish,' but since it does sometimes travel in groups ('prides,' I guess) and since it is an ambush predator with a serious lazy streak, I suppose the comparison to the famous African cat is reasonably apt. This fish, though inarguably striking in appearance, always seemed to me to have an attitude problem. The eyes (and the drooping lower jaw) in Wally's photograph above are more eloquent than me. Not that I want to slander the whole of subfamily Pteroinae, but if you've ever had a few of these freeloaders snapping up shrimp at the edge of your flashlight beam on a night dive—and always lurking right up next to your face— you might agree.

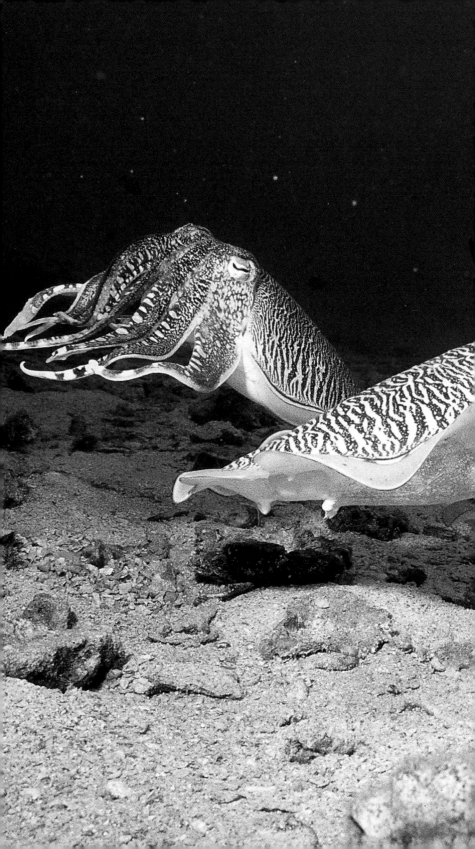

The broad-armed cuttlefish is the only large cuttle in the tropical Pacific. This group appears to be two males, attempting to win the affection—or at least the acquiescence—of a dusky-colored female.

WALLY SIAGIAN Sepia latimanus; Menjangan

Juvenile batfish rely on mimicry for protection, either as a form of camouflage (a mangrove leaf) or deception (a toxic flat-worm). The Batavia batfish—the most rarely seen of the genus—has evolved a pattern that is both disruptive and allows it blend in with crinoids. The species name of this fish comes from the old Dutch East Indies capital, now renamed Jakarta.

Bali's first diving area of note suffered the twin indignities of a crown-of-thorns starfish outbreak and El Niño bleaching, but the best sites here—from rugged, gorgonian-covered walls to strangely fecund bays—remain healthy and beautiful.

The Northwest

MOST GENERAL-INTEREST TRAVEL guides, when they mention the subject at all, state that the best diving on Bali is to be found off Menjangan Island in the far northwest of the island. My copy of Bill Dalton's *Indonesia Handbook,* for example, states: "Pulau Menjangan…boasts the premier scuba diving and snorkeling spot on the whole island, frequented by fish of every size, shape, and color." And Anthony Mason and Felicity Goulden's Cadogan guide to Bali concurs, albeit more calmly: "The best diving is around Menjangan Island."

If you dove Menjangan a few years back, you would have seen what the guidebook writers were talking about: calm, gin-clear water, a steep, craggy reef wall that in areas extends down to forty or fifty meters, and a broad reef flat ringing the island's western extent, so dense with branching and table acroporid corals that you could snorkel over it for an hour without finding a bare patch. It was, by most people's definition, a textbook example of a healthy reef, and one of Indonesia's world-class sites; of the same caliber as, say, Bunaken Island in North Sulawesi. You could imagine an equipment manufacturer choosing the Menjangan reef flat as the setting for a photo shoot: in the foreground, a pretty girl wearing a thin suit, bright pink fins, and too much makeup holding a starfish or some other hapless creature; in the background, the sun streaming down over an unbroken field of coral.

Today, nobody in their right mind would shoot an advertisement here. In fact, the setting would make a pretty good poster for a "Save the Reefs" campaign.

In the time since those guidebooks were written, the reefs around Menjangan and the other

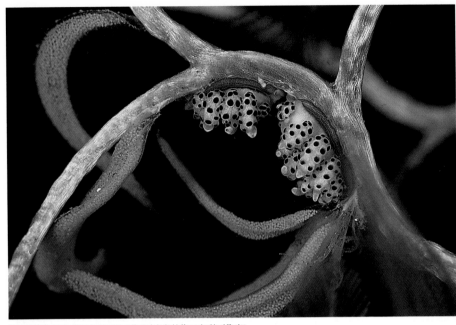

MIKE SEVERNS Unidentified dendronotid nudibranch; hydroid: Macrorhychia philippina

This pair of nudibranchs have laid their eggs on a stinging hydroid. Many nudibranchs live on and even eat stinging cnidarians, but few pick so virulent a host. Macrorhychia (many texts still refer to the genus as Lytocarpus) is one of the worst stingers of all the hydroids.

Graph of the relationship between coral cover and coral diversity. Note that the 'sweet spot'—maximum species diversity—is around 55 percent coral cover. Menjangan's approximately 80 percent put it at the less diverse end of the curve. Data from the Banda Sea.

areas of northwest Bali have been struck by catastrophe—twice. In 1997, a population explosion of the coral-eating sea star called the crown-of-thorns swept through the area, devastating Menjangan's shallow reef flat (see "Crown-of-Thorns," pg. 49). And in the late spring and early summer of 1998, a rise in water temperature brought on by the southern oscillation of El Niño caused much of the remaining shallow-water coral in this area to bleach—that is, lose its symbiotic algae—and die (See "Coral Bleaching and El Niño," pg. 108).

IT ONLY LOOKS BAD

As of the summer of 1999, when Wally and I were completing the fieldwork on this book, the Menjangan reef flat, all of the inshore sites in Terima Bay, and most of the Pemuteran bank reefs remained heavily damaged. In some areas, such as Pemuteran, the damage is spotty; in others, such as inside Terima Bay, once living reefs are now wastelands of rubble and sand.

Although the destruction is real, for a diver the situation is nowhere near as dire as it sounds (a snorkeler will be disappointed, however). The crown-of-thorns damage was almost completely limited to the hard corals growing in the shallow areas, particularly the branching *Acropora* of the reef flats. Similarly, the El Niño bleaching followed a temperature isotherm, which means that the further inside a bay, and the shallower the depth, the more severe was the damage. For the most part the bleaching was limited to the top fifteen meters.

The good news is that Menjangan Island's famous gorgonian-covered walls, as well as the reefs along the mainland Bali coast that drop off quickly to deep water, are still extremely healthy. These sites were always the best that the area offers, and they continue to be as rich and interesting as they ever were.

Personally neither Wally nor I ever much liked the shallow reefs of northwest Bali. The Pemuteran bank reefs, even when they were still

WALLY SIAGIAN Amphiprion ocellaris in Heteractis magnifica

perfectly healthy, were never exceptional—shallow, somewhat patchy, leather- and fire-coral dominated mounds that ran out of steam at about twenty-five meters. And while it may have made a dramatic photograph, the reef flat of Menjangan always seemed barren to us. True, there was healthy coral as far as the eye could see. But all this growth represented a mere handful of species. It was rich in volume, but not in diversity (see graph at left). The fish population was similarly limited: the clouds of damselfish and basslets swarming over the coral, though great in numbers, were all representatives of just a few common species. This reef was close to a monoculture, which is one of the reasons, I believe, it was so devastated by the twin shocks of the starfish and warm water.

RESHUFFLING THE DECK

At the risk of sounding perverse, both Wally and I think the shallow reefs, at least at Menjangan, are now better off. We did enough decompression diving on the Menjangan wall to become intimate with the condition of the reef flat. Everywhere, the scene was the same: old, dead tables and coral heads being colonized by sponges, hard corals, gorgonians, tunicates, and every other sessile member of the reef community. Growing on one dead *Acropora* table no bigger than a dinner plate, I noted the following: three species of sponge, two hydroids, two hard corals, three gorgonians, and two types of tunicates. This is twelve different animals where previously there was just one. In four or five years, and definitely within a decade, I think Menjangan's shallow reef will be a more interesting place than it was before.

In the meantime, stick to the deeper sites, particularly the Menjangan walls and the drop-off reefs just outside of Banyuwedang Bay. Or, if you are interested in rare animals, try Kisik Pegemetan or Gilimanuk Bay. Do not be discouraged by the surface damage. There is still some very fine diving here.

The clown anemonefish is perhaps the most familiar of the genus, and this colony has picked one of the showiest hosts, the magnificent anemone. All anemonefish are protandrous hermaphrodites; born as males and then, if conditions warrant, sex-changing to females. In any group, the largest fish is the functional female. Her partner, often the second-largest, is the functional male. The others, in various stages of adulthood, are all non-functional males. If the female is taken away, her partner switches sex, and one of the junior males becomes sexually functional and assumes the new female's former duties.

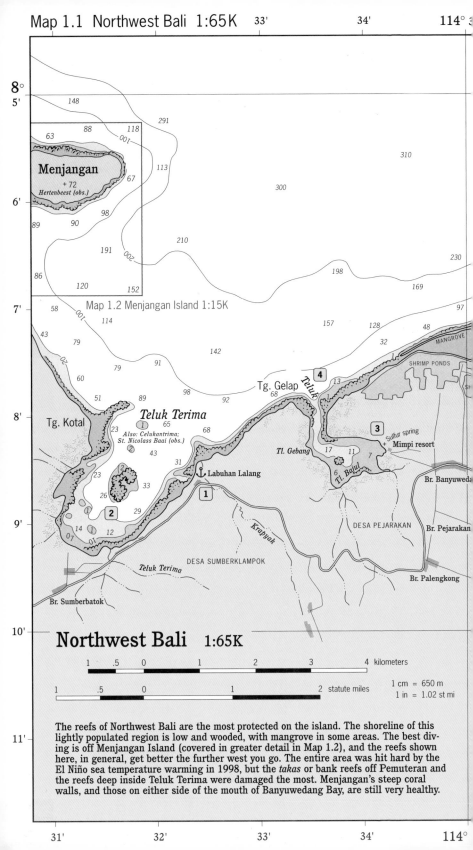

Map 1.1 Northwest Bali 1:65K

Menjangan
+ 72
Hertenbeest (obs.)

Map 1.2 Menjangan Island 1:15K

Tg. Gelap

Teluk Terima

Tg. Kotal

Also: *Celukantrima;*
St. Nicolass Baai (obs.)

Labuhan Lalang

Tl. Gebang

Tl. Bajul

Sulfur spring

Mimpi resort

MANGROVE

SHRIMP PONDS

Br. Banyuweda

DESA PEJARAKAN

Br. Pejarakan

Krapyak

DESA SUMBERKLAMPOK

Br. Palengkong

Teluk Terima

Br. Sumberbatok

Northwest Bali 1:65K

| 1 | .5 | 0 | 1 | 2 | 3 | 4 kilometers |

| 1 | .5 | 0 | 1 | 2 statute miles |

1 cm = 650 m
1 in = 1.02 st mi

The reefs of Northwest Bali are the most protected on the island. The shoreline of this
lightly populated region is low and wooded, with mangrove in some areas. The best diving is off Menjangan Island (covered in greater detail in Map 1.2), and the reefs shown
here, in general, get better the further west you go. The entire area was hit hard by the
El Niño sea temperature warming in 1998, but the *takas* or bank reefs off Pemuteran and
the reefs deep inside Teluk Terima were damaged the most. Menjangan's steep coral
walls, and those on either side of the mouth of Banyuwedang Bay, are still very healthy.

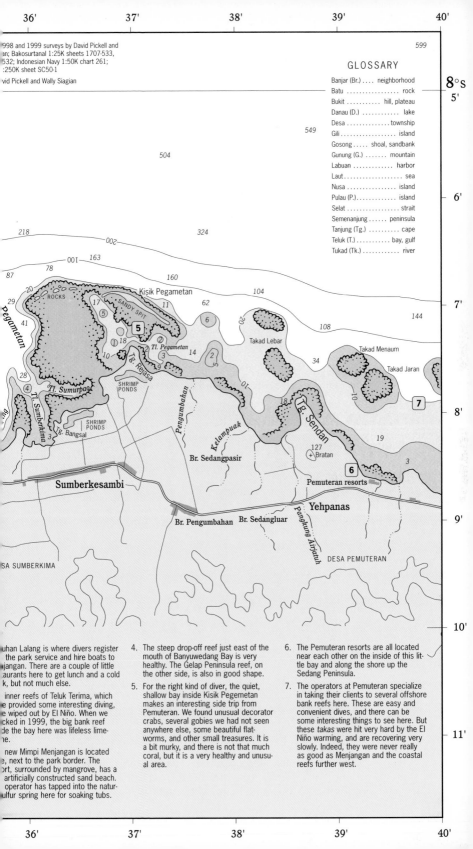

GLOSSARY

Banjar (Br.) .... neighborhood
Batu .... rock
Bukit .... hill, plateau
Danau (D.) .... lake
Desa .... township
Gili .... island
Gosong ..... shoal, sandbank
Gunung (G.) .... mountain
Labuan .... harbor
Laut.................... sea
Nusa .... island
Pulau (P.)............. island
Selat .... strait
Semenanjung ...... peninsula
Tanjung (Tg.) .... cape
Teluk (T.) .... bay, gulf
Tukad (Tk.) .... river

998 and 1999 surveys by David Pickell and
an; Bakosurtanal 1:25K sheets 1707-533,
532; Indonesian Navy 1:50K chart 261;
:250K sheet SC50-1

vid Pickell and Wally Siagian

uhan Lalang is where divers register the park service and hire boats to jangan. There are a couple of little aurants here to get lunch and a cold k, but not much else.

inner reefs of Teluk Terima, which e provided some interesting diving, e wiped out by El Niño. When we cked in 1999, the big bank reef de the bay here was lifeless lime- ne.

new Mimpi Menjangan is located e, next to the park border. The ort, surrounded by mangrove, has a artificially constructed sand beach. operator has tapped into the natur- ulfur spring here for soaking tubs.

4. The steep drop-off reef just east of the mouth of Banyuwedang Bay is very healthy. The Gelap Peninsula reef, on the other side, is also in good shape.

5. For the right kind of diver, the quiet, shallow bay inside Kisik Pegemetan makes an interesting side trip from Pemuteran. We found unusual decorator crabs, several gobies we had not seen anywhere else, some beautiful flat- worms, and other small treasures. It is a bit murky, and there is not that much coral, but it is a very healthy and unusu- al area.

6. The Pemuteran resorts are all located near each other on the inside of this lit- tle bay and along the shore up the Sedang Peninsula.

7. The operators at Pemuteran specialize in taking their clients to several offshore bank reefs here. These are easy and convenient dives, and there can be some interesting things to see here. But these *takas* were hit very hard by the El Niño warming, and are recovering very slowly. Indeed, they were never really as good as Menjangan and the coastal reefs further west.

Menjangan Island

WALLY FIRST DOVE MENJANGAN IN 1978, during a jamboree organized by the Indonesian Navy, and including a group of the nation's pioneer diving clubs—POSSI, Ganesha (Wally is member #041), Nusantara Diving Club, and Trisakti.

The Indonesian dive community was in its infancy back then, and these meetings were as much social events as diving opportunities. These divers were the founders of Indonesian diving, and some went on to start operations in Java, Bali, and North Sulawesi. Dive equipment was very thin on the ground in

Clear, calm water, a mysterious old wooden shipwreck, and rugged, gorgonian-covered walls make this island Northwest Bali's premier dive site.

Indonesia in the late seventies, and when available at all, was prohibitively expensive, so the divers had to make do with the bare minimum.

"In those days," Wally said, "my regulator was still Barracuda, with a hose only this long [he indicated something about the length of a soda straw] so if it became lost from my mouth it was impossible to find. We had no B.C.'s at all. My wetsuit, like everybody else's, was by Levi Strauss."

This jamboree put Menjangan on the map, and it subsequently became Bali's first recognized dive destination, to be followed in a year or so by the *Liberty* wreck at Tulamben.

THE NATIONAL PARK

Menjangan is part of the West Bali (Bali Barat) National Park, a 19,000-hectare tract that covers the coastal area from Banyuwedang Bay around the Prapat Agung Peninsula to Gilimanuk, as well as Prapat Agung itself and a broad swath of the West Bali highlands. This area, which includes pristine rain forests, dry savanna, mangroves, and rich marine habitats, was first established as a game preserve by the Council of Kings, just after Indonesian independence in 1950. Menjangan Island was first famous for its deer, a fact reflected in its name: Menjangan is an old Javanese literary word for "deer," and Hertenbeest, which is what the Dutch called the island, means the same thing.

When the West Bali park was first proposed in the 1970s, it was meant to cover 77,000 hectares, but when the the borders were formally declared, in 1982, they enclosed only the 19,000 hectares of the old game preserve. Subsequent efforts to extend the park boundaries to those in the original proposal have failed, and negotiations between the national park service and the provincial park service, which has direct jurisdiction over Bali Barat, have generally been unproductive.

Since the island is within park borders, the park service controls entry to and diving on Menjangan. Divers arrive at Labuhan Lalang, a small harbor on the southeast shore of Terima Bay. Lalang is a slightly ramshackle little outpost, with, in addition to the park service kiosk and office, a few simple restaurants, a small store, and a toilet and shower facility. From the harbor, divers and their guides head out to the island on park service boats. These are simple wooden vessels, seven to nine meters long, running twin forty-horsepower outboards.

The trip to the island is not very long—thirty minutes to an hour, depending on the site—but it can be a bit uncomfortable, because a straight line from Labuhan Lalang to Menjangan almost always forces you to run parallel with the waves. On the other hand, the ride offers a splendid view of Prapat Agung, and in the distance, the towering volcanoes of East Java.

CLEAR WATER, CALM CONDITIONS

Menjangan is one of the most protected dive sites in Bali. If you think of the one-thousand meter line, which rises north from Singaraja, as the mouth of a great bay, then Menjangan is deep inside it. This yields the clear, still conditions that prevail here. A current of even two knots is unusual around the island, and although the wind can produce chop and some rough conditions, you can dive Menjangan any time of year, choosing sites on the north or the south depending on the direction of the wind. In general, the best diving is during the southeast monsoon, from about April to November, but the area is protected enough to provide good diving even during the rainy season.

The visibility at Menjangan is, on average, the best of any site in Bali. The tail end of the dry southeast monsoon, in October and November, brings the clearest water, with horizontal visibility sometimes reaching fifty meters, although water clarity is good from

April through November. In November, as the seasons change, the waves pick up, which churns up the water and cuts the visibility. January and February can produce very heavy waves, which make it hard—or impossible—to get out to the island on the park service's small boats. Most operators take their

Bali's Endangered Mynah

The most famous denizen of the Bali Barat park is the island's only endemic bird, a beautiful white mynah called the Bali starling. It was discovered in 1911 and named *Leucopsar rothschildi* in honor of Baron Walter von Rothschild, the famous financier of plume hunters and bird collectors, and founder of the Tring museum in England. This bird has now almost vanished

A Republic of Indonesia stamp featuring the Bali starling

from the wild. Although it once inhabited the whole of coastal northwest Bali from Prapat Agung to Lovina, its range is now limited to a few enclaves on Prapat Agung. Perhaps two hundred wild birds existed when the park was established, but the population crashed in the eighties, and the last census I've seen, from 1993, shows just 34 wild birds. Several thousand Bali starlings live in captivity, both in Jakarta and overseas, and a captive breeding program has been started. The park service also plans to introduce a population of the birds to Menjangan Island.

clients out for two dives, spending their surface interval at "Pos I," a small ranger post and dock at the westernmost extremity of the island. Pos I, which houses a ranger and his family, is the island's only facility.

Menjangan is a low, dry, limestone island, like a little piece of Bukit Badung somehow transported to the north, with patches of mangrove growing along the northwest shore. The western extent

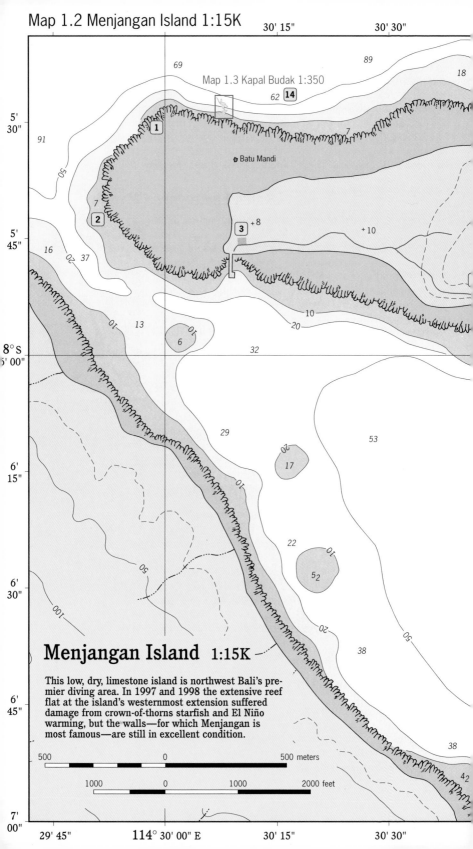

Map 1.2 Menjangan Island 1:15K

30' 15"   30' 30"

69

89

18

Map 1.3 Kapal Budak 1:350

62   **14**

5'
30"

1

7

91

50

Batu Mandi

7

2

5'
45"

3 +8

+10

16

20

37

10

13

10

6

20

8°S
6' 00"

32

29

53

6'
15"

10

17

20

50

22

6'
30"

50

52

10

100

20

6'
45"

38

50

Menjangan Island 1:15K

This low, dry, limestone island is northwest Bali's premier diving area. In 1997 and 1998 the extensive reef
flat at the island's westernmost extension suffered
damage from crown-of-thorns starfish and El Niño
warming, but the walls—for which Menjangan is
most famous—are still in excellent condition.

38

500	0	500 meters

1000	0	1000	2000 feet

42

7'
00"

29' 45"   **114° 30' 00" E**   30' 15"   30' 30"

88

63

100   118

13 11

12

ngan   + 53

62+   **10**

+ 43   **9**

+ 72   67

11

50   **8**

3

5   **7**   + 24   100

6   20   98   8°S 6' 00"

50

200

5' 30"

5' 45"

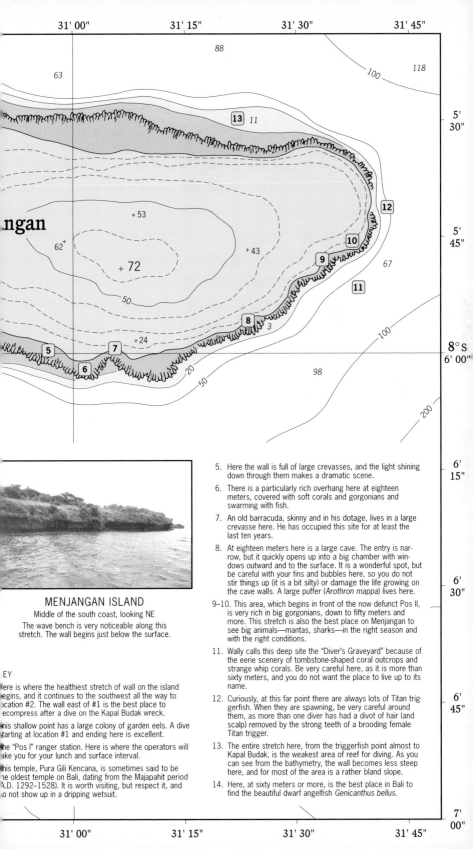

MENJANGAN ISLAND
Middle of the south coast, looking NE
The wave bench is very noticeable along this
stretch. The wall begins just below the surface.

.EY

lere is where the healthiest stretch of wall on the island
egins, and it continues to the southwest all the way to
>cation #2. The wall east of #1 is the best place to
ecompress after a dive on the Kapal Budak wreck.

nis shallow point has a large colony of garden eels. A dive
tarting at location #1 and ending here is excellent.

he "Pos I" ranger station. Here is where the operators will
ake you for your lunch and surface interval.

his temple, Pura Gili Kencana, is sometimes said to be
ne oldest temple on Bali, dating from the Majapahit period
\.D. 1292–1528). It is worth visiting, but respect it, and
o not show up in a dripping wetsuit.

5. Here the wall is full of large crevasses, and the light shining
down through them makes a dramatic scene.

6. There is a particularly rich overhang here at eighteen
meters, covered with soft corals and gorgonians and
swarming with fish.

7. An old barracuda, skinny and in his dotage, lives in a large
crevasse here. He has occupied this site for at least the
last ten years.

8. At eighteen meters here is a large cave. The entry is narrow, but it quickly opens up into a big chamber with windows outward and to the surface. It is a wonderful spot, but
be careful with your fins and bubbles here, so you do not
stir things up (it is a bit silty) or damage the life growing on
the cave walls. A large puffer (*Arothron mappa*) lives here.

9–10. This area, which begins in front of the now defunct Pos II,
is very rich in big gorgonians, down to fifty meters and
more. This stretch is also the best place on Menjangan to
see big animals—mantas, sharks—in the right season and
with the right conditions.

11. Wally calls this deep site the "Diver's Graveyard" because of
the eerie scenery of tombstone-shaped coral outcrops and
strange whip corals. Be very careful here, as it is more than
sixty meters, and you do not want the place to live up to its
name.

12. Curiously, at this far point there are always lots of Titan triggerfish. When they are spawning, be very careful around
them, as more than one diver has had a divot of hair (and
scalp) removed by the strong teeth of a brooding female
Titan trigger.

13. The entire stretch here, from the triggerfish point almost to
Kapal Budak, is the weakest area of reef for diving. As you
can see from the bathymetry, the wall becomes less steep
here, and for most of the area is a rather bland slope.

14. Here, at sixty meters or more, is the best place in Bali to
find the beautiful dwarf angelfish *Genicanthus bellus*.

6' 15"

6' 30"

6' 45"

7' 00"

THE NATURE CONSERVANCY Menjangan, 1994

This photograph, circa 1994, shows Wally drilling through the reef rock to set the footing for a permanent mooring, a program financed and conducted by The Nature Conservancy. This particular mooring, still in use, is on the reef shelf near Kapal Budak.

thing in common: gorgonians. Gorgonians, if they can grow at all, can't grow very large in an area whipped by three-knot currents or plagued by swell, even if conditions are calm during part of the year. They also can't grow big if the water isn't rich with plankton—which means rich with fish and other life as well. Thus a site with lots of gorgonians, particularly if they are of unusual size, is both protected and rich. And the steep, craggy drop-off reef that rings Menjangan has, overall, the greatest diversity of gorgonians of any area on Bali.

Gorgonians are not the only indicators of underwater conditions. If wire corals and whip corals dominate the cover, and the only gorgonians are small and clinging to the inside of crevices, then you are in an area that regularly sees strong current, which can produce difficult conditions for diving. Many sites in Nusa Penida are like this. They are certainly healthy and rich, but you'd better be ready for a ride. If the cover is mostly pink coralline algae, with a few tough leather corals, you are in an area that is regularly battered by strong swell, and you probably do not want to stay there long.

Menjangan is not the best place in Bali to see large pelagic fish like molas, mantas, and whale sharks, although they visit here occasionally. Nor is it really the richest site on the island in terms of the sheer variety of fish and invertebrate life. And of course the reef flat is still recovering from crown-of-thorns and El Niño damage. None of this matters, however. What makes Menjangan worth diving is its clear water, calm conditions, abundance of gorgonians and soft corals, and that nice rough wall with its striking crevasses, overhangs, and caves.

There are plenty of dive sites around Menjangan, but the best area is a stretch along the southeast (from three o'clock to maybe six

ends in short limestone cliffs marked by an eroded bench, and a wide reef flat protects the shoreline of the rest of the three-kilometer-long island. Where there is any beach at all, tiny waves gather a swarf of mangrove leaf litter and seaweed onto a narrow strip of sand.

There is no fresh water on Menjangan, and consequently wildlife is scarce. Rugged little land hermit crabs patrol the shoreline, and the sandy soil near the ranger post is pocked with ant lion traps. In just a short walk north you can reach some clumps of mangrove trees growing on a sandy flat.

THE GORGONIAN THEORY

Dive sites offering good, easy conditions—by which I mean lots of life and light current—have one

thirty, if you can imagine such a narrow island as a clock), and from the far northwest down into the channel between Menjangan and the Prapat Agung peninsula (see Map 1.2, pp. 44–45.) Most of the north is a sand slope and sloping wall, and is not particularly interesting for diving, although in the time before it became a protected national park this stretch was a very rewarding place to hunt lobsters.

A SLAVE SHIP?

Our favorite site off Menjangan is an old wooden shipwreck Wally has dubbed "Kapal Budak," the slave ship (see Map 1.3, pp. 50–51). The site does not cover a lot of territory—the timbers spread out across about sixty meters of sand—nor is the ship in very good shape, since wood does not keep well in shallow, tropical water. But this strange, dark shape, half buried and lit only by the twilight of forty-five meters, is atmospheric and beautiful.

Even when we were diving this site repeatedly over a several-day pe-

riod to make our map (a frustrating task that can make you hate any site), we always enjoyed ourselves.

We had long decompressions after our mapping dives, and we always had plenty of time to wind slowly along the edge of the wall at six to ten meters. We sometimes saw other divers here, but never on the wreck itself. On one occasion, as we were heading back to our boat, we saw a group heading east, and quickly, along the edge of the wall.

"Did you see that?" Wally said, as we climbed aboard. "Talk about Mickey Mouse diving!"

These divers bypassed the best site on the island, were heading the wrong way—away from the richest part of the wall—and were going way too fast to appreciate anything even if they did see it. When we first saw them, they were flying right over a little hollow where we had just seen a green turtle resting, and they did not even notice. It is not really the divers' fault, however.

Dive guides have always called this site the "Anker" wreck, pre-

The dartfish are colorful and nervous little gobioids that hover over the bottom, often in pairs, snapping up plankton as it drifts by. This species, the decorated dartfish, prefers deeper water (more than thirty meters), and Menjangan is one of the best places in Bali to find it. This fish was first described by John E. Randall and Gerard R. Allen in 1973.

sumably because of the large, encrusted anchor in the shallows. This always struck me as a poor choice, since pretty much every ship in my experience has had an anchor. It was only during our repeated dives here in 1998 that I learned the real reason they call it this: the "Anker," in six meters of water, is the only

colonies of *Dendronephthya* and gorgonians appreciated it, though.)

Although past guidebooks have mentioned this wreck, almost nobody dives it. I understand a guide's concern in taking clients to depths of more than forty meters. But here the conditions are calm, and the water is clear. An experienced diver should have no problem visiting this site.

Every skipper knows the location of Kapal Budak, and there is a permanent mooring set not ten meters from the shallow anchor that marks the location of the wreck. Make sure your skipper uses the mooring, and the others around the island. Although the condition of the reef flat now makes the mooring program seem unnecessary, at the time they were set every anchor drop left a painful gash in the shallow fields of *Acropora*. The reef here will come back, as long as divers and skippers respect this special environment—and the park rules.

JUST FOLLOW THE CHAIN

Once underwater, the wreck is quite easy to find: from the shallow anchor, just follow the encrusted chain down the wall—really a steep, terraced slope—to thirty-three meters, where the coral yields to sand. Here stands a second anchor, also beautifully encrusted, and the first few timbers of the wreck itself.

Kapal Budak is more a palimpsest than a wreck. Over the last hundred and fifty years, the waterlogged timbers have slumped into the sand, to the point where the ship has become almost two-dimensional. Still, the dark shapes, so out of place on the sandy white bottom, seem appropriately eerie, a mood enhanced by the big reef white-tip shark that always lurks at the deep end of the wreck.

In places the old spars and deckboards rise up two or three meters from the bottom, and gorgoni-

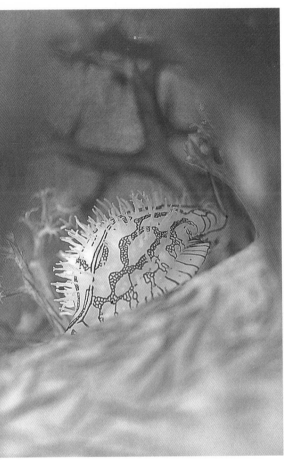

WALLY SIAGIAN Unidentified ovulid (perhaps Serratovolva) on Dendronephthya sp.

These ovulids possess remarkable camouflage. Here the animal's mantle mimics the stippled pattern created by the soft coral's stiffening spicules. These gastropods are sometimes, slightly inaccurately, called allied cowries.

part of the ship they have ever seen.

(On one of our dives, we spent about twenty minutes cutting and unraveling a long piece of rope that had become snarled around the shallow anchor. This was satisfying work—we had a lot of time to kill, anyway—but our fingers itched for days after from all the stinging hydroids. I'm quite sure the beautiful

A Starfish with an Image Problem

I have always found *Acanthaster planci* to be one of the most beautiful echinoderms on the tropical reef. It is certainly dramatic: huge, up to half a meter across, and covered with wild, fierce spikes. The colors vary, but the starfish is usually a subtle azure, pale green, or tan, a bit mottled in the center, with spines that are burnished copper, bright orange, or even red. *Acanthaster* often hosts the tiny shrimp *Periclimenes soror,* and if you get your mask close to the spikes, to see things from the shrimp's point of view, you find yourself in a surreal forest, glowing with color.

However, mine is the minority opinion. Most divers consider this animal a noxious pest. Worse than a pest, really. More like pure evil. I have seen divers bash them with stones, kick them with their fins, and poke at them with dive knives. (In some cases the starfish gets its revenge. Wally likes to call this animal "hammer-finger," a reference to the painful, lingering, disfiguring wounds that contact with its toxic spines yield.)

The crown-of-thorns eats coral. A single adult, it is said, can consume five square meters of reef each year. The animal everts its stomach through its mouth and spreads it in a thin sheet over a patch of living coral, digests the polyps and tissue over a period of several hours, and then pulls its stomach in and moves on. What it leaves behind is nothing but dead, white coral skeleton.

It is not unusual to encounter a crown-of-thorns star on a dive in Bali. They prefer the sun-lit shallows (almost always less than fifteen meters), and are usually found on the reef flat or in the back reef, almost always near *Acropora* coral. It is definitely unusual to encounter three or four on a dive. In 1997, on the reef flat of Menjangan, you could find a hundred on a dive. This was a classic outbreak, or "epidemic" of crown-of-thorns.

NOT THE APOCALYPSE

Scientists are still debating exactly what causes these "plagues." The first theories suggested the cause was human disturbance of the reef, particularly the removal of natural predators of *Acanthaster.* This list always includes the Triton conch, the Napoleon wrasse, and the harlequin shrimp. I always found this explanation unconvincing. In particular, that the harlequin shrimp—a small, secretive, and uncommon species—could be an important predator of *Acanthaster* is, frankly, absurd. (This nonsense comes from research on captive specimens by the Max Planck Institute for Behavioral Physiology in Bavaria, at a time when hysteria over the crown-of-thorns damage to the Great Barrier reef was at its height. Please, scientists, delete this from your citations.*)

Thanks to drill core data, which shows

MIKE SEVERNS Acanthaster planci Hawai'i

evidence of regular *Acanthaster* outbreaks dating back millennia, and the fact that recovery from these events, on a healthy reef, is very rapid (sometimes just five years), many scientists now consider the crown-of-thorns to be part of a natural cycle to maintain reef diversity and long-term stability, although this information has not yet filtered down to the divers hacking away at every poor *Acanthaster* they see.

The starfish prefers *Acropora,* a genus whose competitive advantage on a reef comes from its fast growth. Under certain conditions (and I would maintain Menjangan's reef flat falls into this category) this coral becomes something like a weed, choking out other species. The crown-of-thorns thus gives the slower-growing species (like *Porites* and *Diploastrea*) a leg up, helping to establish a truly diverse reef.

*On the other hand, the fierce little coral crabs *Trapezia* spp. and coral-associated Alpheid shrimp, *do* successfully chase off *Acanthaster...*

Map 1.3 Kapal Budak 1:350

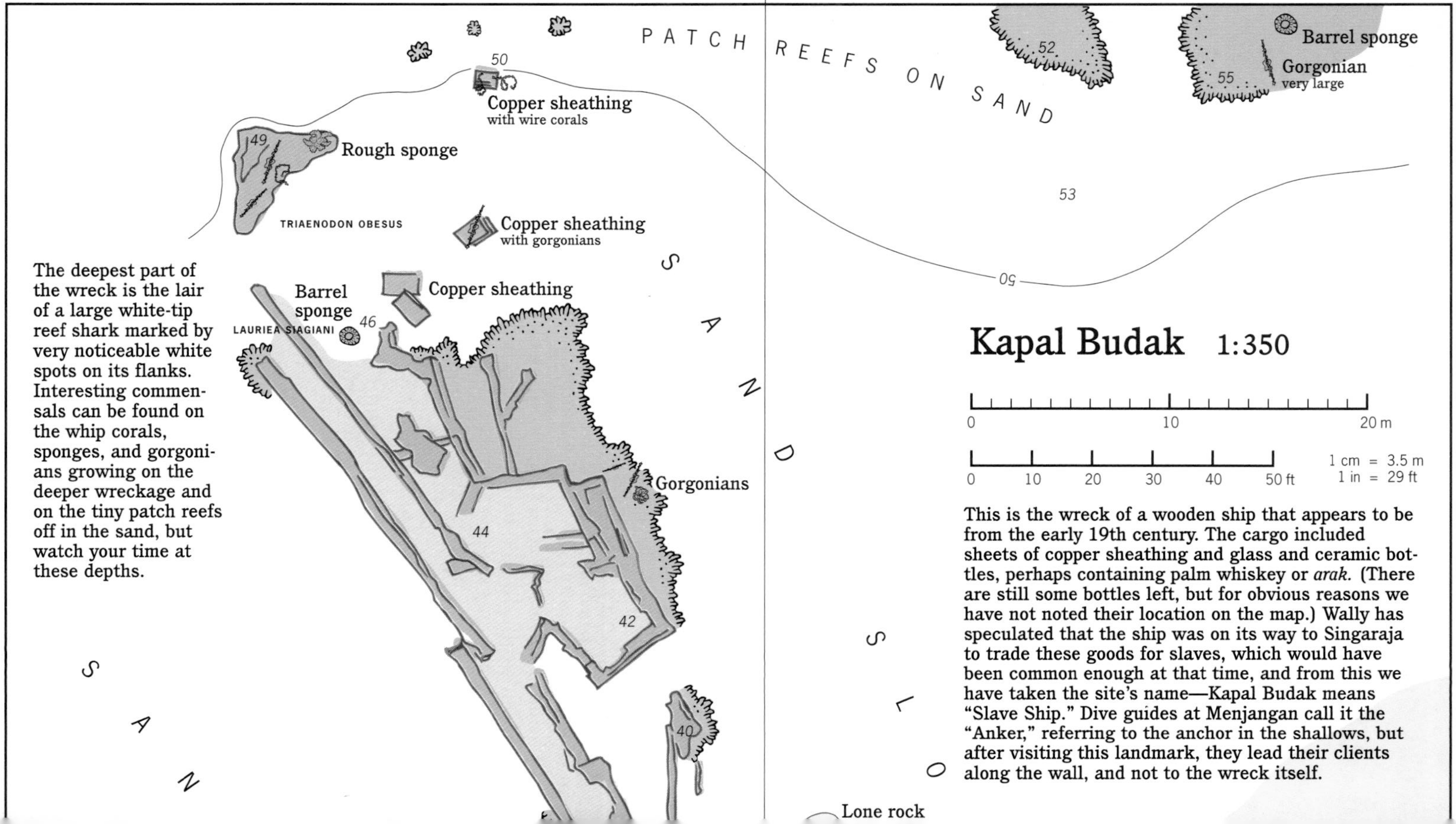

Kapal Budak 1:350

1 cm = 3.5 m
1 in = 29 ft

This is the wreck of a wooden ship that appears to be from the early 19th century. The cargo included sheets of copper sheathing and glass and ceramic bottles, perhaps containing palm whiskey or *arak*. (There are still some bottles left, but for obvious reasons we have not noted their location on the map.) Wally has speculated that the ship was on its way to Singaraja to trade these goods for slaves, which would have been common enough at that time, and from this we have taken the site's name—Kapal Budak means "Slave Ship." Dive guides at Menjangan call it the "Anker," referring to the anchor in the shallows, but after visiting this landmark, they lead their clients along the wall, and not to the wreck itself.

PATCH   REEFS   ON   SAND

Barrel sponge

Gorgonian
very large

55

52

53

50

Copper sheathing
with wire corals

Copper sheathing
with gorgonians

50

Rough sponge

TRIAENODON OBESUS

Copper sheathing

Barrel
sponge

46

LAURIE A. SAGIANI

Gorgonians

44

42

40

SAND

N

SAND

SLOO

Lone rock

The deepest part of the wreck is the lair of a large white-tip reef shark marked by very noticeable white spots on its flanks. Interesting commensals can be found on the whip corals, sponges, and gorgonians growing on the deeper wreckage and on the tiny patch reefs off in the sand, but watch your time at these depths.

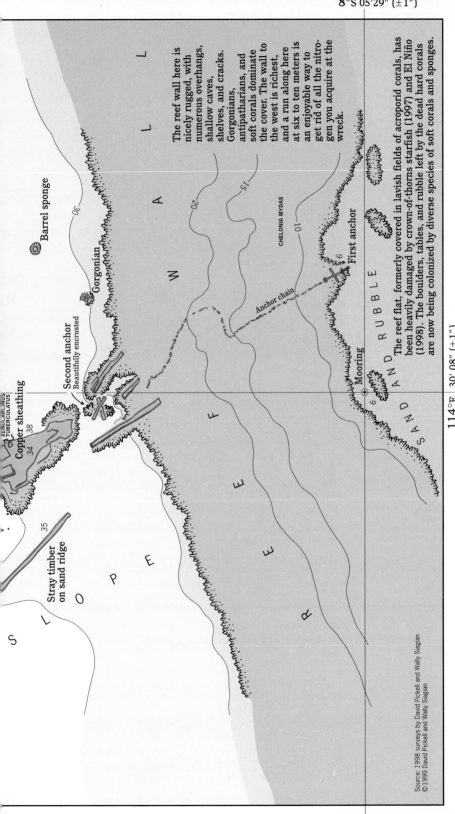

8°S 05'29" (±1")

114°E 30' 08" (±1")

The reef wall here is nicely rugged, with numerous overhangs, shallow caves, shelves, and cracks. Gorgonians, antipatharians, and soft corals dominate the cover. The wall to the west is richest, and a run along here at six to ten meters is an enjoyable way to get rid of all the nitrogen you acquire at the wreck.

The reef flat, formerly covered in lavish fields of acroporid corals, has been heavily damaged by crown-of-thorns starfish (1997) and El Niño (1998). The boulders, tables, and rubble left by the dead hard corals are now being colonized by diverse species of soft corals and sponges.

W A L L

R E E F

S L O P E

S A N D A N D R U B B L E

S

CHELONIA MYDAS

Barrel sponge

Gorgonian

Second anchor
Beautifully encrusted

Copper sheathing

AEOLIARCINUS
TUBERCULATUS

Stray timber
on sand ridge

First anchor

Anchor chain

Mooring

30

20

15

10

6

9

9

34

38

35

Source: 1998 surveys by David Pickell and Wally Siagian
©1999 David Pickell and Wally Siagian

WALLY SIAGIAN Kapal Budak wreck

An old glass bottle, photographed in situ at Kapal Budak (note the whorl of nudibranch eggs at its tip).

A long time ago, Wally collected one of these wine bottles, which he kept as a curio (those were different times). Years later, a friend noticed it and suggested they sample the contents. The friend knew a sommelier who possessed a special device to gently open ancient bottles with questionable corks, and Wally agreed.

On the appointed night, the friends gathered expectantly for their first taste of century-old wine. The device was applied, and the cork came out. Immediately the room filled with the choking, eye-watering fumes of hydrogen sulfide, and the would-be gourmands rushed outside gasping for air.

ans and black corals grow in their cracks. Sheets of copper sheathing, part of the ship's cargo, lie in piles on the wood and sand. Some glass and brown ceramic bottles remain as well, and please don't take any as souvenirs.

THAT PECULIAR INSTITUTION

We don't really know if this wreck was a slave ship, but the run between Buleleng (Singaraja) and Batavia, the old Dutch colonial capital which is now Jakarta, was a famous one in the history of the trade in human beings. And from the location of the wreck, it seems certain that it was headed to Buleleng, historically Bali's most important port.

Bali had traded in both Balinese and Eastern Indonesian slaves since at least the 10th century. By the time the Dutch established themselves in the archipelago, in the early 17th century, Bali had become the most important slave entrepôt in the Indies. In Batavia alone, 17th-cen-

tury estimates suggest that out of a total slave population of 15,000 to 18,000, almost two-thirds were Balinese. Prices were good, running £70–£80 for an unskilled man or woman, to almost double that for a skilled male laborer or beautiful woman (or one especially handy at cooking or weaving).

Balinese women were particularly coveted, and not for erotic reasons. Chinese entrepreneurs were an important part of the Dutch trade network, making it possible to efficiently triangulate shipments of spices and trade goods to China. These entrepreneurs prized Balinese woman as servants and mistresses for the simple reason that as Hindus they would willingly cook pork, something that a Muslim woman could be made to do only under great duress.

Bali's direct trade in slaves with the Dutch East India Company lasted less than a century. In 1665, the Company banned the ownership of Balinese. slaves by its employees, nd in 1688, banned their import into Batavia. This ban did not derive from any humanitarian concerns, however. It was just that after several well-publicized incidents in which shiploads of Balinese slaves ran *amuk* and seized the ship (and their freedom), the Balinese were deemed to be too much trouble. The Dutch continued to buy slaves, of course—they simply sought more malleable victims.

By the early 19th century Britain formally distanced itself from the "peculiar institution," and in 1830 even the Dutch ended their trade in slaves. The Balinese, however, did not answer to the Dutch at this time, and had been running a steady trade in slaves with Mauritius and other French colonies since the time of the Company ban.

Bali infuriated the Dutch by completely ignoring the stipulation that all trade in the archipelago be handled through Dutch ports. In the 1820s and 1830s, for example, Buleleng was conducting a direct, and growing, trade (although not primarily in slaves) with the new British colony of Singapore. Independent traders—the Dutch called them "pirates" and "smugglers"— from the Indies, the southern Philippines, and even French colonies stopped regularly in Buleleng, and the slave trade flourished here until about 1860.

Was the boat that foundered on the reef edge of Menjangan a century-and-a-half ago, with its cargo of palm whiskey, wine, and copper sheathing, on its way to Buleleng to trade these goods for slaves? We'll probably never know.

THE FAMOUS MENJANGAN WALLS

Kapal Budak is not the only dive on the island, and the southeast flank and western tip of Menjangan offer very rewarding diving as well (see MAP 1.2, pp. 44–45). These are all wall dives, and the nooks and crannies are rich. I have never seen so many of the beautiful little Paccagnella's dottyback—half bright magenta, half glowing yellow—as along the south coast of Menjangan. Angelfish, butterflyfish, anthias, gobies, whatever your interest in reef fish, you can find them here. Probably the most unusual specimen at Menjangan is the rarely seen *Geni-*

WALLY SIAGIAN *Xenocarcinus tuberculatus*

canthus bellus, certainly the most beautiful member of this deepwater genus of dwarf fork-tailed angelfish. You will have to go to sixty meters or more to find it, however. The big animals—sharks and rays—are generally quite deep here as well, although one often sees turtles in the shallower areas along the walls.

The area of wall with the best relief is along the south. Here there are

These peculiar, weevil-like crabs live only on black coral whips. This is a pair, with the male clambering on top of his much larger mate, who is gravid with eggs. To better match her host, the female has plucked some polyps from the black coral and planted them on her brow.

A coral grouper (depending on your nationality and background, you might call it a trout, cod, or hind) being cleaned by a transparent palaemonid shrimp. Experiments have demonstrated that cleaning, which the fish seem actually to enjoy, has a measurable positive effect on the health of the the fish. The cleaner shrimp (Urocaridella, although still called Leandrites in many texts) hover in front of caves or among rocks, waiting for their clients.

Swarming over the algae-covered rocks in back are hinge-beaked shrimp, very common in caves and crevices in Bali and elsewhere in the Indo-Pacific. At night these creatures are responsible for the million sparkling eyes reflecting your flashlight beam.

several big crevasses, some leading all the way to the surface, as well as caves and overhangs. In one big split, almost exactly at the midpoint of the island, there lives a single large barracuda. He looks a bit skinny and forlorn to me, but Wally, who has seen this old soldier in exactly the same spot for the past decade, says he has always been this way.

One of the most dramatic, but challenging, areas on Menjangan is the far eastern tip. Here the gorgonians are the biggest on the island, and the wall continues all the way down to fifty meters and more. The deep here gives you your best chance in the area to see big animals like mantas, molas, and sharks. A little further north, in the very deep (sixty-two meters), is an area Wally calls the "Diver's Graveyard." This is a spooky place, full of tombstone-shaped coral heads and strange whip corals.

Perhaps the richest and healthiest wall on the island overall is in the far west, running from the point just west of Kapal Budak around the tip

and almost into the channel between Menjangan and the mainland. One of the nicest things about this dive is that you end in a shallow area full of garden eels.

DANGERS OF A VERTICAL PROFILE

Although current conditions at Menjangan rarely cause problems, the depths can. The deep areas around this island are forty and sixty meters, and these depths are not for everyone. More sport divers get decompression sickness at Menjangan than anywhere else on Bali. The ones that do are mostly good divers, but they had been pushing their computer and diving over multiple days (and perhaps carousing over multiple nights).

Dive conservatively at Menjangan. Watch your time at depth, and do not be impatient at the end of a dive. Now that the shallows are damaged, people are more anxious to get back to the boat. Don't make this mistake. Burn off a lot of air, and don't just rush up because your computer says you can.

The Pemuteran Area

WE REACHED PEMUTERAN LATE ONE afternoon after a long, hot ride from the south. All morning we were thwarted in our errands by the choke of Denpasar traffic, and by the time we finally could leave, we had to fight the whole way with homicidal tour buses, suicidal Vespas (these dart sideways with the jerky unpredictability of a cockroach), and the real monsters of the road: outlaw gravel trucks, grossly overloaded, their sick air-brakes sneezing on every downhill, their rotten exhausts spewing black, poisonous clouds that turn daytime to night with every upshift. Once we made it to Pemuteran, we did not even bother to unpack. We walked straight down the path to the Pondok Sari's little restaurant, right on the quiet curve of beach inside Pemuteran Bay, ordered two beers, and plopped ourselves down at a little table in the sand.

In the golden afternoon light, the village kids splashed around in the water naked, completely disregarding the "PLEASE NO TOPLESS BATHING THANK YOU" sign the hotel management had tacked to a tree, perhaps after some bold Italians had inadvertently shocked the community in their pursuit of a more even tan. (The area is populated by Madurese and East Javanese immigrants, and is one of the few Muslim areas on Bali—there is a mosque not half a kilometer away.) A few men, their lines spread out on the sand, smoked and chatted while they patched broken floats and tears in the netting. A slight breeze came off the bay. Our beers were ice cold.

It is at times like this that the logic of the Pemuteran area resorts becomes incontrovertible. The Pondok Sari, about six years old, was the first, and now there are a handful, all clustered next to each other, with the new Mimpi Menjangan just a few kilometers down the road inside Banyuwedang Bay. In the old days, diving Menjangan and the northwest meant a hassle-

The resorts in this quiet area are cozy, but the nearby bank reefs, though convenient, are bland. Explore a bit, however, and you will find some fine walls and a rich and curious little bay.

ridden, four-hour-long trip from the south in the wee hours of the morning, and after a long day of diving, the same trip back. Many divers stayed in Lovina (Kalibubuk) instead, but this is still at least an hour away. At the Pemuteran resorts or the Mimpi you can step off the boat, take a quick (and hot) shower, and begin your real decompression stop right away.

The Pemuteran Takas

In Indonesia, a *taka* (*takad* or *takat*, on some maps) is a bank reef or atoll. I don't know the etymology of the word, but my guess is that it originates with the Bugis, the archipelago's famous seafarers from South Sulawesi. Although operators will also send you to the inshore reef at Pemuteran, particularly for night dives or snorkeling, basically diving here means diving *taka*s: Taka Lebar, Taka Jaran, Taka Menaum, and the recently named "Close Encounters" and "Napoleon Reef," among others.

These reefs are all quite similar: coral-covered sea mounds, roughly half a kilometer in diameter, rising from a sandy bottom (Note: *Taka* specifies a coral mound or bank; if it is a sandy mound or bank, it is called a *gosong*.) The tops are generally shallow, maybe six to eight meters, and the coral runs out and becomes sand at twenty to thirty meters.

The visibility here is good, but not excellent, and unlike at Menjangan, it varies considerably. The Pemuteran *taka*s are relatively shallow and close to shore, which makes them vulnerable to degraded visibility from heavy waves stirring up the bottom, or rainy season runoff from mainland Bali. Current is rarely an issue.

April through August is a good time to dive Pemuteran, and September through October is probably the best. During the northwest monsoon, roughly December through March, conditions are not as good as they are the rest of the year. January and February bring high waves, and conditions here (like the rest of the north coast) can be very poor at this time.

Operators in Pemuteran like to take their clients to these reefs rather than to Menjangan. You may even hear claims that these *taka*s are just as good, or even better than Menjangan's walls. Diving Pemuteran is certainly convenient—the boat rides can be as short as ten minutes, depending on the site—and it is possible to do night diving here, which is something than can

not be done on Menjangan. But the tops of these banks were hit very hard in 1998 by the El Niño warming, and when Wally and I checked again in 1999 they were still quite battered. The deeper areas were better, but in general the damage here was much more severe than at Menjangan or the walls at the mouth of Banyuwedang Bay.

Even before the El Niño disaster, these were pretty average shallow water banks: a reeftop covered with a mix of tough, shallow-water soft corals (*Lobophyton, Sarcophyton, Sinularia*), fire coral, and hard stony corals (*Acropora, Porites*) with some sponges, gorgonians and black coral spirals showing up in the deeper areas. The underwater structure is rather plain, a simple bank with little relief, and the fish and invertebrate life, though generally good, is simply not as diverse or rich as at premier sites like Menjangan or Tulamben. Like anywhere, you might get lucky and see something special, like a whale shark or a manta, but the chances are very poor. Even reef white-tip sharks are scarce here.

I think Pemuteran is a splendid place to stay, but if it were our diving vacation, we would spend most of our time at Menjangan, or other points west. A couple dives on the Pemuteran *taka*s can be rewarding, especially if you are willing to look closely for interesting small animals in the gorgonians and little bommies along the edges where the coral turns to sand, or if you want to night dive. Otherwise, have the operator drive you the fifteen kilometers to Labuhan Lalang and get a boat to Menjangan.

Kisik Pegemetan

We were in about a meter-and-a half of water, and the seagrass bed we were diving over began to thin. First it went to a forest of tiny algae tufts, and then just ahead and a little

AL MULLER   Phyllorhiza punctata; Caranx sp. 'Napoleon Reef,' Pemuteran

le bit deeper, plain sand. Peering at one of the tiny tufts of algae, I was delighted to find that it was, instead, a little majid crab who had planted a bit of seaweed on its head as a disguise. As I turned to point this out to Wally, who was at my side, I caught him in the process of pointing another one out to me. Then, as we looked again at our field of algae tufts, the realization hit us both at the same time: every one of these, covering an area of maybe ten square meters, was a crab.

This was just the first of many surprises for us at a strange site we stumbled on in the most protected area of Pegemetan Bay (see MAP 1.1, pp. 40–41). We had been diving Menjangan and the Pemuteran *taka*s, and we were a bit bored. Grabbing our charts, we looked for a likely area for a seagrass bed, or a mangrove edge, or something other than a coral wall or a bank reef. We settled on the backside of a sandy spit called Kisik Pegemetan, deciding there must be a seagrass bed

there, and hired a *jukung* near Pemuteran to take us out.

The boat ride was a lot longer than it looked from the map, because we had to motor all the way along a line of rocks to the main opening of Pegametan Bay, go deep inside the bay to Teluk Sumurpao, and then back up to the sandy spit of Kisik Pegametan itself. When we got there, we did find a seagrass bed, but then found our crabs, and continued for a short ways over the sand to encounter a strange, silty, back reef wall. The bottom was never deeper than nine meters, usually less than six. It was dead calm, but the visibility was terrible, occasionally three or four meters, but in places dropping to one or two.

The coral, covered in a light dusting of silt, had grown in forms that were extremely fine and lacy, with branches so thin that I wondered how they could even support the tiny red-headed gobies resting on them. I'd guess that even a quarter-knot current would blow the

This rhizostome jelly can be found in warm waters around the globe, and is said to grow to a bell diameter of nearly a meter. The fish sheltering in its tentacles are juvenile jacks. Unlike an anemonefish, they have no protection from the jelly's sting. Instead they rely on their thin shape, quick wits, and supreme sense of body position (any athlete would love to have a sense organ like a fish's lateral line) to avoid contact with the tentacles.

Madame, Some Cyanide with Your [

WE HAD OUR SKIPPER STOP HIS ALUMINUM skiff at the very edge of the Tanjung Gelap reef, just where the green water of the battered reef flat ends and the blue-black begins. We rolled off, and even before I got my ears settled, Wally gave a yelp through his regulator and dropped like a stone to thirty meters.

When I caught up with him, he was holding a huge Javan moray in his arms. The eel was as big around as my thigh, and when stretched out, even longer than Wally and his long free-diving fins combined, or more than two meters. It was a beautiful animal, mottled bronze, with a huge, toothsome maw, and that soft, rippling, infinitely flexible flesh that morays have. It was also stone dead.

We were saddened and puzzled by this discovery. The eel could not have been dead long. There was not a trace of rigor mortis, and its eyes were clear and bright. A cleaner wrasse continued weaving in and around

the moray's mouth, as if it too could not un derstand its best customer's sudden death Wally gathered up the eel, carried it down to a cave at forty meters, and gently placed it in side. We both, silently, wished the old soldie a safe journey.

It was at this point that I found a clue: small hand-made dip net (see photograph a right). The moray was at thirty-two meters the net at thirty-six. It, like the eel, was fresh there was not so much as a tuft of algae or bryozoan growing on it. This net told me tha the eel had died of cyanide poisoning.

'CUT FLOWER INDUSTRY'

A cyanide fisherman chases his quarr into a crack in the reef, and with a squirt from a plastic bottle, stuns it. He scoops up th quivering fish, places it in a collecting bag and moves on to the next target. Th process is much faster than trying to net th specimen, and competent fisher man can probabl catch every fish h sees this way. Potas sium cyanide is common industria chemical—it i used, for example to clean jewelry an ceremonial *kri* knives—and yo can get it very easi ly in Indonesia.

The fisherman who dropped hi net at Gelap wa seeking specimen for the aquariun trade. A former re gional director o WWF in Indonesi once told me tha he considered th trade in "marin ornamentals" to b equivalent to a "cu

DAVID PICKELL Saikung Harbor, Hong Kong, circa 1991 Moray: Gymnothorax favagineus

The ziggurat-like holding tanks at Saikung Harbor rival a good public aquarium in the range of their offerings. Here, in just one corner of one vendor's display, you can see honeycomb morays, two species of lobsters, flower crabs, horse mussels, scallops, and whelks. Elsewhere the same vendor had stomatopods, myriad varieties of shrimp, cuttlefish, abalone, parrotfish, rabbitfish, at least half a dozen species of grouper, and Napoleon wrasse.

In between the fishmongers are restaurants, which—this being Hong Kong—cook your order to perfection. My host suggested the polka-dot grouper Cromileptes altivelis, known here as the "rat-faced grouper," together with courses of shrimp, abalone, and other shellfish. Unlike many Hong Kong residents, he considers the much-esteemed Napoleon wrasse to be a lackluster eating fish, and the morays, whose appeal is strictly their dragon-like appearance, to be a wasteful folly unfit even for stew. The Cromileptes, on the other hand, deserves its reputation. The tab for our party of eight, by the way, came to US$1,800.

ed Grouper?

ower industry," and it caused him little con-
ern. With the increased use of cyanide, this
may no longer be the case. The poison stuns
he fish, but it kills the surrounding coral.

Wally and I used to occasionally dive a
hallow, isolated reef along the north coast we
all "The Place of Nowhere." This is not a
pectacular reef, but there were some inter-
sting fish (*e.g.* sea moths) that lived there.
We stopped diving it a couple of years ago.
The site had always been heavily fished by
quarium fish collectors, but it was only in
he last few years that the cyanide began to
ake its toll. A fresh cyanide wound on the
oral is a blistered patch of black slime; an
ld one is just dead coral rock.

This trade in Indonesia is dominated by
inerant Madurese, and Madura—an island
ff northeast Java about the same size as
ali—is just a stone's throw away from north-
vest Bali. The National Park is legally off-
mits to fishing (Tanjung Gelap, for exam-
le, is inside the park), but we saw
Madurese collecting boats, even at Menjan-
an Island, every day we were there in 1999.

The huge moray was obviously not a tar-
et species for our unknown collector. Per-
aps he poisoned the eel out of malice or, as
like to think, fear. Chasing a dottyback, he
urns his head and suddenly there is this
reat maw. In panic, he squirts his cyanide
nd bolts for the surface. He drops his net in
ll the commotion, but there is no way he is
oing back down to face that monster again.

AN UNUSUAL MARINADE

Cyanide is also used to collect table fish,
articularly several species of groupers and
he Napoleon wrasse (although export of this
atter was formally banned by Indonesia a
ew years back), which are prized in Hong
Kong and elsewhere in East Asia (see photo
t left). Indonesia has now surpassed the
Philippines to become the world's largest
upplier to the live food fish trade, and most
f these are caught with cyanide.

It seems at first rather odd to serve up a
oisoned fish, especially one for which you

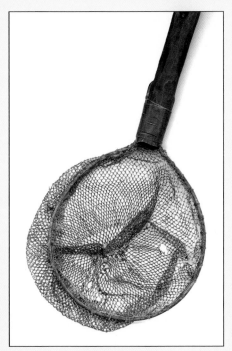

DAVID PICKELL

This hand-made collecting net was dropped on the reef at
Tanjung Gelap, where I found it at thirty-six meters. Note
the proportions: it is ten centimeters in diameter, but only
four deep. It is not a net, but a scoop, and to catch a fish
with this it would have to have been stunned with cyanide.

are charging $500. But cyanide in less than
a lethal dose is rapidly detoxified (by both
fish and humans), and all evidence suggests
that it is not carcinogenic.

I don't think there is anything inherently wrong in collecting either aquarium or
food fishes from the reef, and their value is
high enough to accommodate ecologically
sound collecting methods. For example, a
live dottyback, at an aquarium store in New
York City, retails for $60. A live polka-dot
grouper, in Hong Kong, *wholesales* for $100
a kilogram, and can retail for five times this
amount (even less vaunted grouper species
wholesale for more than $40 a kilogram).

But the Indonesian collector, risking decompression sickness and daily contact
with poison, receives $1 for his dottyback,
and the last I checked, about $3 a kilo for
groupers. This, of course, is the problem. It
is the cheap scoundrels in the middle, not the
poor fisherman whose net now hangs on my
wall, that are the enemies of the reef.

whole reef to powder. This magical little reef was full of healthy fish: fat blennies, each appearing to have swallowed a pea, cardinalfish in swarms of thousands, and great shoals of juvenile fusiliers. We saw what we call the biggest lettuce coral in the world, an unlikely tower three meters high built of tissue-thin whorls, and found little curiosities like shrimp gobies, urchin clingfish, and coral gobies, and lots of fat honey-headed damselfish, which are more beautiful than the pictures communicate, but also very aggressive little devils. (I always tell people that if damselfish grew to even half a meter in length, the tropical seas would be undiveable.)

One of the strangest animals we encountered was a red sponge, which doesn't seem so exceptional except that these sponges were covered with white polyps. I gently squeezed one of these animals which just made me more puzzled—they surely had to be sponges, but just as surely, sponges don't have polyps. I later learned that what I had been seeing was probably the polyp stage of the jellyfish *Nausithoe punctata,* which is known to live in sponges. The sponges were also encrusted with tunicates and hydroids, and the pretty little flatworm *Pseudoceros bifurcus*—lavender, with a white stripe edged in black down its back, and a splash of red near its head—was everywhere.

Wally told me later that he was a bit edgy during the dive worrying about bull sharks. I'm glad I didn't think of this, but actually a murky, inshore back reef like this is just about to a bull shark's taste. Still, we were both surprised and very pleased with this dive.

I know a site like this is not to everyone's taste. Two-meter visibility? Bull sharks? For what, a few crabs? A *flatworm?* We include it here just to encourage people to explore a bit. There are lots of different habitats to dive, and lots of sites.

Banyuwedang Bay

Deep inside Banyuwedang Bay is a tiny, white sand beach, complete with coconut trees. The little beach is quite startling, since this bay, just east of Teluk Terima, is muddy and lined elsewhere with mangrove. It reminded me a bit of a Hollywood set, an impression helped by the bamboo stakes propping up the coconut trees, and a plywood wall—in a touch of whimsy, painted to look like a forest—erected to block the sight of ongoing construction from the beach and nearby restaurant. The beach, restaurant, and construction are part of the Mimpi Menjangan, a tony resort just opening when we visited in 1999.

The Mimpi lies barely outside the national park boundary, and right next to a natural sulfur spring, which is why the operator built here in the first place. The word "banyuwedang," from Old Javanese, makes reference to the spring, and people have been coming here to take the waters for a very long time. The spring smells strongly of sulfur, and its water is said to cure all manner of skin ailments. The resort's rooms are air-conditioned and very well appointed, and the better ones each have a walled-in garden, complete with a private hot tub fed with water from the famous spring. It is not a cheap place to stay, but if you have the means it is awfully luxurious to soak in one of these tubs after a long day of diving.

All of the operators in this area can take you to any of the sites, but the Mimpi is in a better position than the Pemuteran resorts to reach Menjangan, as well as two sites at the mouth of the bay.

The reef in front of the Gelap Peninsula, on the southwest side of the Bay's mouth, is a steep wall that drops down to more than forty meters. This site has much of the character of the better sites on Menjangan itself, and was quite rich. In one deep cave, I encountered a beautiful little diorama: clumps of *Halimeda* algae, a pair of big stenopid shrimp, a bright little dottyback, and a beautiful baby foxface rabbitfish, not much bigger than a silver dollar. Richness like this at such a small scale is a sign of a healthy reef.

Unfortunately, one of the most interesting animals we found, a huge Javan moray eel, was dead, probably the result of cyanide fishing, which has become a serious problem in this area (see "The Live Fish Trade," pg. 58).

We also dove on the opposite side of the bay's mouth, on another steep wall, which appears even healthier than Gelap. This site, at least in 1999, was one of the very best in the whole area, equal to the best Menjangan sites. The wall is rough and fissured, with a more interesting structure than that at Gelap, and gorgonians were everywhere, in great variety. This reef has that somewhat indefinable glow that you see only on reefs that are very rich and healthy.

We found tiny groupers, jet black with pearly spots; anglerfish; a juvenile *Chelmon* butterflyfish hiding in a bright blue tube sponge, and the striking brittle star *Ophiomastix variabilis*, its arms decorated with bright rings and curious warts.

The reef flats on both sides, like the other shallow reefs in the area, show signs of damage, but they also show signs of recovery. The reef flat on the Gelap side is very blanched and sandy, but even there we saw groups of shrimpfish picking at amphipods, and a tiny ghost pipefish mimicking a blade of seagrass. This particular specimen, the first I have ever found, was a more remarkable mimic than those I have seen pictured. It *was* a brown, broken-off

piece of seagrass, right down to the rough edge of the break. I even found it lying sideways on the sand, swaying in the light surge with the other bits of seagrass and mangrove litter. Only its tiny bill gave it away: seagrass, it slowly dawned on me, does not have a stem.

On our second dive we encountered a clue as to why this reef is still

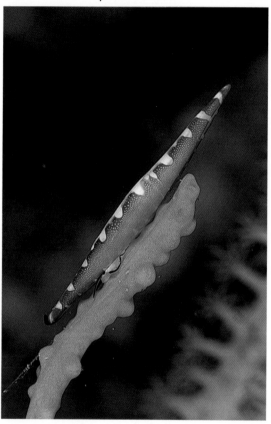

MIKE SEVERNS Phenacovolva sp.

so healthy. At twenty-four meters we hit a thermocline, beneath which the water was very cold, maybe 24°C. (Cold enough, anyway, to cut our time in the deep short). If cold water rolls in here regularly, it could explain why these reefs remained so healthy, while the *taka*s off Pemuteran were hit hard by the El Niño warming, and even now, more than a year later, are recovering slowly.

The spindle ovulids are a diverse group, with about thirty species so far described in the genus Phenacovolva alone. This one may be new.

Gilimanuk Bay

WHEN WE WERE CONDUCTING THE final fieldwork for this book in May and June of 1999, the buzz in the island's diving community was about a place called, mysteriously, "Secret Bay." I know dive operators are not poets, which is probably a good thing, but the lack of imagination displayed in the proprietary names they give to sites is a pet grievance of mine. For example, how many "Blue Corner"'s are there

This unlikely site, a mangrove-lined bay off the Bali Strait, is a trap for plankton, yielding extremely healthy fish and some rare macro-scale treasures.

in the world? A hundred? A thousand? And what, really, does it mean to call a dive site "The Aquarium"?

The other common mode, after the silly name, is the "Secret Place That Only We Know." I understand that the interests of the writers of a diving guide and those of an operator can easily clash on this subject, but it has also been my experience that the operators who are most open about the locations of their sites, and what they've seen there, are also the best ones.

These are people who understand that you cannot own a dive site, and in any case, their enthusiasm and love of diving and the underwater world would make it impossible for them not to share their discoveries.

The operator who is trying to make Gilimanuk Bay into a kind of private pond shall remain nameless here, because he is far from being alone in this kind of attempt. In any case, it seems almost laughable to call this bay a "secret"—Gilimanuk is where the ferry to and from Java lands, and the narrow Bali Strait and Gilimanuk Bay are one of the best mapped parts of Bali's inshore waters. For the record, the Dutch vessel *Van Gogh* first surveyed the area in 1902, and one might confidently assume that the Balinese had some knowledge of these waters even before this.

A MANGROVE-LINED BAY

Gilimanuk Bay is about two kilometers across and very shallow, most of it less than five meters deep. A reef north of the bay's mouth makes the opening even more narrow than it appears on a land map, and creates a channel that sweeps in and hooks around two islands in the bay's center (see MAP 1.4, pg. 65). These islands, and parts of the shoreline, are lined with mangrove. The islands get their names from the animals that roost there—Kalong, the near island, bears the Indonesian word for the flying fox (sometimes *keluang*), and these large fruit bats spend their days in Kalong's mangroves; Burung, the inner island, means "bird."

According to the reports we had heard, this bay offered a number of rare jewels for the macro-photographer, including odd gobies and dragonets, and such rarities as the

juvenile Batavia batfish, a beauty with zebra stripes and ragged fins that seems to want to make itself look like a crinoid (see photograph pg. 36). The particular prize was the dragonet *Synchiropus picturatus,* a comical little bottom-feeder marked in bright and unlikely rings of green and orange. *S. picturatus* seems far more difficult to find than the closely related mandarinfish, and fish identification books always illustrate it with photographs of aquarium specimens, a situation guaranteed to present a challenge to any good underwater photographer. (*S. picturatus* is very common in the aquarium trade, so the collectors in the Philippines, whence the specimens come, must have their own Secret Bay.)

Gilimanuk is the only bay off the narrow Bali Strait, which is subject to a semi-diurnal tidal stream that can reach a strength of seven knots. The seasons have a marked effect on the direction of this fierce flow. During the southeast monsoon, the current tends almost constantly south,

simply becoming weaker on a falling tide; during the northwest monsoon, the north-tending current is the strongest, although it can reverse and head south when the tide shifts. During the transition months the current direction reverses with the tides, and is only a bit more sane, generally staying below five-and-a-half knots.

This strong flow through the Bali Strait is what makes Gilimanuk Bay an interesting place. The bay becomes a kind of refugium, a catch tank, for all the larval fish and other plankton sweeping along between Bali and Java.

A MAKESHIFT CREW

Wally and I drove down to Gilimanuk Bay from the Menjangan area, a twenty-minute trip that leads across Bali's northwest peninsula and through the heart of the Bali Barat National Park. In the old days, when there was no place to stay near Menjangan, Wally would often pull over to the side of the road and sleep in his car here after a long day of div-

Garden eels are common around Bali, particularly at Menjangan and, as shown here, in the Tulamben area. They are very skittish, and withdraw into their burrows at the slightest excuse. The best way to approach them is slowly and steadily, keeping very low to the ground. (It helps even more if you don't breathe—they hate bubbles—but this, eventually, becomes impractical.) Ichthyologist Jack Randall researched these animals at Tulamben with James Tyler, who poured epoxy down the burrows to determine their shape and extent. As it turned out, they are not straight, but form sinuous curves.

ing. On these occasions, he would see birds of all kinds, including the rare wild chicken or green jungle fowl (*Gallus varius*), a beautiful and clever bird that makes its domesticated cousin look like the pea-brained fool that it is.

We picked up Wally's old friend Engkol, who was going to join us on our dive, and stopped at the park service office to get a permit to dive there (Gilimanuk Bay is formally part of the park).

Engkol works for the park service, and has the good health and humor of somebody who works outdoors and likes what he does. His name, a nickname, really, means an engine crank or wrench, and although nobody wanted to relate the circumstances to me, he has been stuck with it since he was a kid. Physically, at least, it suits him, and Engkol's build is as efficient and solid as a Crescent wrench. He also has a real commitment to, and understanding of, conservation work. (Wally simply calls it "heart.")

Wally and Engkol have been in a number of scrapes together, many of them having to do with people who were, to be polite, a little unclear about the purpose of a national park. When we visited his house, Engkol had about a hundred one-, two-, and three-year-old seedlings of a rare variety of sapodillo tree that still grows in a few scattered areas of the West Bali park. By distributing these for people to plant outside their homes, he hopes to increase the range of this almost extinct tree.

We reached the bay at the point just across the peninsula from the ferry landing, near an old Dutch-built lodge that the dive operator has partially converted for diving visitors. The shore here is dead quiet, and mudskippers hopped about on the fine sand. Without warning a kingfisher flew down and hovered for an instant, like a hummingbird, then snatched up one of the mud-skippers and flew off. We watched him repeat this move about three times. It was like picking food off a plate, and we felt sorry for the hapless fish. "They're young ones," Wally said. "The old ones know better, and wait until that bastard is gone before they come out."

The dive operator keeps a boat, but the best one available, we discovered, belongs to Pak Haji, who runs a modest pearl oyster collecting operation based here. Pak Haji and his crew know these waters intimately, and they are all very experienced divers. We negotiated a rate for the day and climbed aboard. Neither the captain nor the crew speaks any English, and the nine-meter traditional wooden boat has no tourist amenities. But the engine is strong, the crew knows their job, and overall the vessel suited our purposes just fine.

A BIT LARGE FOR PLANKTON

Rather than comb the shallows deep inside the bay, we decided to dive the channel that forms the literal and figurative mouth of the bay, and enter the bay the same way the plankton does. We anchored over the shallow reef flat north of the Gilimanuk peninsula, and dropped into the water at the very end of the flood tide. The current was ripping at more than three knots, and we fought our way across the reef flat and then down to the bottom of the sandy channel, not quite ten meters. There we gave up fighting, and let the current sweep us inside the bay.

The bottom here is fine volcanic sand, salt-and-pepper gray with some glittery specks of mica. The channel itself is barren of coral, but bommies and clumps of tough leather corals and *Porites* line either side. The bommies were swarming with damsels and cardinalfish, with some of the inshore species of angelfish and butterflies.

The sand bottom provided the

Map 1.4 Gilimanuk Bay 1:40K

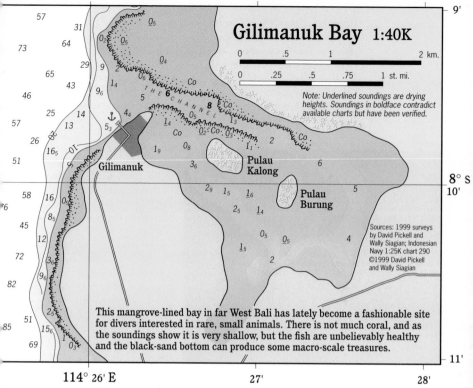

most interesting scenery. We were swept along over fields of long-spined diademnid urchins, their black spines alive with cardinalfish and dancing little clingfish, and at one point I brushed past a huge bed of the very toxic flower urchin *Toxoneustes pileolus*. This latter encounter was a bit unsettling, as they came up on me very suddenly while I was working close to the bottom. There had to be more than a hundred of them spaced out across the sand like mines. These urchins usually lug around bits of coral rubble and stones as a partial disguise, but in this setting all they could find were old mangrove leaves, sticks, and even bits of paper and plastic.

At one point we followed a huge school of the hinge-spined shrimpfish *Aeoliscus,* an odd seahorse relative that spends its life looking downward, prowling for small crustaceans. Juvenile plotosid cat-

fish, striped black and white, swirled and formed huge balls of hundreds of individuals.

The fish and invertebrates in this bay were the healthiest Wally and I have seen anywhere. The fish were fat to the point of bursting; the damsels looked like tennis balls, and even the cleaner wrasse were as thick as a Cuban cigar. The diademnid urchins had half-meter-long spines, and the toxic urchins were the size of pomelos. Even the shrimpfish, usually as two-dimensional as a shard of glass, were downright fat. And the colors of the fish just glowed. The explanation for this good health seems simple: they are all extremely well-fed by the strong tidal current that daily flushes the bay.

On the incoming tide, the water was crystal clear, with more than thirty meters horizontal visibility. Everywhere were bits of trash—

Rinso wrappers, plastic water bottles, and the like. Although the ferry terminal is nearby, I don't think its passengers are necessarily to blame for this. The current is so strong here that this plastic could probably have come from anywhere in the Java Sea. I became fascinated with how even a small piece of trash,

©BURT JONES/MAURINE SHIMLOCK *Kentrodoris rubescens*

These two nudibranchs are mating. Nudibranchs are hermaphrodites, and the exchange of gametes takes place through a kind of tubular organ on the animal's starboard side, near the bow (the end with the horn-like rhinophores).

combined with the strong current, could change the shape of the bottom. Investigating a crater almost a meter across, with an accompanying mound of the same size, I found that this large structure was created by a small, sand-filled plastic Aqua bottle no bigger than a beer can.

Toward the end of our dive, as the tide slowed, visibility dropped

dramatically. At this point we were inside the bay, just north of Kalong Island, and had reached the area where the bay water and strait water were mixing. The churned area looked like an underwater storm cloud, and when we hit it we were shocked by the sudden drop in temperature, which is the reverse of what you might expect. The water, already quite cold, dropped suddenly to 23°C. After a few minutes of this Engkol, wearing only a thin Lycra suit, surrendered and returned to the boat. Wally and I retreated to the center of the channel, where we could still bask in the relatively warm strait water.

Although it was May, over the previous week the west of Bali had been experiencing cold winds, enough that sitting outside along the coast at night, we wished we had brought sweaters, which is quite unusual. Perhaps these winds had cooled the shallow water of the bay, producing temperatures more typical of a deep ocean upwelling.

While warming up after our dive, we began a conversation with Pak Haji and his crew that distracted us for hours. On the way back we motored along behind the ferry terminal. We waved to the prostitutes, who were washing clothes and chatting during their afternoon time off, and they good-humoredly wagged their behinds at us.

NOT FOR EVERYONE

Gilimanuk Bay is not a dive for everyone. Nowhere will you find a sounding of even fifteen meters. There are no rich stands of coral. It is a specialty site for photographers and for divers who are looking for something different. One does not see species like shrimpfish just everywhere, and considering the conditions here, I do believe that with time one could find treasures like *Synchiropus picturatus* here. Some animals, while not rare, are

MIKE SEVERNS   Goby: Amblyeleotris sp.; Shrimp: Alpheus randalli

asier to photograph here, such as he shrimp goby *Stonogobiops,* which can be found in six meters at Gilimanuk (you can also find them t Tulamben, but not in less than eighteen meters).

If we had more time, in addition o the channel, we would have ried the inside reef edge where Pak Haji stores his live pearl shells, which is roughly halfway in a traight line between the tip of the peninsula and Kalong island. We would also have tried some diving or snorkeling along the mangrove edge, or in the silt-bottomed backbay areas. This is our taste, however. Yours might be different.

YOU DIDN'T HEAR IT FROM US

Another potential dive site exists here, although I am reluctant to even mention it. A ferry, with trucks aboard, went down just north of the signal light marking the edge of the shallow reef that forms the northern part of the bay's mouth, not far from where we started the dive de-

scribed above. The exact location of the wreck is marked on both the Indonesian and British Admiralty charts. Pak Haji and his crew have dived it, but I don't think anyone else has. According to them, the ship sits at about thirty meters, and is full of sharks and other large fish, including a giant grouper.

It sounds enticing, but I'm not sure how quick I would be to attempt this dive. Remember, the tidal current reaches seven knots in this strait. If I did try it, I would only go with Pak Haji and his crew (I'd bring along a couple extra sets of good equipment and tanks for them), and I would be very, very picky about the conditions—the right season, full slack tide, etc. A mistake here would be very costly. Consider this: from this site, a seven-knot current will take a drifting diver north around the point of Bali into no-man's land in less than forty-five minutes; heading south, it will do the same thing in an hour. Better stick to the bay, really.

This flag-tailed shrimp goby has not yet been named. Shrimp gobies live in association with several species of alpheid or snapping shrimp. The relationship is considered commensal, although at first the shrimp—which work continuously, clearing the shared burrow—seem to get the worst end of the deal. But the shrimp's eyesight is poor or non-existent, and the sharp-eyed gobies are excellent watchdogs. The shrimp tend to keep one antenna resting on the fish, so they can sense its every twitch.

Harlequin shrimp, though undeniably beautiful, have rather grisly feeding habits. They eat the arms of starfish, working from the tip to the central disk, thus keeping their dinner alive for as long as possible.

The wreck of the Liberty, a World War I–era cargo ship outfitted with cannon for World War II duty, lies in just ten to thirty meters of water, just off the beach at Tulamben. This might be the world's easiest wreck dive.

Since the Liberty wreck first brought divers here twenty years ago, the Tulamben diving area has outgrown the confines of the bay itself. The excellent sites here, some recently discovered, now extend almost all the way to Bali's eastern tip.

The Tulamben Area

WITH EACH OUTGOING WAVE, THE heavy cobbles of Tulamben's beach clack and rattle as they inexorably wear each other smooth. It is a pleasant and comforting sound, and even as I write this, sitting on the other side of the Pacific in Berkeley, California, I can hear it. What I see, if I squint a little bit, is the smooth blue surface of the Tulamben Bay, with, I think, a streak of current showing about three-quarters of a kilometer out. My view is framed by a scruffy *Plumeria* tree growing up through the floor of the Sunrise restaurant. A dripping wetsuit has been draped across the much-abused branches of this poor tree, and somebody's puffed-up B.C. is sitting on the concrete terrace nearby, looking like it is about to explode in the hot sun. What I smell is the incense of a freshly lit Dji Sam Soe clove cigarette, mixing with the perfume of frying onions

and garlic drifting out from the kitchen door. And what I taste, of course, is ice-cold Bintang beer.

Tulamben is now the most famous diving area in Bali, and attracts divers from all over the world. It is Tulamben Bay that provides the iconic images of Bali diving: the sweep of cobbled beach, with bright white, blue, and red *jukung*s pulled up beneath the trees under a hilltop temple; divers in neoprene boots wincing as they step gingerly across the stones, while smiling girls in torn flip-flops stride confidently on ahead with thirty kilos of tanks and gear balanced on their heads; the dramatic black sand bottom, mysterious, almost forlorn, that makes the colors of the fish glow like neon; and the great, broken-backed *Liberty,* now a castle of gorgonians, sponges, and black corals, so close to the shore that you could skip a stone to its stern.

It is Tulamben where Bali's diving community, both visitors and expatriate and local guides, is concentrated. The restaurant at the Sunrise or at the Paradise or at Mimpi—popularity and fashions change—is the island's informal divers clubhouse. Here is where you will hear news about conditions in the different parts of the island or

WALLY SIAGIAN Anomalops katoptron

Photoblepharon palpebratus

The flashlight fishes possess a biochemical light organ—the light is produced by symbiotic bacteria— that seems to function to attract plankton, and may also be used to confuse predators. Two species (in two genera) can be found at Tulamben. In the chamber deep on the seaward side of the wreck is Anomalops (photographed above) and on the drop-off, very deep, is Photoblepharon (line drawing). The two fish differ in the flashing mechanism used in their light organs: in Anomalops, the organ rotates on and off; in Photoblepharon, a flap of skin serves as a shutter.

exceptional events like the sighting of a whale shark or mola, gossip about love affairs within the guiding community (both budding and failing), or about diving operations (both budding and failing), and here is where you will most likely encounter celebrity underwater photographers and writers. This little village lives and breathes diving.

Diving started here in 1979, with the discovery of what a rich dive site the wreck of the *Liberty* had become. At first divers would visit only occasionally, and on day trips from the south. In the mid-eighties, as the site became more popular, the first resort opened, allowing divers to stay overnight. Today there are at least six diving operations here.

It quickly became apparent that there was more to Tulamben than just the wreck. This bay harbors an almost puzzlingly diverse underwater ecosystem (See "Why is Tulamben Rich?" pg. 91) and today divers can choose from among

more than a half-dozen excellent and distinctive sites.

THE FAMOUS BLACK SAND

For many divers, Tulamben's black sand bottom is a novelty. If you have never dived over this type of substrate, you must try it. Photographers in particular love the way it makes the colors of their subject snap, like matting a photograph in black board. (On the other hand, it can wreck havoc with light meters and your own exposure instincts— remember to compensate.) The black lava spurs of the wall, and the hulk of the *Liberty*, rising from a bed of coal-dark sand, provide unforgettable tableaux.

This said, not everybody finds the effect to their liking. It is quite different from the bright world of a normal limestone reef. Particularly if the visibility drops off, the dark bottom can create a gloominess that wears on a diver. I have felt myself, after a week of diving in the bay, that I was trapped in a kind of perpetual olive-drab world of late afternoon.

The water clarity here is good, but not great—there is usually too much water movement and plankton for exceptional visibility—and because the bottom offers no reflective assistance, you are better off diving when the sun is bright.

And on a nice, bright day, Tulamben is stunning. These reefs are so healthy that they offer rewards at any scale: from a distance, you see the huge school of big-eye jacks swirling across the wreck like a great silver storm cloud; closer, you see mops of black coral and bright blue sponges, peppered with anthias, butterflyfish, and little sharp-nosed puffers; closer yet you see big scorpionfish tucked in among the rusted decking, or fields of garden eels, dancing nervously in the shallows; still closer, you see the rare comet, its tail mimicking the face of a moray, or a prawn goby and its blind, shoveling partner, or the sudden, bright display of a flasher wrasse; and finally, with your mask against the bottom, you see the ghost pipefish hidden in the crinoid, the furry crab in among a tangle of brittlestars, and the tiny anglerfish, like a wad of pink chewing gum pressed against a rock.

Although sharks, molas, mantas, dolphins, tuna and other pelagics visit Tulamben, these are occasional and unpredictable events. It is the sheer richness of Tulamben that is always there, and this is what inspires people to dive here again and again. It is a wonderful place to learn about underwater life. You could come here with a good underwater field guide, and over the course of a week's diving, find most of the animals listed just by exploring the wreck, the patch reef in front of the resorts, and the wall.

BEYOND THE DROP-OFF

Until recently, "Tulamben" meant the sweep of bay from the wreck to the wall. Divers staying in Tulamben who wanted a change of pace would drive to Jemeluk, about forty minutes down the coast, to dive the bay there. Unfortunately, the coral bleaching brought on by the El Niño warming of 1998 hit Jemeluk very hard, and its shallow water corals, once among Bali's best, have been decimated (although recovery has started).

Because of the damage to Jemeluk, and the increasing popularity of Tulamben, Wally and I decided to explore the coast southeast of the wall, hoping to find new sites. What we learned, after traveling several kilometers down the coast by *jukung*, was that the best area was hiding right under our noses. It turned out that the stretch of reef beginning just around the corner from the Tulamben drop-off was remarkably healthy (see MAP 2.1, pp. 74–75). The finest site we located in

the time we had was Batu Kelebit, a beautiful set of coral-covered ridges leading down to ninety meters. This may be the very best site in the area to see big animals, and although it is barely a kilometer from the Drop-off, the bottom here is bright white sand.

We also took a boat from Jemeluk, heading east toward the

KAL MULLER

very tip of Bali island. Here we revisited the shipwreck and reef at Lipah Bay, a site Wally had not dived for several years, and found it to be in excellent condition.

I am quite sure these are not the only sites worth diving along this coast. The area between the wall and Kelebit, in particular, deserves further exploration. Why not get a *jukung* and try it out yourself?

The superstructure at the stern end of the Liberty lies just a few meters below the surface.

Map 2.1 Tulamben Area 1:7K

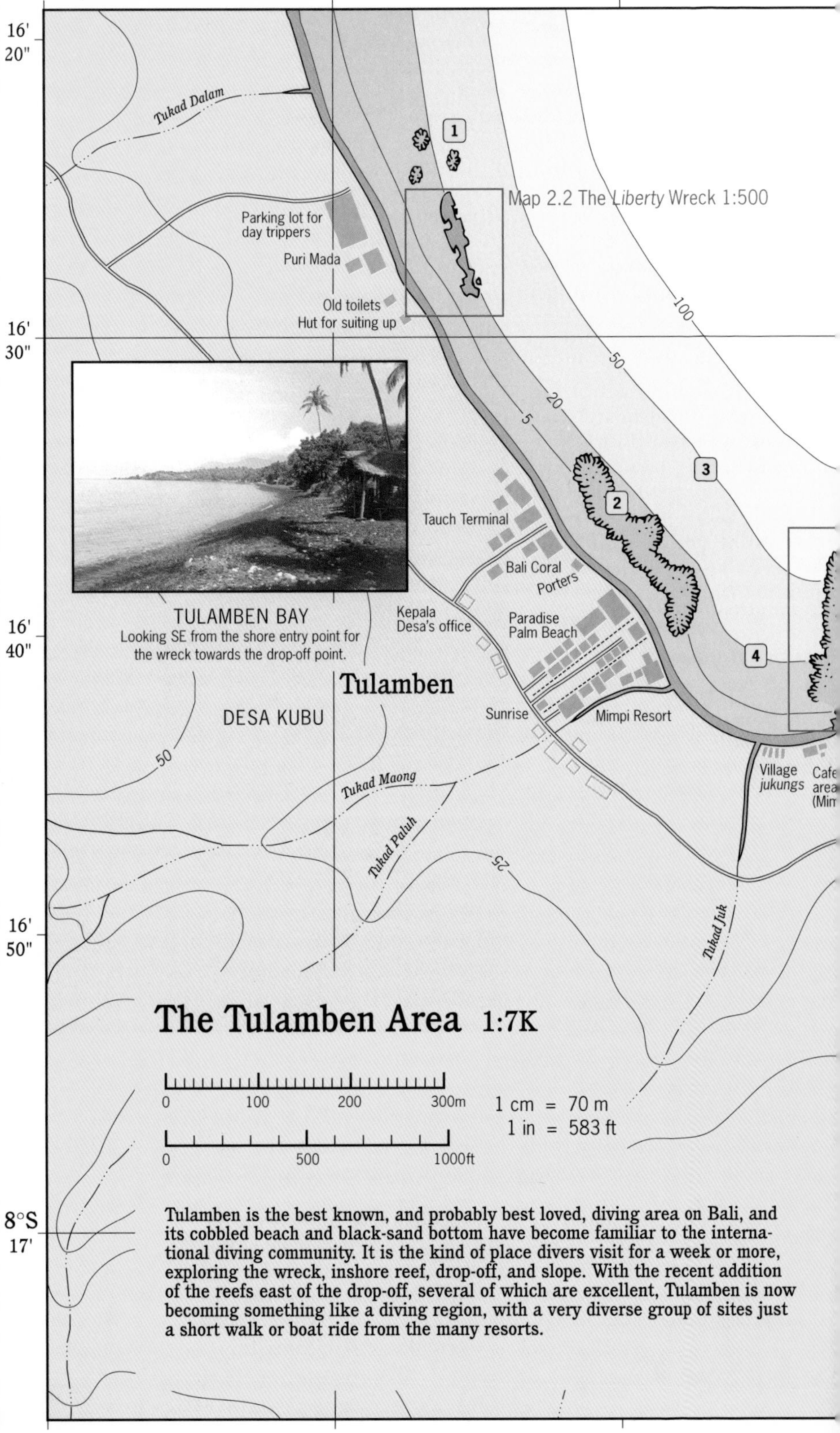

16'
20"

Tukad Dalam

1

Map 2.2 The *Liberty* Wreck 1:500

Parking lot for
day trippers

Puri Mada

Old toilets
Hut for suiting up

16'
30"

100

50

20

5

TULAMBEN BAY
Looking SE from the shore entry point for
the wreck towards the drop-off point.

Tauch Terminal

3

2

Bali Coral

Porters

Kepala
Desa's office

Paradise
Palm Beach

4

Tulamben

16'
40"

DESA KUBU

Sunrise

Mimpi Resort

Village
jukungs

Cafe
area
(Min

Tukad Maong

50

Tukad Paluh

25

Tukad Juk

16'
50"

The Tulamben Area 1:7K

0	100	200	300m	

1 cm = 70 m
1 in = 583 ft

0	500	1000ft	

8°S
17'

Tulamben is the best known, and probably best loved, diving area on Bali, and
its cobbled beach and black-sand bottom have become familiar to the international diving community. It is the kind of place divers visit for a week or more,
exploring the wreck, inshore reef, drop-off, and slope. With the recent addition
of the reefs east of the drop-off, several of which are excellent, Tulamben is now
becoming something like a diving region, with a very diverse group of sites just
a short walk or boat ride from the many resorts.

35' 20"   35' 30"   35' 40"

...EY

...f the bow of the wreck is a steep
...nd slope carved out by the current
...weeping around the wreck. The cover
... a patchy reef of sponges, small
...lumps of whip corals and black coral,
...nd small coral colonies. It is a surpris-
...ngly rich area, and worth exploring up
...ose for small commensals. The deep
...ea behind the wreck is similar, and
...so worth exploring. Seaward of the
...reck, in forty meters or more, is
...here mola-mola and other pelagic fish
...e sometimes seen.

...he Patch Reef (sometimes called "The
...aradise Reef") in front of the original
...esorts is quite young, only having
...eveloped over the last dozen years or
...o. It is not very big, but it is quite rich
...nd is shallow enough to snorkel over.
...his reef makes a perfect, and very
...asy, night dive.

...ehind the Patch Reef is a deep sand
...ope, with small clumps of coral creat-
...g islands of life. There are some spe-
...al fish in the deep here, including
...teene's dottyback (fifty-five meters),
...nd interesting soft corals and sea
...ens. Be careful, however, as these are
...erious depths, and it is not uncommon
... face a downcurrent here.

ap 2.3
lamben Drop-off 1:800

4. This site is usually called "The River,"
because the dry river mouth near the
temple is where you set up your gear.
Underwater, it is basically a sandy bowl
carved out by the rainy season action
of the two intermittant rivers here. The
bottom consists of shifting ridges of
fine sand, covered with crinoids, black
coral bushes, sea pens, and other small
tufts of life. This site is always full of
surprises—mimic octopus, ghost
pipefish, harlequin shrimp—and is one
of our favorites.

5. The little bay just past the Drop-off is
muddy and uninteresting, but the reef
further east is healthy. A big gorgonian
sits on the outer point of a coral-covered promontory, and the bay east of
here is covered in a shallow turf of
healthy staghorn coral. The tiny pocket
beach formed by this bay has salt-and-
pepper sand.

6. This reef is also quite interesting. It is
not so rich in coral, but the structure is
good—the lava spurs here have broken
up into jagged pillars of black rock. If
you are ambitious, you can reach this
and the following site by swimming from
the Drop-off.

7. Like site #6, of which this reef is really
still a part, the underwater scenery
here, because of its rocky emptiness,
reminds me of Hawai'i. This is a very
steep, narrow canyon of white sand,
flanked by sharp spurs of black lava
rock. Although not rich in coral cover,
this site is stark and mysterious, a
mood enhanced when a couple of
sharks appear in the depths (not an
uncommon occurrence here).

8. This is a very rich area, which unfortunately we were not able to explore to
the extent we would have liked before
this edition came due. In 1999, in any
case, the gorgonians here seemed bigger, healthier, and more diverse than at
any other area along this stretch, which
considering the size and condition of
the sea fans at the Drop-off and at Batu
Kelebit, is saying quite a bit. This is a
beautiful stretch of reef, and highly recommended. Like Batu Kelebit, the bottom is white sand. If you are good with
your air and do not mind a bit of a
swim, you can reach this area from
Kelebit, but it is really too far to reach
by swimming from the Drop-off.

9. Just northwest of Batu Kelebit, the reef
is rough and relatively uninteresting. If
you want to reach the good area, be
patient. When you see a large, lone
Porites coral head you can begin to
cheer up, and when you begin to get
into an area of bommies, you are in the
good reef.

10. This area, which we explored quickly, is
rough and rubbly, and the whole stretch
here seems not worth diving.

11. This is "Emerald Bay," or at least that is
what the resort operator on the hill here
calls it. Some maps call this Cape
Muntig, so if the bay has a name it is
probably Teluk Muntig. The resort specializes in training Japanese divers, and
to that end has built a special dock,
marked off swimming areas with floats,
and even sunk its own wreck (a Toyota).
It is a bit silly, really, and in any case
the reef here is small and rough, and
not as rich as the sites listed above.

Map 2.4 Batu Kelebit 1:800

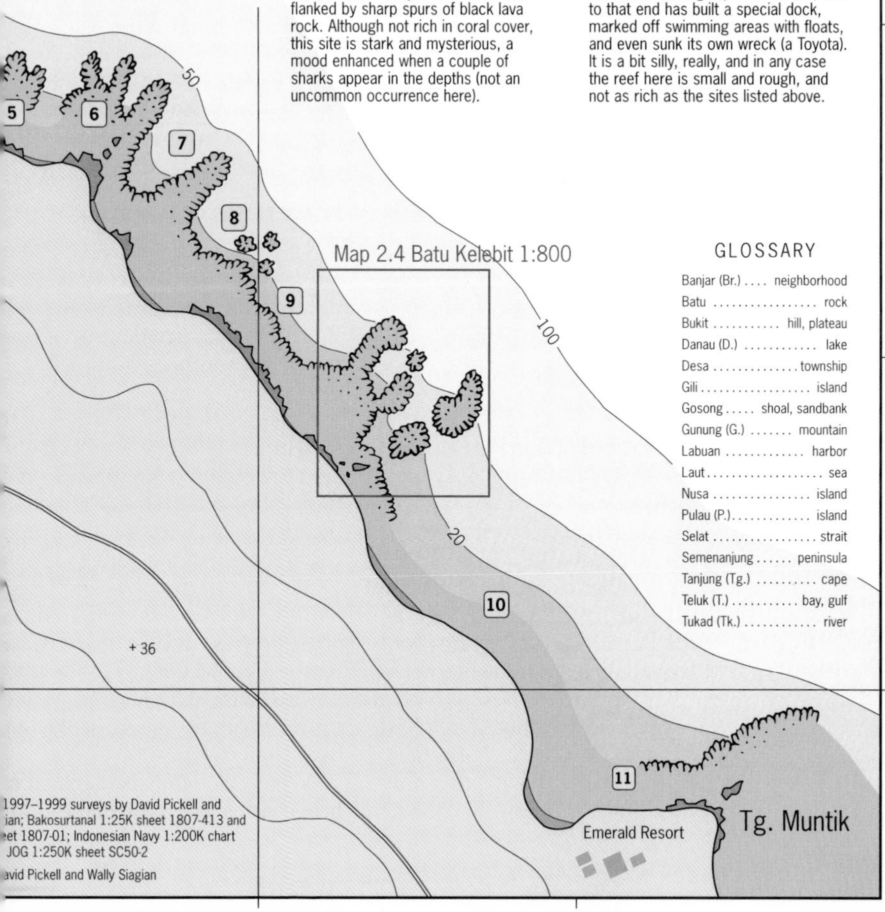

GLOSSARY

Banjar (Br.) .... neighborhood
Batu .... rock
Bukit .... hill, plateau
Danau (D.) .... lake
Desa .... township
Gili .... island
Gosong ..... shoal, sandbank
Gunung (G.) .... mountain
Labuan .... harbor
Laut................... sea
Nusa .... island
Pulau (P.)............ island
Selat .... strait
Semenanjung ...... peninsula
Tanjung (Tg.) .... cape
Teluk (T.) .... bay, gulf
Tukad (Tk.) .... river

+ 36

1997–1999 surveys by David Pickell and
...ian; Bakosurtanal 1:25K sheet 1807-413 and
...eet 1807-01; Indonesian Navy 1:200K chart
...JOG 1:250K sheet SC50-2

...avid Pickell and Wally Siagian

Emerald Resort

Tg. Muntik

Tulamben Bay

THE WATER WAS STRANGELY WARM, and glowed dimly under a full moon. With our flashlights off, our fins threw off spirals of blue phosphorescence. The great hulk of the wreck soon loomed in the near dark, and we rounded the stern and glided down into the deep. Here Wally played his light about some, to keep us from crashing into the wrecked booms and broken decking, and then we came to rest on the sand. We kneeled on the soft bottom, and peered through a crack into the belly of the broken vessel. Wally cut the light. Twenty-five

With a 120-meter shipwreck at one end, a dramatic drop-off reef at the other, and rich sand slopes and a bank reef in between, this bay can keep a diver happy for weeks.

meters down and in the shadow of the wreck, we saw only inky black. Then, so suddenly I did not know if I had really seen it, a short dash of light. Then another. Then three or four together. Soon, a whole school of flashlight fish darted back and forth before our eyes, writing scribbles of light against the blackness.

This dive, maybe seven years ago now, was the first time I saw flashlight fish. It was at Tulamben. I could also describe the first time I saw a ghost pipefish. That would

also have been at Tulamben. Or the first time I saw a harlequin shrimp, or a comet, or a tiger garden eel, or a skeleton shrimp, or the first time I found myself in the middle of a school of thousands of jacks, or the first time I saw coral spawn, or the first time I ever encountered any of a hundred interesting animals or behaviors. All of these were while diving Tulamben.

It is true that I have dived many times at Tulamben. It is also true (and certainly more salient) that almost all of these dives have been with Wally. But it is the place itself that made these experiences possible. If you dive here for a while, you can almost believe that sooner or later, just about every creature in the sea is going to show up.

THE SEASON OF EAST WINDS

In 1999, a La Niña year, it was not until the very end of May that the east wind started blowing steadily in Bali, signaling the official start of the southeast monsoon (the dry season). I was in Tulamben at the time, and was finding it very hard to get to sleep. All across the island the children had brought out their kites, and although the temperature was about the same, you could sense that something was different. Down by the dry rivermouth, dragonflies gathered in great swarms. And—this being the reason I could not sleep—the cats yowled all night long, as if the wind brought with it some kind of feline Spanish fly beetle.

What this wind also seemed to bring with it was some of the clear-

KE SEVERNS

st water we have ever seen at Tulamben. Horizontal visibility off the wreck reached something like forty meters, and even from the shore the water was a deep, pure blue. Although Wally and I took this opportunity to work some sites to the east, in our absence molas were seen regularly off the wreck and the wall for a week-long period.

The northeast coast of Bali is, in general, unprotected, and the one-thousand meter line lies just offshore. From Tulamben, you hit a sounding of 875 meters just two kilometers away. This is part of what makes the diving so good here, but it also insures that this coast is quite vulnerable to wind and waves. The northwest monsoon (the wet season), which lasts from December to about April, brings squalls and can really churn up the Bali Sea. I have been at Tulamben on a New Year's Day, and the waves pounding the beach, if they were not breaking so close together, would have been surfable. Nobody was thinking about

diving. (Well, actually two people were. I can report that visibility at the surface over the river was approximately three centimeters, but things cleared up by ten meters, and at twenty meters depth the visibility was maybe ten or fifteen meters. It was very strange diving under these conditions, like swimming under a cloud, but interesting.) Although late December through March is a bad time to plan a trip here, conditions usually improve in late March and April, as the west winds die down.

Good conditions usually come to Tulamben with the first part of the southeast monsoon, May through June, and last into July. In August and into September, during the height of the southeast monsoon, wind and high waves can pound this coast, making diving difficult. In September, as the southeast monsoon calms down, conditions improve again. In fact, the very best time to dive here is during October and November, the interim

A view from the hill above the temple at the southeast end of Tulamben Bay. The radio towers—telephone lines did not reach this village until mid-1999—mark the location of the resorts. It is rare that the top of Mount Agung is visible.

period before the northwest monsoon begins.

Current is not generally a problem. Tulamben is on the Lombok Strait side of the current break in North Bali (the actual break point is Tanjung Gulah—west of there you are essentially in Bali Strait water) but it is outside the narrows, and the flow is more predictable and less

©BURT JONES/MAURINE SHIMLOCK   Micromelo undata

The bubble shells, unlike other opisthobranchs (sea slugs), retain an adipose shell. Micromelo is a widespread, shallow water species that feeds on poisonous worms, and then incorporates their toxins into its own tissues as a protection against predators. Tulamben's black sand makes this beautiful animal glow with color.

fierce here than it is at the East Coast sites or at Nusa Penida. The typical current during the good diving season flows northwest, parallel to the coast here. During the southwest monsoon, the current flow through the Lombok Strait tends southward, so the current affecting Tulamben should really be considered an eddy, albeit on a large scale. In any case, a northwest tending flow is what is felt here, and it usually causes few problems. In general—and this is true everywhere, of course—the calmest conditions occur at slack tide.

A VERY POPULAR SITE

Wally and I were conducting the final fieldwork for this book in May and June of 1999, in the midst of what was feared to be a fractious election campaign (Indonesia's first democratic election in three decades). Actually, things were remarkably calm, but since foreign governments had issued travel warnings, tourists of all nationalities

stayed away from Indonesia in droves. Restaurants in Jakarta locked their doors nervously at eight o'clock (which is as inconceivable as a New York restaurant doing the same) and Indonesians with means decided that it was a good time to vacation overseas.

Despite this, Tulamben seemed still to be bustling. Groups of Japanese divers took their courses up near the wreck, and the more-or-less usual contingent of Germans, Australians, and Japanese (and the odd Italian, French, British, or American) suited up and hit the reefs. I'm sure occupancy was below expectations for this time of year, but even in such adverse conditions it was clear that the popularity of this place has grown dramatically in the seven years since I have been visiting.

Wally first dove Tulamben in 1979, and at that time there were no diving facilities at all. In 1986 the Dive Paradise, Tulamben's first operation, went up. Today the Paradise is squeezed in among a handful of competitors. A diver can now choose accommodations ranging from an air-conditioned suite with a private garden and fancy European shower knobs to a spartan little concrete-block room where the only bourgeois distractions are a plastic fan, a trickle of cold water, and a stale-smelling rectangle of cloth on the bed.

Actually, development of tourist facilities here was hampered for many years by the people of Tulamben village itself. Not that they did not want divers or dive businesses here. The successful and well-run porter collective (see "The Diving Helper Club," pg. 81), and the village's vigilance in keeping net and line fishermen, live fish collectors, and other destructive itinerants out of this bay prove otherwise. The problem is that the people of Tulamben are serious about their pol tics. The village has been on the electricity grid for only three years, and telephone lines were installed in June 1999, just a few days before the election. The lack of these government-controlled services was a form of punishment, because throughout the Suharto era Tulamben repeatedly and resolutely voted against the government party. (As it turned out, the largest plurality of this diverse nation agreed with the people of Tulamben, and P.D.I. Per-juangan won the biggest vote total.)

THE DIVING AREAS

There seems to be a pattern to a new diver's discovery of Tulamben. First, of course, the diver encounters the charms of the *Liberty* wreck, and falls in love. He or she might dive the drop-off a time or two, but usually finds it underwhelming in comparison. After a while, the love affair with the wreck winds down, and the diver begins choosing the drop-off more and more often. By paying more attention, the diver begins to realize just how special this wall is, and becomes a drop-off partisan.

After a very long time diving the wreck, the drop-off, and the shallow inshore reef, the diver "graduates" (as the most senior dive operator in the area put it) to the sand slope in front of the river. This, on its face the most unlikely dive site in the area (a sandy bowl with no hard coral at all), is almost always the favorite area of divers who have been coming here year after year, particularly underwater photographers and biologists. In deference to this curriculum, as it were, I will take up the sites in this order.

The Liberty Wreck

The first experience most people have at Tulamben is limping out into the shallows at the north end of the bay, desperately trying to look competent as they don their fins and get their B.C.'s adjusted. Usually

they fail, instead banging their knees and tanks as they come to grips with those awkward, rounded rocks and cobbles, as well as their own jet-lag. As soon as they get underwater and head outward, however, all of this ceases to matter. The stones become sand at five meters, and even before this happens, the diver is surrounded by goatfish,

KAL MULLER Solenostomus paradoxus in Antipathes sp. Tulamben sand slope

brightly patterned wrasse, and dozens of electric blue damselfish, so bold and demanding that they bump right up against his or her face plate.

It is at this moment, perhaps, that the magic of Tulamben's black sand is strongest: it makes you see one of the most common reef fish in the Indo-Pacific, the blue damsel, as something of almost ethereal beau-

The ornate ghost pipefish can be found hiding in crinoids, zooanthid colonies, or (as here) black coral bushes. These interesting fish are seasonally quite common at Tulamben.

ty. The difference is so striking that the first time I saw these fat little specimens I made a mental note to check and see if they were not a different species.

One of the nicest things about the wreck, and the area around it, is how tame the fish are here. From the moment you put your fins on, the wrasse and goatfish swarm around, looking for treasures kicked up by your fins. If you feel generous, overturn a rock and they will immediately snap up any worm, small crab, or brittle star that is thus exposed. Do not overdo it, however. Just have a look at how fat they are and you will realize they get enough to eat. Actually, this can be a great irritation to a photographer trying to get a picture of, say, a small, beautifully marked shrimp. As soon as he or she pushes away the rocks to get the lens in position, the subject has vanished—usually into the belly of the clever—some would say "criminal"—wrasse *Thalassoma lunare*.

Even the big fish are tame, particularly up around the shallow parts of the wreckage, especially the rudderfish (*Kyphosus*) and surgeonfish. It can be downright startling when a big unicornfish suddenly whirls from out of your blind spot and passes two centimeters in front of your mask.

And then, of course, there is the wreck itself: one hundred and twenty meters of twisted steel, lying in shallow water in some of the most fertile waters in the entire Indo-Pacific. What is the best thing about this site? The numbers of healthy, near tame fish, including schools of sweetlips, batfish, unicornfish, fusiliers, and a huge, swirling, ball of big-eye jacks? The sheer variety of fish species, approaching three hundred according to some surveys, including some very rare specimens? The good condition of the wreck itself, including the bow gun, boilers, and other recognizable structures? The rich invertebrate life here, which includes unusual nudibranchs, shells, crabs, and other small wonders? The ease of the dive, and generally calm conditions? I guess the answer to this depends on a diver's own interests, but it really has to be: "All of the above." Perhaps the highest compliment Wally and I can pay to this site is that despite the many times I have dived this wreck, and the thousands of times Wally has dived it, every time we dive here we find something new and interesting.

Wally and I have prepared an annotated map of the wreck (see MAP 2.2, pp. 84–85) to guide you to some of our favorite places and residents, but the best advice might be just to get up there and dive on it for a few days and discover your own favorites.

There is no real trick to diving the wreck. The current can pick up a bit, particularly later in the afternoon, which can stir up the bottom and spoil the visibility. It almost always blows northwest. If you find yourself in these conditions, do not go swimming out in the midwater behind the wreck, where the current is strong. Get inside or close to the structure, which will protect you from the current. The visibility will be better here as well, and you can entertain yourself looking at smaller animals living in the encrusting growth.

If the conditions are calm, and particularly if the moon is full, you should try a night dive here. It is truly an eerie and memorable experience, and there are not too many wrecks in the world that you can safely dive at night.

A FATEFUL HISTORY

Early in the morning of January 11, 1942, the *Liberty* was motoring across the Lombok Strait as part of a convoy of ships bringing war matériel from Australia to aid the Al

THE DIVING HELPER CLUB
Are You Man Enough to Let a Girl Carry Your Tank?

A BIG PART OF THE CONVENIENCE OF DIVING TULAMBEN comes from the Diving Helper Club, a collective organized by the village of Tulamben to haul divers' equipment to the wreck, the Drop-off, or wherever else on this kilometer-long stretch of beach you want to dive. The porters are so well organized that even if you carry your own gear (something only a few testosterone-charged Europeans seem to want to do), you have to pay anyway. The occasional cheap fool grumbles about this, but the fee is very reasonable, the money goes directly to the village, and negotiating those loose cobbles is a frustration best left to a professional.

Pak Kari Yasa founded the collective in 1978, and today there are thirty members, with twenty on call every day. In true democratic fashion they pool their income and split it equally at the end of each day, with twenty percent going to the club. In 1993, the collective used its savings to buy a beautiful set of gamelan instruments, giving the village an additional source of both recreation and income.

Wally and I always opt for the full "automatic program," giving our porters a nice tip to wash our gear and to look after our sunglasses and cigarettes while we're under. Don't forget: you are on vacation. And that smiling girl with your tank on her head is quite happy to do her job.

1. Nengah Tulamben 2. Nyoman Tirta 3. Wayan Selamat 4. Ketut Susilawati 5. Nyoman Dana 6. Ketut Darma 7. Gede Tunas 8. Wayan Cocong 9. Nengah Toya 10. Nengah Rana 11. Nengah Remsun 12. Ketut Cara 13. Luh Kadek 14. Luh Arsini 15. Nyoman Kartini 16. Ketut Suriyati 17. Luh Suartini 18. Nengah Santi Dewi 19. Luh Cepe 20. Nyoman Kecil 21. Nyoman Suardana 22. Ketut Sumiati 23. Komang Suartini 24. Nengah Cepe 25. Luh Tini 26. Ayu Suartini 27. Dasning Sih 28. Nyoman Intaran

lied effort in the Philippines. According to some sources, the *Liberty*, a freighter conscripted into wartime service, was carrying rubber and railroad parts. At 4:15 a.m., the ship took a torpedo from the Japanese submarine I-166. Although crippled by the blow, the *Liberty* did not sink. Two destroyers that had been chaperoning the convoy—the U.S. *Paul Jones* and the Dutch *Van Ghent*—made fast to the *Liberty* and began towing the ship toward Singaraja, where it was hoped she could be repaired. The damaged ship took on too much water, however, and was beached at Tulamben. (A postscript: the sub that torpedoed the *Liberty* was itself sunk off Penang, Malaysia, on July 17, 1944 by the British submarine *Telemachus*.)

According to Merchant Marine records, there were no casualties among the *Liberty's* crew, but their was no time to recover the cargo before the Japanese reached Bali.

The *Liberty* was built as a freighter by the Federal Shipbuilding Company in Kearny, New Jersey. She was 395 feet (120 meters) long, 55 feet (17 meters) in beam, drafted 24 feet (7.3 meters), and grossed 6,211 tons. The ship was powered by a 2,500 horsepower steam turbine engine. For World War II service, the *Liberty* was outfitted with bow and stern guns.

Dive guides and guidebooks often refer to this ship as a Liberty class ship, which is incorrect. The so-called Liberty ships, all of which were named after people, were built later and were bigger: 441 feet (134 meters) long and grossing approximately 10,000 tons.

MOUNT AGUNG AWAKES

The *Liberty* sat grounded in the shallows of Tulamben Bay for more than two decades, during which time her cargo, and valuable items like her propeller, were salvaged.

Then, in 1963, Bali's highest and most holy mountain, Gunung Agung, erupted, creating powerful earthquakes that rolled the ship into deeper water and broke her at the bow and stern.

The eruption of Agung was one of the greatest tragedies of Bali's recent history. On March 17, 1963, the volcano exploded, showering whole villages with ash and sending great rivers of lava down across eastern Bali. At least two thousand people are thought to have died, and one hundred thousand made homeless. The roads in East Bali were blocked for weeks, making it hard to get help in. Also, the political atmosphere in Indonesia was tense at this time, and the government did not broadcast the scale of the tragedy, making international aid slow to arrive.

The eruption actually began in February, when Agung became active for the first time in three centuries, spewing forth smoke and ash. Just downslope of the crater, at Besakih, Bali's holiest temple, priests were preparing for Eka Dasa Rudra, a very important ceremony in the Balinese calendar that takes place just once every hundred years. Some priests had disputed the timing of this event, and the rumbling volcano gave their position a lot of popular support. However, since President Sukarno was expected to attend, as was as an international group of travel agents, preparations went ahead.

On March 8th the ceremony began. Agung was now in the throes of what could only be called a full-blown eruption, shooting hot mud and rocks into the air, and raining ash down on the island. The travel agents showed up for the ceremony (Sukarno did not) but then left as quickly as they could. A few days later, Agung's vent plugged, and blew, unleashing earthquakes, lava, and destruction.

AGORAPHOBIA

The wreck is the only dive site in Bali that is so popular it can actually become crowded. One day I loaded a camera with high-speed black-and-white film and swam out to the open water past the wreck to get some rough pictures to help with the rendering of our map. It was a nice sunny day, and the water was quite clear. It was at this moment, hanging in fifteen or twenty meters and with the backside of about the rear third of the wreck in view, that I realized how popular this dive was—from this vantage point, the only pictures I was going to get would be of bubbles. No matter what I did, I always had at least ten divers in my frame (and those great streams of bubbles blocking my view of the wreck itself).

A few years back, you could beat the rush by staying at Tulamben and diving the wreck in the morning. Since most people were driving up from the south, you had at least a three-hour head start on the crowds. Now, however, since many more people stay at Tulamben itself, it is harder and harder to find some solitude at the area's premier site. If you dive in the late afternoon you are usually alone, but the conditions are not as good then either. The light is fading, and the current often picks up. Better just to expect to see a few people there, and dive when conditions are best.

Once, the morning after I arrived in Bali, Wally rushed me out to the wreck to show me a special commensal crab he had found the day before. We hit the water and made a bee-line right for it. It wasn't there. In fact, the black coral spiral it was living on wasn't there either. All we could find was a little broken spot in the coral cover where somebody's fin smacked against it. At that moment, in fact, the little beast was probably riding his broken twig of

antipatharian toward Lombok. This was probably an accidental event, but it was still irritating (and our friend *Xenocarcinus tuberculatus* was probably even more angry than us).

This was not the first time Wally has taken me to see an animal that was not there. The time before it

MIKE SEVERNS   Macolor macularis; Caranx sexfasciatus

was to see a special *Solenostomus*, a favorite genus of mine. In this case, Wally himself was to blame. His mistake? He mentioned the fish and its location to a photographer.

A pair of midnight snappers at the Tulamben wreck.

BUT WORTH A THOUSAND CRINOIDS?

In this instance, one photographer's persistent and insensitive attentions scared off a fish. But it can

Map 2.2 The *Liberty* Wreck 1:500

The *Liberty* was a cargo ship, hastily armed with a bow and stern gun for World War II service, that was disabled by a Japanese torpedo in the Lombok Strait early in the morning of January 11, 1942. She limped towards Buleleng (Singaraja) under tow, but made it only as far as Tulamben, where the vessel was beached to keep it from sinking. It was the *Liberty* off the beach and finally sunk her. When she motored away from the Kearny, New Jersey dock in 1918—powered by a then-novel steam turbine engine—the ship was 395 feet long (120 meters) and grossed 6,211 tons. Although writers and dive guides continue to traffic in this misinformation, the *Liberty* was not a ship of the Liberty *class*, all of which were built later and were powered by more primitive piston engines.

This wreck offers a rather rare combination in a dive site: easy conditions and great richness. Lying less than forty meters offshore in generally calm waters, this may be the world's safest large wreck to dive. It is also very rich, particularly in the kinds of rare animals that have made the Tulamben area so famous. The number of divers visiting the *Liberty* is beginning to show, as errant fins and clumsy photographers erode the finer encrusting life, but it is still a very rewarding place to dive.

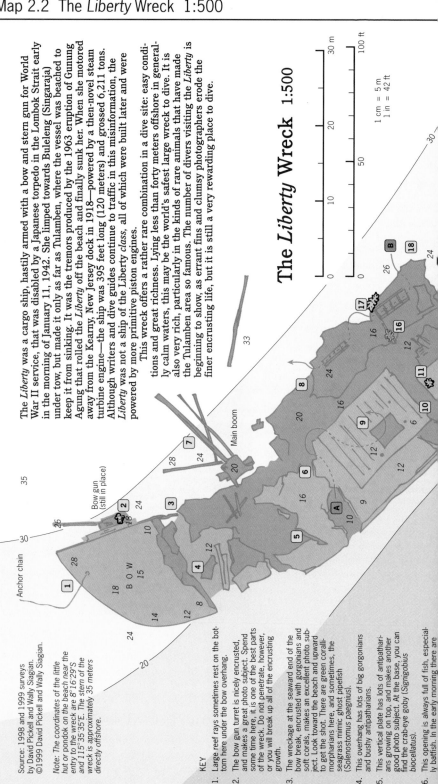

The *Liberty* Wreck 1:500

1 cm = 5 m
1 in = 42 ft

Source: 1998 and 1999 surveys
by David Pickell and Wally Siagian.
©1999 David Pickell and Wally Siagian.

Note: The coordinates of the little hut or pondok on the beach near the entry to the wreck are 8°16'29"S and 115°35'35"E. The stern of the wreck is approximately 35 meters directly offshore.

KEY

1. Large reef rays sometimes rest on the bottom here under the bow overhang.

2. The bow gun turret is nicely encrusted, and makes a great photo subject. Spend some time here, it is one of the best parts of the wreck. Do not penetrate, however, or you will break up all of the encrusting growth.

3. The wreckage at the seaward end of the bow break, encrusted with gorgonians and soft corals, makes an excellent photo subject. Look toward the beach and upward to get the shot. There are green corallimorpharians here, and sometimes, the seagrass mimic ghost pipefish (*Solenostomus paegnius*).

4. This overhang has lots of big gorgonians and bushy antipatharians.

5. This vertical plate has lots of antipatharians growing on top, and makes another good photo subject. At the base, you can find the crab-eye goby (*Signigobius biocellatus*).

6. This opening is always full of fish, especially batfish. In the early morning there are

of flashlight fish (*Anomalops katoptron*). On a night dive, turn off your lights to see them.

9. The view from underneath here is great, with the light coming in through the old busted-out decking. It is always protected from the current, and the fish gather here. Antipatharians grow here on the posts, and some are wrapped by colonies of *Nemanthus* anemones.

10. The wall here, towards the bow, is often covered with pink patches of Sergeant Major eggs, especially near full moon. Also, at about eight meters, there is an entertaining pair of furry red "orangutan crabs" (*Achaeus*) living on a bubble coral (*Physogyra*).

11. This patch of fire coral serves as a cleaning station. Lots of fish, including fusiliers, snappers, and groupers, stop here to be cleaned by the wrasse. A very beautiful nudibranch (*Nembrotha kubaryana*) lives among the tunicates here.

12. If you look carefully, you can find a commensal pygmy helmet shell living on the snowflake coral (*Carijoa*) here.

13. The shelly rubble and sea urchin spines on the sand under this plate marks it as a dining area for the Titan triggerfish.

14. A group of sweetlips always line up underneath and in the lee of this boom, which lies just off the sand. Together with a gorgonian, which is growing upside down, they make a nice photo composition.

15. This old post is covered with soft coral. It is a good place to find decorator crabs and the *Dendronephthya* commensal crab (*Hoplophrys oatesii*).

16. The top edge of this vertical plate is covered with life: a large table coral, tunicates, soft corals, and snowflake coral.

17. This is another place to find the flashlight fish. Kneel on the sand bottom (at twenty-five meters), turn off your light, and wait a few minutes. The fish will come to you. It is a little deep, but it is easier to see them here than at location #8.

18. In a patch of coral rubble off the wreck here, there is a harem of what look like square-spot anthias (*Pseudanthias pleuro-taenia*) led by a single male two-spot anthias (*P. bimaculatus*). The fish in this school are thought to be hybrids between the two species.

19. The rubbly sand bottom here is a good place to find jawfish (*Opistognathus sp.*).

20. The sand bottom here is a good place to find blue-spotted stingrays (*Dasyatus kuhlii*).

21. The small overhang here, just above the sand bottom, is a wrasse cleaning station. This is also a good spot to look for pipefish.

22. On the ledge here is a glowing red anemone (*Entacmaea quadricolor*) with a single clownfish (*Premnas*). The anemone has been here for five years, and Wally has watched it grow from the size of a coin. (It is now as big as a small plate). As of 1999, no mate has stumbled by for the anemonefish, and he is still a batchelor.

23. The wall here is covered with tunicates and orange cup corals. You can find *Nembrotha* nudibranchs here, as well as the snail *Epitonium billeeanum*, which blends in with, and eats, the orange *Tubastraea*.

24. The area of broken decking here is very rich with small gorgonians, sponges, ascidians, and other encrusting life. With the nice structure, good life, and shallow water, this makes a good setting for photography.

25. The barrel sponge here always has Wally's galatheid crab on it (*Laurea siagiani*).

26. On the turret here is a cleaning station. Wally has trained these *Lysmata amboensis* to clean his teeth. If you try this trick, be patient. Also, do not let your chin touch the ledge, as there is a very large carpet anemone (*Stichodactyla*) here, and you will regret any contact with this animal.

27. The wall and overhang here is very rich, with big soft corals and black coral bushes full of winged oysters. The saw-toothed *Lopha* oysters grow here as well, and when we last looked it was covered with young blue tube sponges. This is a good area to find scorpionfish. Also, there are now (1999) a group of four baby crocodile fish living under the plate on the sand. Sweep under it gently with your hand to bring them out.

28. The rock pile here, erected as a marker for divers, is a good place to find sand divers (*Trichonotus*). There is also an old pair of stonefish who live here. They are quite placid, but please don't bother them too much, or they will find somewhere else to live. Also, of course, do not put your hands on the rocks without looking first.

THE SWIM-THROUGHS

A. There is nice light through the opening here, and the chamber is tall, maybe twelve meters, so there is plenty of space. Lots of hanging soft corals and fish, at modest depths.

B. Remember to look up if you do this one. The scene makes a nice composition for a wide-angle lens. The first section, in particular, is very nice. Enter from the backside of the wreck, not the narrow, coral- and hydroid-encrusted opening facing astern. (This latter, as long as nobody breaks it up, is your photo subject.)

C. It is best not to attempt this swim-through. The deck plates are cracking badly, and this is now a risky penetration. Especially if it is choppy, you can see the metal moving around.

Booms

Stern gun

STERN

Rudder

Wooden planks

Boom

Garden eels

Garden eels

CAUTION: SEE NOTE

©BURT JONES/MAURINE SHIMLOCK   *Pseudochromis steenei*

Steene's dottyback was discovered at Tulamben, living on a bommie on a deep sand slope. At first it was thought to be a color variant of Moore's dottyback from the Philippines, but the fish was eventually determined to be distinct, and named for Australian photographer Roger Steene in 1993.

P. steenei has the facial aspect and personality of a junkyard dog, and divers are lucky it only grows to about twelve centimeters. These dottybacks—a family related to the groupers—live in pairs, and always seem to be near crinoids, as here. Only the male has an orange face; the female is brown with a bright yellow tail. Her personality is no sweeter than her partner's, however.

be far worse. Photographers, in fact, are a measurable source of reef erosion. Hot on the trail of their subject, they lose track of their body position, crunching coral with their knees and elbows, and excavating small gorgonians with their fins. Even without their cameras, you can always tell a photographer when they come back on shore: they are the ones wearing all the oddly placed crinoid corsages.

This clumsiness can sometimes approach cruelty. A French photographer, the last time I was in Tulamben, darted around the wreck, poking the framing wires of his viewfinder Nikonos into sea anemones, delicate sponges, and other fragile and beautiful creatures, with a technique reminiscent of a mentally disturbed surgeon. His horrible probing produced gusts of milky protoplasm and torn coral polyps, nauseating everyone who happened to dive with him. Although his attitude and dinner table claims suggested he was a famous photographer, his methods

(and equipment) proved otherwise. You obviously have a backscatter problem when torn bits of your subject are floating around in the water.

The damage from each instance of photographic or buoyancy control clumsiness is small, but the net result is that the wreck is definitely looking a bit worn, with a patina like that of an old wooden chair—or a car in which three brothers and a sister have learned to drive. "In the old days, I remember eleven big table corals on the wreck," Wally said. "Table, table, table, table, table. And I remember when every one of them came down." Even the superstructure is continuing to crumble—though perhaps less from wear and tear than simply age.

The *Liberty* is still a wonderful place to dive, and it is still very much alive, as its rapid recovery from the El Niño bleaching of 1998 showed. But with so many divers now visiting, everyone needs to be more careful. Please do not stumble around here like a kid in a playground. Take your time, and learn your way around this special reef. Be respectful of how fragile it can be. There are individual animals here that Wally has watched for a decade, and they have not moved even a centimeter. Do not let your fins or a dragging second stage give them an unexpected eviction notice.

THE BOW REEF AND SLOPE

Over the years, the current sweeping past the wreck has changed the natural contours of the bottom, scouring a noticeable bowl off the bow, which is the lee of the wreck (think of the way an outgoing wave digs a little hole seaward of a seashell lying on a beach). A patchy covering of life has grown up in this area, and in the shallower areas this has become a true hard-coral reef. Perhaps because of the swirls of plankton-carrying current eddying out from the wreck here, this area is very rich, particularly down at twenty meters or more. It is the kind of place where a whip coral will not have a single commensal ovulid, but three—and they will all be different species. Interesting commensals of all kinds are very common here.

A thin reef also radiates out from the wreck toward the deep, in thirty to fifty meters and more, where the sand has sprouted a spotty covering of barrel sponges, gorgonians, black coral bushes, cerianthids, and crinoids. Each of these has become a kind of minature ark of life on the sand. Places to hold on to are at a premium here, and a diver encounters some surprising assemblages: a beautiful *Dendronephthya* smothered in crinoids of all colors; a fallen gorgonian on which four species of tunicates, three species of sponges, and two colonies of soft corals all battle for a space the size of a person's hand; a big barrel sponge made almost unrecognizable by a clinging rabble of black coral bushes, crinoids, soft corals, and tunicates. (A biologist, more neutral-ly, would call these squatters "epizoic organisms.")

It is well worth at least a short run out to this reef, or the shallower reef northeast of the wreck. Take a close look at what is living in the gorgonians, and peer into the folds of the big barrel sponges and see what has hidden itself there.

By the way, the large Indo-Pacific barrel sponge (*Xestospongia testudinaria*), which is so common in Tulamben and other plankton-rich sites in Bali, is not necessarily the ancient animal some people believe. In Wally's experience, the specimens on the sand around the wreck last only about five or six years. When they are about to die, he said, they become infested with something like a small amphipod or copepod. These eat away at the sponge until it becomes soft, at which time a swarm of angelfish, butterflyfish, and triggerfish descend on it and devour the rest.

If you happen across the spent remains of a barrel sponge, be very careful. The sand around it will be full of extemely irritating spicules. In fact, Wally suggests, if you would like to torment someone, take a handful of these and put them down his or her wetsuit. Be careful, though: your victim will hate the world for only a couple of days, but will hate you forever.

The Drop-off

Diving the Drop-off a few years back, I rounded the corner and hit a stiff current blowing dead against me. It was late in the afternoon, and the light was poor. It was my third dive of the day. The water was cold. Frankly, I was not enjoying myself.

Wally was back at the restaurant, merrily drinking beers and telling lies with some old friends. I was on chaperon duty. A young friend of mine and a group of recent graduates of Wally's certification course wanted to get a dive in (the new divers

Solenostomus paegnius

If you see a robust ghost pipefish at the Tulamben wreck, be careful whom you tell.

were leaving the next morning), and somehow I let myself be talked into going along. Although my friend is a good diver, and Wally's students all passed with flying colors, I'm not used to looking after new divers underwater, and it makes me a bit nervous. Also, of course, I wanted to be back there with the beer and the lies.

When the graduates hit the

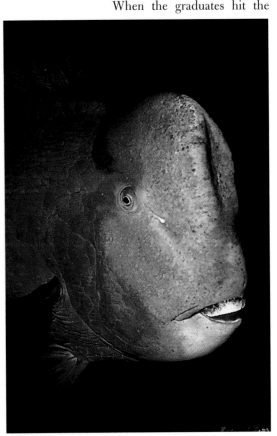

WALLY SIAGIAN   Bolbometopon muricatum

The bumphead parrotfish is the largest of its family, and one of the few that feeds almost exclusively on live coral. The strong, fused teeth of this animal are clearly visible here.

point, they did not like what they encountered one bit. They quickly signaled that they were going to turn around and head back along the wall. We parted, and I thought at this point of taking my friend to the deep, but decided I was too crabby and that we had been in the water too long for that, so we should head back, too. In the course of my indecision, the current had worked us

up onto the reef flat a bit, where the surge was quite strong. It was at this point that we noticed we were not alone in the water.

We were in a group of five big bumphead parrotfish, the largest one being not a whole lot smaller than me. We were swaying back and forth with the surge, the lot of us, but on average we stayed over the same patch of reef. These huge, wild-eyed creatures were placidly eating coral, in audible bites, and did not even deign to acknowledge our presence. Periodically, with what seemed like great satisfaction, one would expel a great plume of yellowish calcium dust from its vent. I could have touched the closest fish without even extending my arm the whole way.

I had never before gotten such a good look at their big green scales, each the size and approximate shape of a scallop shell, or their huge beaks. They are very special creatures, really, and seem so different that one thinks they do not just come from another world, but another *time*. It was a beautiful experience, and we stayed with them for at least five minutes before they moved off downslope. Then we swam back to shore.

The Tulamben Drop-off often produces pleasant surprises like this. Once, Wally and I were inspecting the base of the big gorgonian, which was loosened at the roots a bit by a storm, and immediately found a comet, in classic pose: tail out, doing its best to make us think it was a spotted moray. Little boxer crabs on the reef flat, a big shark in the deep, soft coral crabs, an octopus—none of these could even be considered unusual here.

GUNUNG AGUNG'S TOES

The basic structure of the Dropoff—Wally and I always call it the "wall," but the porters and many of the operators say "drop-off," so I se the latter here—is a spur of volcanic rock leading out from the rise on which the temple sits. It is an old lava flow, or, in another manner of speaking, one of Gunung Agung's many toes. The reef is actually three separate spurs, with the one closest to the bay being the longest and most interesting. (See Map 2.3, p. 92–93).

It is the dramatic topography of this reef that makes it so interesting. From about fifteen meters to about forty, the bay side of the main spur forms a wall—rough, steep, and even undercut a bit. In the shallow part, just as the wall begins, several small spurs lead off into the bay. Past the point is a steep channel, and then another small spur. Even the shallows of the back reef are nice, with huge black outcrops jutting out, and underwater, big split boulders worn smooth by the surge.

The bearing of the main spur at first caused some controversy between Wally and me. He, and most divers who have been here a lot, instinctively think the drop-off comes out from the little hill at an angle heading back into the bay, maybe thirty degrees or so west of north. Actually, the compass says the wall runs just about due north.

Throughout this area, the iron in the lava wreaked havoc with our compass readings, in many cases making them just about useless. Still, in this case we came to the conclusion that it was not the compass, but one's mental picture of this bay that causes the problem. When you look out from the resorts, you cannot help thinking that you are somehow looking north. Actually, the coast here runs at a forty-five degree angle, and if anything, you are looking more east than north. I think of it this way: it is the coast that angles back toward the drop-off, not the other way around (Map 2.1, pp. 74–75, makes this easy to see).

What this means is that if you are diving deep on the spur past the wall, it is shorter to swim straight back to the resorts rather than come back in along the wall. In fact, this is what Wally and I usually do, finishing our dive in the shallower areas of the sand slope at the edge of the patch reef.

Although the top and back-reef near the temple are dominated by

MIKE SEVERNS

The porter system is one of the real luxuries of diving at Tulamben. The fee is small, but it makes a big difference to the economy of this village. This is Nyoman Kartini and her child.

hard corals—and, because of the surgy conditions here, generally tough species—the wall itself is a great hedge of gorgonians and, particularly, black coral bushes. This is a kind of cover more often associated with deeper reefs and wrecks, and the wall is one of the more convenient places to see big antipatharian bushes. The picture of this site that I most readily call to

MIKE SEVERNS Lutjanus gibbus Tulamben

Along rich reef slopes, like Tulamben, humphead snappers gather in large schools. They are common in Bali.

mind is of great mops of black corals growing out horizontally from the black rock, swarming with schools of damselfish and anthias, and hiding bright juvenile butterflyfish, sharpnosed puffers, hawkfish, dottybacks, and other gems.

THE BIG GORGONIAN

For Wally, the large gorgonian that marks the corner of the Drop-off is the site's definitive underwater landmark. When he describes the location of something he has seen on the wall, it goes like this: "On the small terrace, ten meters down and straight out from the Big Gorgonian," or "Just past the Big Gorgonian, around the corner and down the ridge a few meters on your way to the deep slope." This sea fan, almost two meters across, is the crown jewel of the Drop-off.

The Drop-off, perhaps, served as Wally's Galapagos Islands in his formation of the Gorgonian Theory. The protected run of wall on the bay side of the spur is where the large gorgonians and bushy black corals flourish. Deeper on the spur, where the reef receives more current, the cover goes to small fan gorgonians, gorgonian whips, and black coral spirals.

The area on the main spur past the wall we call the Deep Slope, and though it lacks the big fans that distinguish the wall proper, it is a

sparkling world of bright blue tun cates, blood-red sponges, jagge corkscrews of black coral, and "turf" of myriad small animals cov ering the rocky ridgeline. Here an there bent branches of wire cor grow in patches, like haunte forests. The spur goes to sand sixty-eight meters, but the pate reefs continue down to near abyss depths. The scenery is similar o the second, smaller spur, which run to sand at a much more manageabl depth. The sparkling beauty both these reefs is helped in n small measure by the onset of n trogen narcosis—please be sensibl and brief, in your visits here.

AN EASY DIVE

On a good day, at slack tide, vi ibility at the Drop-off will reac twenty meters, and there will be a most no current at all. More typ cally, you will encounter horizont visibility of about ten meters (b cause of plankton in the water) an a small, but manageable, bit of cu rent. Because of its structure th reef is inherently protected, and it rare that it is not diveable at all.

Standing at the beach in front the resorts, you can quite easily se the conditions at the wall. If th water is bright blue and the surfac is quiet, conditions will be good. you can see signs of current an swell, and the water has gone over the green side of blue, underwat conditions will be poor. In the latt case, you can still dive, but you w likely find yourself limited to the b side of the spur.

The typical situation faced by diver on this site when the curre picks up is the one we encountere when we met the parrotfish: on you round the corner, you face strong current pushing you back t ward the bay. This does not crea a hazard, but it does limit the are you can comfortably cover. The be thing to do is to go back to the pr

A Prime Location—and Some Help from Agung

ULAMBEN IS FED BY A VERY DIRECT EDDY f the main branch current of the Indonesian hroughflow, pulling plankton-rich water om the Pacific Ocean to the Indian Ocean ee pg. 130). It is just eight degrees from the quator, in the world's richest marine bio-ographic zone. It is dry, and has no serious ltation or run-off problems. The wreck, cky wall, and sand slopes provide a wide riety of physical habitats. These factors, ken together, may be sufficient to explain hy this single bay harbors more species an, say, the entire Hawai'ian island chain. ut I think there is something else.

BALI'S SPECIAL WATER

The best way to understand Tulamben, think, is to suit up down by the river, spit your mask, and follow the bottom out until ou are under no more than three meters of ater. Then pick up one of the round, fist-zed stones from the bottom.

The top of this stone will be covered by scruffy, brownish turf of algae, with a few hitish streamers of hydroids mixed in (okay, ur hand might itch a bit later, but don't rop the stone just yet). Along the sides there ight be a bit of stony coral, like somebody uck a piece of chewing gum to the rock, or aybe even a branching colony the size of a ne. Then turn the rock over. The bottom ill have a whitish or orange patch of en-rusting sponge, a bryozoan colony, and aybe, a small snail or chiton or nudibranch.

Now, consider this: come the season of gh waves, this same rock will be tumbled nooth. And, when the weather calms, it will ;ain begin to grow its yearly coating of algae, onges, corals, and other encrusting life. If u were to pour a couple dozen yards of oncrete out here, to lock the shifting rocks gether, this area would become a full-blown ef in a matter of years.

This, in a more natural way, is what hap-ened in front of the Paradise—the corals ere were able to grow enough, perhaps be-use of a few mild seasons, to cement the undation rocks together and begin an ac-al reef. Once this happened, the coral just

kept advancing, forming today's reef.

Many texts maintain that stony corals grow at a very slow rate, just a centimeter a year or even less. Some of these same texts suggest that coral reefs require extreme oligo-trophic ("nutrient-poor") conditions to prosper. I think Tulamben proves both of these statements false. There are two-and-a-half-meter–wide table corals growing in

KAL MULLER Pterois volitans Tulamben, The River

It is always a shock at Tulamben to see reef fish in a setting that seems more appropriate to a mountain stream. This juvenile lionfish was found in two meters of water, hiding beside a tangled clump of tree roots that had washed into the bay during the rainy season.

front of the Paradise, and they were not there twenty years ago. (Do the math.) I also think that this bay, far from being oligotrophic, is actually being actively fertilized.

Bali's lush rice fields are famous, as is the fertility of its soils. In fact, the soils are not themselves particularly fertile. It is the water, which percolates through the relatively unweathered, mineral-rich ash produced by Agung, that is fertile. Farming, in Bali, is re-ally a type of hydroponics, and you could probably grow a crop of rice in a bathtub if you filled it with Bali water.

Now, you can put the rock back where it came from. Get your mask down low, against the bottom, and look toward the shore. Here and there you will see small, glassy spumes created by freshwater mixing with salt. This is the subsurface river flow—Bali water—percolating up through the cobbles, fertilizing the algae and everything else that depends on it, adding, I believe, to the strange richness of this special bay.

Map 2.3 Tulamben Drop-off 1:800

115°E 35' 48" (±1")

The Tulamben Drop-off 1:800

1 cm = 8 m
1 in = 67 ft

After the wreck, the Tulamben drop-off is the area's most popular dive. The main wall is formed by the westernmost of three coral-covered, lava spurs, and the landmark is a very large gorgonian at almost thirty meters. The wall has a nice, craggy structure, and is exceedingly rich. Many divers do not round the corner, and although the westernmost spur is the richest, the small middle reef and, to a lesser extent, the easternmost extent, are also worth exploring.

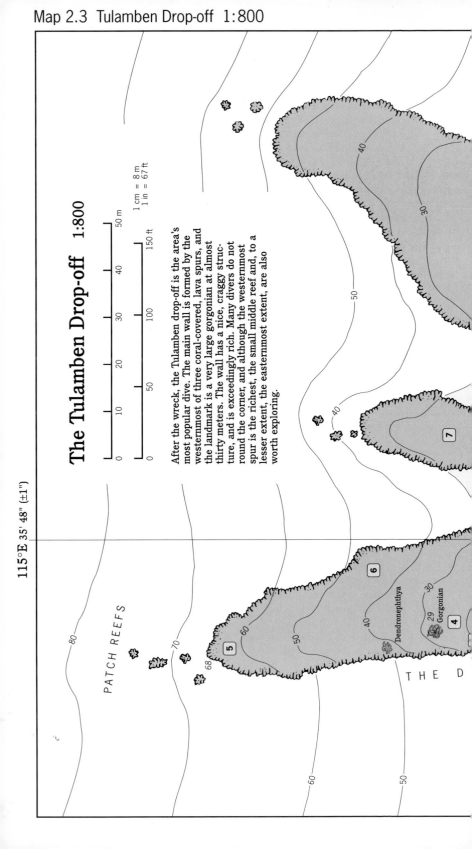

PATCH REEFS

THE D

Dendronephthya

Gorgonian

5

6

7

4

80

70

68

60

50

40

30

29

50

60

40

30

50

40

50

KEY

1. These coral spurs lead into the bottom forming sharp little valleys of black sand. Because of the rivers, even so close to shore the bottom is quite deep.

2. Here begins the drop-off proper, a vertical, fissured wall covered with gorgonians and fine, bushy black corals.

3. At around the twenty-meter line the wall forms a kind of corner here, and rounding this, a diver comes out of the protected lee formed by the wall and can face some current.

4. The drop-off's signature landmark is this large gorgonian, sprouting—rather precariously close to the sometimes currentswept edge of the wall—from a small terrace at 29 meters.

5. The wall becomes more like a ridge at forty to fifty meters, but the coral continues to almost seventy meters. In fact, the ridgeline, covered with tiny patches of life, continues to approximately one-hundred meters, but please don't be a cowboy and try to verify this. Others have, and it was very nearly the last thing they ever did. The fifty to sixty meter area here is beautiful, and plenty deep enough.

6. This area we sometimes call the "Deep Slope," and it is a rich, sparkling world of small gorgonians, black-coral spirals, and bright blue tunicates.

7. The second spur has a similar look to the Deep Slope, and also makes a nice deep dive.

8. A very large *Dendronephthya* on the sand here is a landmark on your way to the third spur. A commensal crab lives on it.

9. The easternmost ridge is the least interesting of the three. A double seamound marks the location of a short, but steep wall on the east flank of the reef. The bay beyond is murky, with a bottom covered with rubble and rough leather corals, but if you cross it you pick up another reef that is quite rich (see Map 2.1.)

10. Many people snorkel here in the back reef. It is surgey, but otherwise protected, and although the bottom is a little worn, the great chunks of rock are dramatic.

11. The reef flat, particularly along the western side, makes a nice place to decompress after your dive. The shallows harbor some interesting animals, such as the boxer crab, if you are willing to be patient and look.

ROCKY BACK REEF

LYBIA TESSELLATA

TEMPLE

THE DROP-OFF

Looking slightly E of N, between the two rocky points, from the bluff by the temple.

Source: 1998 and 1999 surveys by David Pickell and Wally Siagian. ©1999 David Pickell and Wally Siagian.

115°E 35' 48" (±1")

tection of the Drop-off proper, and spend the rest of your dive there.

At times (though not often), a trickier current condition forms at the Drop-off. In this case, an eddy rolls off from the northeast-tending main current, and if this eddy current becomes strong enough it can even penetrate the wall—blowing southeast against the wall and up and over the plateau of the back-reef. This type of current will do its best to push a diver back out along the wall, away from shore, or even carry the diver around the point and to the southeast, away from the bay. If you encounter these conditions, do not go around the point (where it will only get worse). Instead, stay very, very tight to the wall, and using the crannies as refuge, slowly and calmly work your way back toward the river mouth and shore. Never try to fight this current—or any current—in midwater, unless you actually enjoy working yourself into a wheezing panic, or you want to field test the maximum flow rate of your regulator.

The Patch Reef and Beyond

Just in front of the Tulamben resorts, in five to twenty meters of water, is a delightfully rich little patch reef. (See MAP 2.1, pp. 74–75.) This reef, which is the area's favored snorkeling spot, is dominated by acroporid hard corals—including some large tables—and fire corals, but there is a little of everything here: large clownfish anemones, crinoids, leather corals, colonies of coralli-morpharians, and bushy hydroids.

Though less than two hundred meters long, this reef, like the rest of the Tulamben area, also supports a diverse fish population. Parrotfish, wrasse, snappers, angelfish, butter-flyfish, and the rest of the normal complement of inshore reef fishes are always here, as well as some rar-ities, like ribbon eels, frogfish, and

unusual scorpionfish. This reef, because of its proximity to the re-sorts, makes an excellent and very convenient site for a night dive. It begins as patches of coral among the cobbles, becomes a fully devel-oped limestone reef at about eight meters, and runs to black sand at twenty meters or so, where the ba-thymetry begins to steepen.

This reef, sometimes called the "Paradise Reef" from the days when Dive Paradise was the only operator here, is surprisingly young. "Twelve years ago, there were almost no corals just in front here," said Emiko Shibuya, who has been running the Paradise's dive op-eration for more than a decade. "It was just rocks, like the rest of the bay. Also, in those days there were always flashlight fish, even in the shallows. And of course"—she said with a smile—"lots and lots of big lobsters."

Times are different now, and no-body (at least openly) takes lobster or any other animals from Tulam-ben. You can still see a few here, but not many. I'm not so sure how much their decline had to do with people catching them, either, as Emiko seemed to hint. A good lobster area is almost always rough and rocky, and the big bugs do not seem to like areas where the coral cover is thick and rich. I would guess that the change in the reef has had at least as much to do with their decline as poaching.

TO THE DEEP

One of the first dives I ever made with Wally was straight out from the Paradise, past the patch reef, and downslope to fifty meters or so. He was taking me and two of our friends to see a pair of Steene's dot-tybacks (*Pseudochromis steenei*). This fish is quite large for a dotty-back, and although the male has a bright orange face, its overall aspect (and personality) is less beautiful

Lybia tessellata clasping Triactis producta

than thuggish, with its spiky teeth and pushed-out lower jaw. Wally continually tries to torment photographer Roger Steene, for whom the fish was named, by saying: "It even *looks* like Roger."

On this particular morning, I felt about how this fish looks, except that the relevant color of my face would have been green. Wally felt no better. We had stayed up until almost four o'clock the night before getting acquainted and exhausting the kitchen's supply of beer. Our friends, however, were insistent that we dive at seven o'clock, which we did. As soon as we found the fish, which ruled a small bommie on the sand at fifty-five meters, I signaled that I had had enough and was heading back. Wally, with relief that was visible even underwater, immediately concurred, and we headed upslope.

It was at this stage, queasy and exhausted, that we found ourselves fighting a stiff current trying to push us downslope. The dottyback was interesting, but I have to say that this was very far from my all-time favorite dive. We put our bellies on the sand, to get what advantage we could from the boundary effect, and gradually fought our way back to the Paradise patch reef, beyond the influence of the downcurrent. I was very happy to see this sunny patch of coral, especially as it provided something to distract us as we waited an interminable twenty minutes or so until we and our computers felt it was safe to get out of the water (and go back to bed).

This downcurrent—it is as if the water is draining out of the bay—is not uncommon out on the sand slope, and seems to occur most often in the morning. It seems as if it should be related to the tide, but it is not always predictable. If you encounter it, do as we did, and get as close to the bottom as you can. It really does make a difference. Also, don't panic, because although it takes a bit of work, it is nothing an average diver cannot handle.

Boxer crabs live under rubble in the shallows. They are not easy to find, although the back reef at the Tulamben wall is a good place to look. Just two centimeters across, these xanthids have very small pincers, and perhaps to make up for this they clench juvenile sprouts of the anemone Triactis, which they brandish like weapons in the direction of intruders. They are sometimes called 'pom-pom' crabs, for obvious reasons, but this seems a bit disrespectful. At a diver's scale these 'pom-poms' might be harmless, but anemones of the infra-order Boloceroidaria are well known for their powerful stings, and they likely serve Lybia quite well.

The River

About three years ago, Wally and I were finishing a dive just in front of the dry river down by the temple. We were in about four meters of water, where the bottom is made up of the same fist-sized cobbles as the beach. Wally was carefully picking these rocks up and away from a

MIKE SEVERNS Pleurosicya boldinghi on Dendronephthya sp.

The soft coral goby lives in small groups on Dendronephthya bushes. It is almost colorless, and furtive, and takes sharp eyes to spot.

bristling colony of black-spined diademnid sea urchins. Then he grunted through his regulator, and I looked where his hand was pointing. There, quivering against the black sand, was a harlequin shrimp (*Hymenocera picta*), brilliantly spotted in blue-edged pink on white.

"The River," or "The Slope," as it is sometimes called, is certainly the most unlikely dive site in the Tu-lamben area. It is a gray bowl of rocks and sand, with no structure other than small sand ridges radiating out into the deep. Although such distinctions are difficult to make, it is also probably our favorite dive site in the area. If you asked the many photographers and scientists who have worked in Tulamben, they would say the same thing. The reason is simple: this is probably the single best place in Bali to find rare and unusual animals.

Here we have found hydroids with tiny caprellid or skeleton shrimp dancing off them, ghost pipefish, translucent baby lionfish no bigger than a coin, rare (and even unidentified) nudibranchs, a blue tube sponge full of bumblebee shrimp, sea pens with tiny crabs, bean-sized frogfish, strange soft corals rooted in the sand, and many, many other treasures.

The River was also the home of "Mr. Smart," Wally's nickname for a mimic octopus that took up residence at Tulamben for a while. This animal, which to my knowledge has yet to be awarded a species name, is one of nature's most remarkable mimics, twisting its body into shapes that replicate sea anemones, crinoids, flounders, lionfish, sting-rays, and other creatures.

Mr. Smart favored a crinoid impression, which was unconvincing only because the other crinoids in the area were so much smaller than the octopus. But Wally was absolutely dumbfounded one day when he found Mr. Smart mimicking a seahorse. (Again, his problem was one of scale—Mr. Smart, should he have deigned to stretch out thus, would have been maybe fifty centimeters long, and the seahorse he made was significantly bigger than any so far known to exist.

A TEMPORARY SANCTUARY

This site is basically a large bowl, carved out by the two *tukads* or rivers, that empty out here. During most of the year, these rivers are dry beds, but during the height of the northwest monsoon, they flow water. This, and the rough weather of December and January, stirs up the sandy bowl, creating a pattern of ridges that create the "reef" here. These ridges have a crest of life—crinoids, algae, tunicates in small clumps, black coral bushes—and for the most part, this thin cover lasts just a single season. Every year the nature of the ridges is different, and every year they attract a somewhat different set of animals, which is why this site is so exciting.

In the summer of 1999, the ridges were especially pronounced (probably because of the rough winter), and had an odd character. The main ridge in the west was cloaked in filaments of red algae, and small forests of the calcareous alga *Halimeda,* which has fronds like chains of green coins. In the east, nearer to the wall, the ridge was a hedge of crinoids. The year before, both ridges had been dominated by small green bushes of black coral.

In fact, the changeability of this site can be downright frustrating. In early May of 1999, we dove the crinoid ridge several times over a three-day period. There were so many ornate ghost pipefish there that one in four of the crinoids contained one of these cryptic seahorse relatives. Three weeks later, we returned with a photographer friend, and could not find a single one. This was just before the east wind started in earnest, and for this or some other reason, the season of the ghost pipefish was over.

Although one cannot depend on finding any single animal here, there will always be something interesting. A dive like this will not be for everyone, but one way to try it is to loop out onto the Slope on the way back from a dive on the Drop-off. Look closely at the ridges, and the life growing there, and we think you will be pleasantly surprised. This is also the most protected part of the bay, and if the view from the resorts is choppy and olive-colored, looking for macro treasures down at the river mouth may be the best dive you can make that day.

Beyond the Point

When we first began exploring the area past the Drop-off, Wally and I hired a *jukung* and motored down the coast, dropping in for short, ten-minute explorations at any likely site. On the way back from one of these outings—it had been pretty fruitless, and we still had air and bottom time left—we decided to try a dive just around the corner from the Drop-off. (See MAP 2.1, pp. 74–75.) This unnamed, rocky point leads off underwater from the southeastern edge of the squared-off peninsula of which the Drop-off forms the northwestern extent. Even from the boat, we could see a white-sand canyon between two volcanic spurs, so we moved out to the deeper area, and decided to roll off with empty B.C.'s and "sky-dive" down into the deeper part of the canyon.

We dropped into a rugged moonscape of sharp, black ridges, with light coral cover, and steep rivers of white sand. We stopped at thirty meters or so, where two reef white-tip sharks whirled and headed off down the canyon to ninety meters or more. We didn't stay long, but we were impressed with the dramatic structure, white sand, and a steep profile that means sharks and other deepwater animals are not going to be rare here.

In the two years since that dive, I have logged a handful in the area between the Drop-off and Batu Kelebit (and Wally many more), but there is still a lot more exploration to be done here. This area is really just one long reef that continues down the coast to at least Tanjung

WALLY SIAGIAN *Pseudanthias squamipinnis* Tulamben wreck

Anthias, always in big schools, are common, and colorful, members of the reef community. Sometimes called fairy basslets, they are closely related to the groupers. Anthias are protogynous hermaphrodites, and the territorial males, which have distinctive markings, are sex-reversed females. The individual in the opening, being cleaned by a wrasse, is a male. The others are females.

Muntig, where there is a small bay and a hillside resort.

A BRIGHT, FRESH WORLD

We made several long dives through this area just as we were finishing the fieldwork for this book in 1999, and found most of these reefs to be remarkably healthy, and in much better condition than they were two years before. The best reefs lie between the Drop-off and Batu Kelebit, and some of these are fantastically rich. Frustratingly, the areas just east of the Drop-off, and just west of Kelebit, are weak, making it less attractive to combine these areas in a single dive.

The best way to get past the Drop-off is by *jukung*, which gives you flexibility in picking your sites. With the growing popularity of Batu Kelebit—even before this book was released, operators began taking clients to Kelebit as we spread the word—some of the Tulamben fishermen have begun working on an intermittent basis taking divers around the point.

Just one year after the El Niño warming, this area was fully recovered, and has the healthy, fresh look of a spring meadow or a young rice field. There were sponges everywhere, spiky blue tubes, big barrel sponges that were so fat they were more like spheres, and the strange, lumpy barrels of *Stelletinopsis*, growing on stilts. There were great stands of soft corals, and areas where the gorgonians were as big and healthy as anywhere in Bali. In the scree of hard coral that had built up in areas between the ridges, the growing edges of the plate corals were bright and pink.

Beginning just past the Drop-off, where there is a small pocket beach with salt-and-pepper sand, the substrate throughout this area is bright white, although the rock is still black lava. So far, although these sites are so close, almost nobody dives here. If you want a change from the dark bottom in Tulamben Bay, and especially if you enjoy Batu Kelebit, get a *jukung* and head out here. You will enjoy it.

Batu Kelebit

IN MAY OF 1998 WALLY AND I SPENT a few days in a small *jukung*, running around the Drop-off and down the coast, looking for promising new dive sites. In a way, it was the worst possible time for this kind of work. After four weeks of the 30°C+ surface water temperatures brought on by El Niño, the coral from Menjangan all the way to Gili Selang was bleaching. Even Tulamben was looking bad, and some of the foreign divers were grumbling. A few even offered inane explanations having to do with trash in the water, pollution from Java, or vague accusations of "bad management" by the Indonesians.

Their tone was that of someone who had gotten bad service at a restaurant, and it was getting on our nerves. We were happy to have an excuse to escape all this ill humor.

I don't know if you've ever looked for a reef from a small boat, with decently clear water but with enough of a wind up to mottle the surface. It's not particularly easy. Usually, it is the white sand that you can see, and you pick out the areas of coral by the absence of white. This "absence of white" could be a thriving reef, but it could just as easily be rubble or gray sand.

Once you get to an area you think is promising—"David, what do you think? That point continues underwater, and it seems protected. Looks like some coral there, too"— you have your skipper stop the boat, and try to get a better look, mostly by squinting and using your mask as a makeshift viewing bucket. If there is any chop at all, of course, this pro-cedure becomes more trouble than it is worth, and basically, you just do a lot of jumping in, looking around for a few minutes, climbing back in the boat, drying your hands with a T-shirt so you can light a cigarette, scratching your head, and moving on to try another place.

SOME HELP FROM EL NIÑO

El Niño, inadvertently, turned out to be a tremendous help to us in our explorations: a bleached white coral head just glows, even if it is fifteen meters down. We could tell right away when we were over living

Just around the corner from Tulamben Bay, this beautiful site consists of steep, coral-covered ridges separated by valleys of bright white sand.

reef because, for once, the coral was the brightest thing down there. We spent the first day working down near Cape Batu Niti, which we eventually determined was too sandy, too unprotected, and too affected by the river to produce a good reef. On the second day we found Kelebit.

Batu Kelebit, literally the Kelebit Rocks, are two large underwater boulders lying just offshore from a point marked by a jagged crest of lava. The smaller of the two rocks is always submerged; the larger has two humps, which are *batu mandi,* "bathing rocks," meaning they are alternately exposed and covered by the tide.

Kelebit is the fishermen's name for the site. Although you might think otherwise, a place that produces good fishing is not always (or even often) a good dive site. Fishermen are up on the surface, and the fact that three- and four-knot currents continually swirl around a point is not so relevant from their point of view. Nor do they care about visibility, or whether there is any coral there.

As soon as we hit the water, we knew we were on to something. The colonies of fire coral crowning the top of the two main ridges were a bit

John E. Randall   Balistoides viridescens

The titan triggerfish is the largest of its family, and these fish—especially nesting females—can be downright ornery. The jaws are very powerful (it eats shellfish and echinoderms) and when that wild eye starts spinning around, be careful. It is always a question of territory, so all you need to do is move away.

bleached and algae covered (which is how we found the reef in the first place) but other than this, the Kelebit reef—at the height of the El Niño warming—was completely undamaged.

The basic structure of Batu Kelebit consists of three coral-covered ridges that fan out from the eponymous rocks (see Map 4.5, pp. 102–103). Between the ridges are sand channels, and the sand is bright white. The bathymetry is one of the best things about this site. The ridges are steep enough to protect the two channels from both sides, making the inside diveable regardless of the current. And their

approximately radiating structure makes it almost impossible to get lost here.

In fact, this structure confused us on our first few dives. Although we always found ourselves back at the rocks at the end, we had difficulty agreeing on the structure, bearing, and even number of ridges. It took about eight dives to come up with a map that we think is relatively accurate. The drop here, whether along the ridges or in the channels, is quite steep, and the easternmost ridge in particular seems to continue all the way to infinity. On one of our early dives we followed this out to almost eighty meters, thinking we could see hard reef picking up again. This turned out to be an optical illusion, brought on by a steepening of the sand slope and, no doubt, more than a touch of narcosis.

THE MOTHER REEF

In fish and invertebrate life, Batu Kelebit is every bit as rich as Tulamben Bay, and perhaps even richer. The ridges are covered with an extremely diverse growth of hard corals, sponges, gorgonians, black corals, and every other encrusting animal it is possible to encounter. Even the fire coral at the top of the ridges, which seemed both bleached and overgrown in 1998, was completely recovered by 1999, now encompassing an area more than fifteen meters across.

The animal life here, because of the substrate and structure, is noticeably different from that in Tulamben Bay. Green *Tubastrea* trees, with their odd, crooked branches, are not common in Bali, and you won't find them in Tulamben Bay. But you can find them at Kelebit. Reef white-tip sharks, also rarely seen inside Tulamben Bay, are almost always at Kelebit. Even among common families of reef fish, like angelfish, butterflyfish, and anemone fish, the species here are slightly dif rent from those at Tulamben.

And Kelebit is probably the sin-
le best site in the area to see big an-
nals (see "Pelagics," pg. 104). The
ottom drops fast and sharp to a
undred meters, there is always
lankton in the water, and the
tructure of the ridges creates an
ddy where the plankton accumu-
ates. These are perfect conditions
or the big dogs. In the first three
ays of diving this site, we saw man-
as, schools of skipjacks, shoals of
arracuda and jacks, dogtooth
una, and in the deep off the east-
rnmost spur, always on the first
norning dive, a large silky shark.

This great richness led Wally to
armise that it was Kelebit, not Tu-
amben, that was the "mother reef"
f this area. I took this as a kind of
eresy, coming from a strong Tu-
mben partisan like himself, but I
nd to agree. Think of it: at a time
hen Tulamben and every other
ef in North Bali was bleached and
urting, Kelebit, except for a minor
ruise on its shoulder, was in the
ink of health, with feeding mantas
nd a great pelagic shark prowling
s depths.

AN EASY, SAFE DIVE

Because Kelebit receives deep,
ffshore water, clarity is generally
ood, and temperatures are a bit
old. Actually, visibility would be
xcellent, except that there is almost
ways plankton in the water, which
f course is why the site is so rich in
he first place. In the deeper areas
ou can usually see about twenty
eters, but plankton can accumu-
te in the middle channel, creating
kind of turbid zone at fifteen to
venty meters. Always remember to
ok up here (the bottom is at thir-
 to forty meters) because this is
here the mantas and other pelag-
s will be.

The current at Kelebit usually
nds northwest (although it can
w east as well), and seems to pick

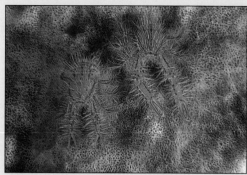

©BURT JONES/MAURINE SHIMLOCK   Laureia siagiani (female on left)

LAUREIA SIAGIANI
Wally's Squat Lobster

Wally first found this little character in the mid-
eighties, living, as it always does, in the outer folds
of the common large Indo-Pacific barrel sponge
Xestospongia testudinaria, deep on the sand slope
behind the Tulamben wreck. A specimen was sent
to Dr. Keiji Baba, of Kumamoto University in
Japan, who named it in 1994.

This crab belongs to family Galatheidae, an
odd group called squat lobsters, or sometimes,
"half-crabs." A galatheid has a pointed snout ("rostrum" to a biologist), long, lobster-like claws ("chelipeds"), and three, instead of the typical four, pairs
of walking legs. The "missing" legs are inside the
gill cavity, where they are used for cleaning the gills.

Photographs do not prepare you properly for
the color of this animal as it appears underwater—
the violet stripes glow like neon. This half-crab is
also quite spunky for being no bigger than your fin-
gernail, and when you get close it will stick its
"chelipeds" out and vibrate in a kind of war dance.

Laureia siagiani is not particularly rare, and is
quite easy to find if you know how to look. It favors larger sponges (always on the outer folds, despite what some texts state), and prefers the lee
side. But the most important clue is the presence
of a brittle star of the genus *Ophiothrix.* It is this
animal—with its hairy arms and flashes of violet—
that *Laureia* mimics. I have never seen this crab
in a sponge that did not also have these brittle stars,
packed in a great tangle into the outer folds.

Actually, there is another crab often found with
the brittle star (and with *L. siagiani* as well), a
smooth-shelled porcelain crab that has not yet
been named—it is also bright violet and pink.

Map 2.4 Batu Kelebit 1:800

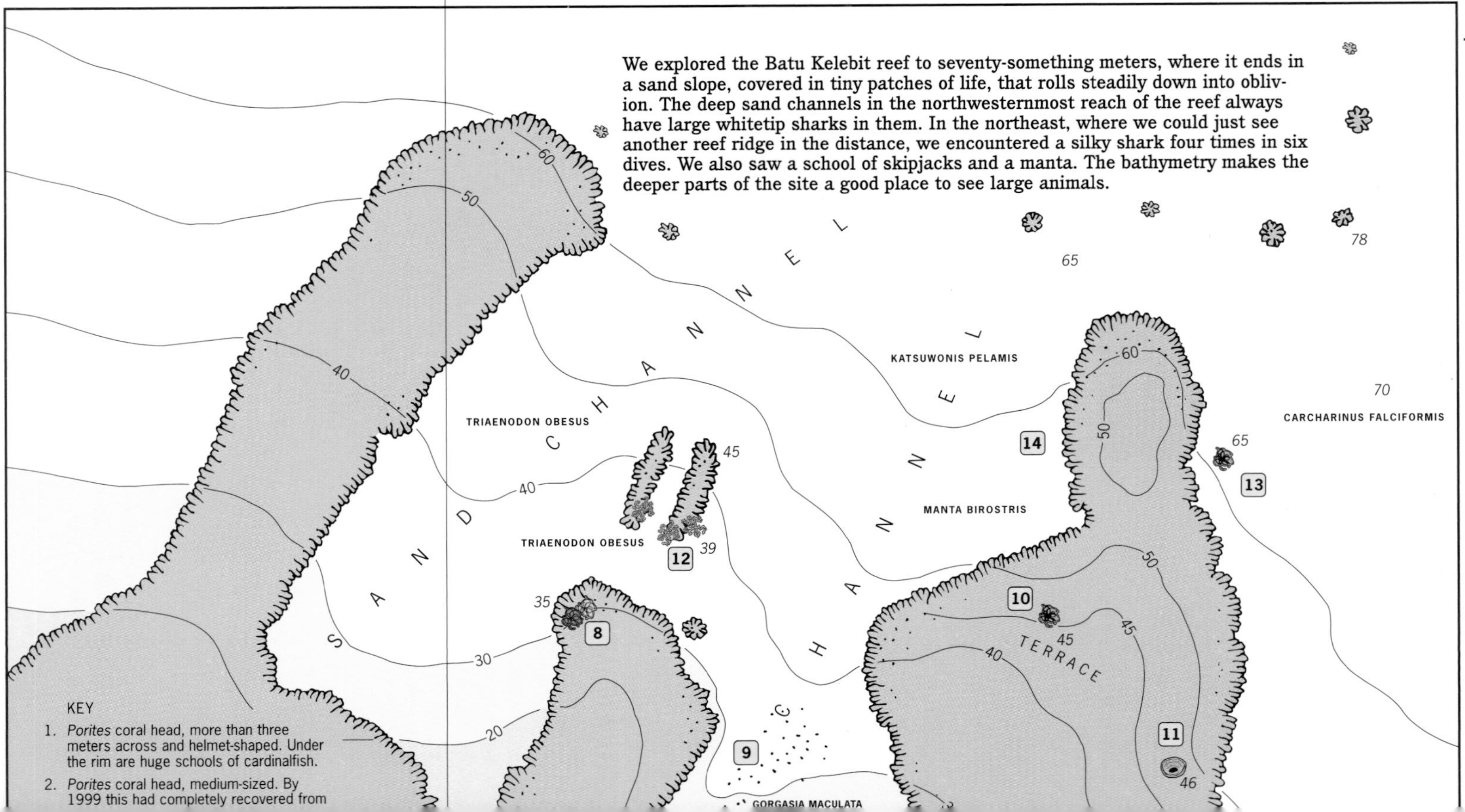
KATSUWONIS PELAMIS
MANTA BIROSTRIS
CARCHARINUS FALCIFORMIS
TRIAENODON OBESUS
TRIAENODON OBESUS
GORGASIA MACULATA
SAND CHANNEL
CHANNEL
TERRACE
8
9
10
11
12
13
14
78
65
70
65
60
50
40
45
39
35
30
20
46

We explored the Batu Kelebit reef to seventy-something meters, where it ends in a sand slope, covered in tiny patches of life, that rolls steadily down into oblivion. The deep sand channels in the northwesternmost reach of the reef always have large whitetip sharks in them. In the northeast, where we could just see another reef ridge in the distance, we encountered a silky shark four times in six dives. We also saw a school of skipjacks and a manta. The bathymetry makes the deeper parts of the site a good place to see large animals.

KEY

1. *Porites* coral head, more than three meters across and helmet-shaped. Under the rim are huge schools of cardinalfish.
2. *Porites* coral head, medium-sized. By 1999 this had completely recovered from

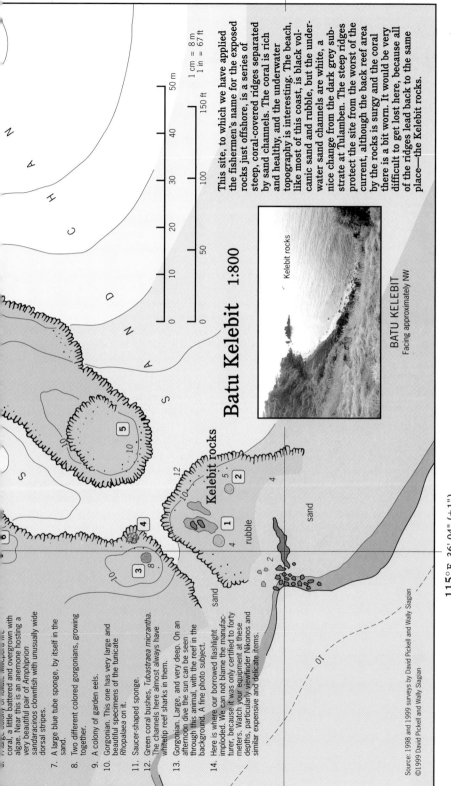

Batu Kelebit 1:800

This site, to which we have applied the fishermen's name for the exposed rocks just offshore, is a series of steep, coral-covered ridges separated by sand channels. The coral is rich and healthy, and the underwater topography is interesting. The beach, like most of this coast, is black volcanic sand and rubble, but the underwater sand channels are white, a nice change from the dark grey substrate at Tulamben. The steep ridges protect the site from the worst of the current, although the back reef area by the rocks is surgy and the coral there is a bit worn. It would be very difficult to get lost here, because all of the ridges lead back to the same place—the Kelebit rocks.

1 cm = 8 m
1 in = 67 ft

BATU KELEBIT
Facing approximately NW

Kelebit rocks

Kelebit rocks

rubble

sand

sand

7. A large blue tube sponge, by itself in the sand.

8. Two different colored gorgonians, growing together.

9. A colony of garden eels.

10. Gorgonian. This one has very large and beautiful specimens of the tunicate *Rhopalaea* on it.

11. Saucer-shaped sponge.

12. Green coral bushes, *Tubastraea micrantha*. The channels here almost always have whitetip reef sharks in them.

13. Gorgonian. Large, and very deep. On an afternoon dive the sun can be seen through this animal, with the reef in the background. A fine photo subject.

14. Here is where our borrowed flashlight imploded. We can not blame the manufacturer, because it was only certified to forty meters. Watch your equipment at these depths, particularly viewfinder Nikonos and similar expensive and delicate items.

...coral, a little battered and overgrown with algae. Near this is an anemone hosting a very beautiful pair of *Amphiprion sandaracinos* clownfish with unusually wide dorsal stripes.

Source: 1998 and 1999 surveys by David Pickell and Wally Siagian
©1999 David Pickell and Wally Siagian

115° E 36' 04" (±1")

8° S 16' 54" (±1")

Where the Big Dogs Swim

BATU KELEBIT IS PROBABLY THE BEST SITE IN THE Tulamben area to see big animals, but they show up on occasion in the deeper areas of the Drop-off and even the wreck. There is no specific season or location for these sightings, and unfortunately we cannot tell you exactly when and where you will be able to see, for example, a hammerhead shark. But Wally's experience is extensive, and the following observations may prove helpful:

WHALE SHARKS (*Rhincodon typus*) are known from the area, but these huge filter-feeders are very uncommonly seen. Scattered, but reliable sightings have taken place at Tulamben and elsewhere along the north coast, even Pemuteran and Menjangan.

GREAT HAMMERHEAD SHARKS (*Sphyrna mokarran*) are probably often around at Tulamben, and at some of the sites further east along this coast. Sightings occur irregularly at all the deeper sites in the area. By "deep" we mean fifty to sixty meters, which is why one does not hear of them every day. The most likely areas to see one of these great, shadowy creatures are Batu Kelebit and the Drop-off.

THRESHER SHARKS (*Alopias vulpinus*), and SILKY SHARKS (*Carcharinus falciformis*) and other large oceanic requiem sharks are also sometimes spotted. A single, large silky shark has been seen at Batu Kelebit on many occasions. It was always deep or very deep (ninety meters) and quite shy. Other large pelagic sharks are seen on occasion in the same areas as the hammerheads, usually so deep and for so brief a period that they cannot be identified with any certainty.

MANTAS (*Manta birostris*) are occasionally seen inside Tulamben Bay, at the wreck and the wall, but this is not a regular occurrence. We saw them on several occasions in June 1998 at Batu Kelebit.

MOLAS (*Mola mola*) appear in the area occasionally, but regularly. A string of sightings took place in late May of 1999, for example, just after the east winds picked up. For about a week, people were seeing these peculiar fish every day. They are most often seen on the slope out behind the wreck, at about forty meters, and off the first spur of the Drop-off.

up more in the afternoon. It doesn't make a lot of difference, however, because the ridges provide excellent protection. You always get some surge in the shallows back near the rocks, but nothing dangerous. It can actually be a bit entertaining, while you are doing your safety stop, to sway with the surge in and among the rocks and the giant *Porites* coral head. The split between the two Kelebit rocks is about a meter wide, and it is possible to swim this as well.

The shallows are a bit worn from the constant surge, but there are interesting animals to find here as well. In 1998, as El Niño was winding down, juveniles of the sea cucumber *Bohadschia graeffei* were everywhere. These are pretty good mimics of the nudibranch *Phyllidia*, although a trained eye will ultimately find them a little too skinny and spiky to be convincing.

The *jukung* ride from Tulamben Bay to Kelebit is only about fifteen minutes, and gives you a good look at the dry, grassy landscape and the raw black lava rock that marks the points here. Once you get there drop in near the rocks and head along the outer flank of the eastern most set of ridges. Stay on this side until you have gone as deep as you are comfortable with, then cut across—the terraced area at forty five meters is a nice place for this—to the protected center channel. From there you should pay at least a quick visit to the little twin ridge off the center spur, where there are always a couple of white-tip sharks lurking, and then wind your way up the second spur, the sand channel by the garden eels, or the first spur—it's your choice—back to the rocks.

Depth is the only hazard to watch out for. The ridges go to more than sixty meters, and even then the "reef" doesn't end. A rubbly slope still covered with life, extends down to the abyss. Be responsible

on this site. Also, pay attention to the depth ratings of your equipment—we didn't, and when a flashlight Wally had strapped to his B.C. imploded with a sharp crack at fifty-eight meters, it just about stopped his heart.

If you are ambitious and good with your air, you can combine a dive at Kelebit with the next reef to the northwest (see Map 2.1, pp. 74–75). You have to swim across a hundred and fifty meters of rubble barren sand to get there, but this reef is also excellent, although the structure is not as dramatic as Kelebit.

Heading in the other direction here is not much to recommend. Although we didn't have the time, a friend of ours tried "Emerald Bay," a little training reef in front of a resort of the same name. There wasn't much of interest there, he said, except for a wreck—a car sunk by the operators, which we here dub the *Toyota Maru.* I hope they at least drained the crankcase and gas tank (and also hope they don't use it to certify wreck divers).

THE SWISS ARMY KNIFE OF SITES

There are as many tastes in dive sites as there are divers, but Batu Kelebit is probably the closest thing to a do-it-all dive site that Bali offers. Do you like sites with lots of coral, lush gorgonians, and plenty of macro-scale life? Batu Kelebit has all three. Do you like sites where you can see big animals? Batu Kelebit has them. Do you like a fun, scenic boat ride on your way to a site? Batu Kelebit offers one. Do you like a site with dramatic underwater structure? Batu Kelebit has it. Do you like a site that is fifteen minutes from a cold beer? Batu Kelebit is. And perhaps most important, do you like a dive site that is safe, inherently protected from current, and diveable in just about any conditions? Batu Kelebit is.

We spread the word about this reef even before this book came out, and the reviews have all been positive. Tulamben Bay is a beautiful place to dive, but if you are here, you should at least give Kelebit a try.

These Nembrotha are among the most strikingly patterned nudibranchs. Picking through the turf of ascidians, algae, and hydroids, these two are seeking bryozoans, which, apparently, is all they like to eat.

THE TULAMBEN AREA
Jemeluk and Beyond

IT WAS A BLAZING HOT, LATE JUNE day, and Wally and I were wedged into a tiny *jukung*, coasting the Seraya Peninsula southeast from Jemeluk. There was only the faintest breeze, and the water was blue glass. Conditions were perfect. Well, not quite perfect, since we had foolishly left our cigarettes in the glove compartment of the Kijang, and after forty minutes we were both jonesing a bit, but this was some of

This quiet bay was heavily damaged by El Niño, but a steady recovery has begun. In the meantime, there is an interesting wreck further east.

the clearest water we had seen in a long time, brought in by the recent shift to the dry season of southeast winds. Visibility at Tulamben the day before was easily forty meters, and with conditions like this, we were looking forward to doing some exploring down this coast.

Then our little vessel's engine began changing pitch, and we quit our conversation and started paying attention to the water.

What we saw was rather worrying. Once we left the calm of Jemeluk Bay, we could already feel the strange energy of the Lombok Strait. There were no waves, and with no wind, no whitecaps or chop. But the current was running wild, sluicing around on the surface

in great silvery streaks. We even en countered whirlpools, like grea dinner plates fifteen meters across which slapped our little woode boat sideways as we slid down int them, and then slapped us again th other way as we climbed on ou The little outrigger had a nev Yamaha motor, but these vessels ru converted generator motors, an eight horsepower was not going t be much help if things got an worse.

Our destination was Tanjun Ibus, a rocky point an hour's rid from Jemeluk. A few days earlier, i a supermarket in the south, we ha bumped into a friend of Wally's, young American adventurer wh likes spearfishing and surfing. H had been up at Ibus a week or so be fore, free-diving for jacks with hi spear gun.

The point was swirling with fish he said, including one huge *Caran ignobilis,* far too glorious (an probably too strong) to take with spear. This fish, the largest jack i the world, can reach a size that is a long, and as heavy, as most adul men. It makes a formidable adver sary. I have heard a reliable story o a spearfisherman being charged b an adult *ignobilis,* and even thoug this particular spearfisherman was two-hundred-and-fifty-poun Hawai'ian, as squat and strong as concrete block, the jack succeede in breaking three of his ribs.

It wasn't the great jack that in trigued us, however, it was the tw dark forms that followed Wally' friend around with such interest tha he finally decided to leave th water. These were great hammer-head sharks (*Sphyrna mokarran*), and our informant—not one given to exaggeration—said that if they weren't five meters long, they were awfully close. I was really looking forward to finding these great hammerheads, but given the wild current, and the modest size and power of our vessel, we decided to exercise the better part of valor, and picked a calmer site about halfway between Jemeluk and Ibus.

DOWN, BUT NOT QUITE OUT

If this book had been written three years ago, this would be the point at which I would wax poetic about the shallow inner bay of Jemeluk, a site with such a variety of healthy hard corals that it could serve as a kind of museum of scleractinian coral diversity. I would be raving about the huge gorgonians and barrel sponges on the bommies, wall, and deep slope on the reef outside the bay. I would go on and on about the reef sharks, big Napoleon wrasses and bumphead parrotfish that are often seen here. But today, I don't quite have the heart for this.

Jemeluk Bay (the site is sometimes called Amed) was hit harder by the April–May 1998 El Niño warming than anywhere else on the island other than Terima Bay and Pemuteran. (See "Coral Bleaching and El Niño," pg. 108.) Its recovery has been puzzlingly slow, and it seemed unclear if the inner bay, in particular, would ever return to its original splendor. When we dove it in the summer of 1998, most of the shallow coral was bleached, and beginning to be overgrown with a scum of brown and red algae. When I returned a year later, I expected to see a great improvement. Wally quickly delivered the bad news: even after a year, little had changed.

The deeper sections fared better, and the gorgonians and corals on the outer reef below about fifteen meters were never hurt, and are still healthy. But overall, this reef was still only a shadow of its former self, and for someone who had enjoyed it in its glory, it is rather sad. The damage to Menjangan, for example, was only on the reef flat, which was ultimately uninteresting. But the reef flat at Jemeluk was one of its major charms.

KAL MULLER   Jemeluk

Wally, working then with Wolfgang Besigk, discovered the reef at Jemeluk—it is sometimes rendered "Cemeluk," although the "J" gets an English speaker closer to the correct pronunciation—in about 1986. It has since grown into a small diving center, albeit one that is not as professional or well-organized as Tulamben. The biggest loss will be felt by snorkelers, as the inner reef at Jemeluk was perhaps the richest, calmest, and easiest to reach snorkeling spot on the island.

We just gave the reef a quick looking over in May of 1999, and in June I returned to the United States to finish the manuscript. In the late summer Wally called to tell me the good news: Jemeluk was coming back. After two months of the clear, cold water brought on by the southeast monsoon, the edges of the coral were beginning to glow with the bright colors of new growth. This is very good news, but at this point we still can't say what condi-

Divers at Jemeluk in the mid-1990's. At one time a common side-trip for divers from Tulamben, Jemeluk was hit hard by the El Niño warming of 1998, and the coral is recovering quite slowly. Still, there were strong signs of life in the late summer of 1999, and within a few years it may become very rich again.

The Delicate Relationship between Coral and Algae

WHILE EXPLORING THE REEFS OF NORTHWEST Bali, we decided to try a *taka* deep inside Terima Bay. Wally hadn't dived there in at least six or seven years, and probably, in their haste to get to Menjangan, nobody else had either. This bank had a coral-rich top, with a bit of seagrass in the middle, and steep walls covered in gorgonians and sponges. It was an excellent place to find seahorses, and some unusual cardinalfishes, and Wally had escorted a photographer and an ichthyologist around the site in the past.

When we rolled off the skiff and into the water, we found a bleached wasteland. The shallow top of the bank looked like a limestone quarry. As we drifted down the steep sides to the thirty-meter bottom, the visibility dropped to just a few meters. Streams of fine white sand were pouring down along the clefts in the wall, rising up into the water like clouds of cement dust. The only living things we saw were a school of fusiliers and a scattered few spiky blue sponges—none bigger than the last joint of my little finger—clinging to the reef's dead white skeleton.

Coral bleaching was first noted by scientists in 1979–1980, on the Great Barrier Reef, the Ryukyu Islands, and at a couple sites in the Caribbean. Since then it has been found to be a global problem, with major, well-studied "events" in 1982–1983 (circumtropical), 1986–1988 (circumtropical, and even more extensive), and 1991–1992 (chiefly French Polynesia). And now, although the scientific jury is still out on this one, 1998 will also have to be added to the list.

A CRUCIAL PARTNERSHIP

Reef-building corals have developed a symbiotic relationship with a dinoflagellate alga called *Gymnodinium microadriaticum,* or more compactly, zooxanthellae. The algae live in the tissues of the coral, where they are physically protected, and receive a steady supply of nutrients and carbon dioxide from the coral animal. What the coral receives from this relationship is oxygen, and more importantly, a waste disposal service. Although reef-building corals receive thirty percent or more of their nutritive needs from plankton and free organics in the water, it is the presence of the zooxanthellae that allows them to excrete fixed calcium at a high rate, thus building their aragonitic skeletons, and eventually, the rich and complex enviroments we call coral reefs. This relationship evolved 250 million years ago, and has long since become obligatory for both parties. It is actually more meaningful to treat the coral-algae assemblage as a single "organism," which scientists call a holobiont.

"Bleached" coral is coral that has lost its zooxanthellae; the coral appears white because the pigment comes from the chlorophyll in the zooxanthellae. This bleaching is a response to environmental stress: sudden changes in temperature, sudden changes in salinity, and sudden changes in lighting. Perhaps appropriately to a case of such extreme co-dependency, scientists are still unsure whether it is the zooxanthellae that abandons the coral, or the coral that kicks out the algae. In any case, under conditions of stress, the zooxanthellae migrate from the surface tissues to the polyp's mouth—where they either escape, or are spit out. And without its symbiont, the coral tissue soon withers and dies.

The coral-algae partnership is designed to function within a very narrow range of temperatures, and even a 3°C rise can cause bleaching. It is not the warm temperature per se that is the cause, but the change. If you were to take a small coral colony from a deep wall and place it in the shallows of the same site, it would certainly bleach—from the suddenly warmer water, and the suddenly brighter light.

Bleaching appears to be an act of desperation—scleractinian suicide—but it is a rational evolutionary response. When the color returns to a bleached coral, it is coming from a *different* zooxanthellae. The coral has changed partners. Corals sometimes need to adjust the "fit" between their particular environment and the particular strain (some phycologists would say species) of zooxanthellae they harbor. During bleaching events, younger colonies are hit harder. Old

©BURT JONES/MAURINE SHIMLOCK   Nudibranch: Glossodoris cincta complex; Shrimp: Periclimenes imperator

The emperor shrimp has catholic taste in hosts, including several genera of sea cucumbers, at least one sea star, and several nudibranchs, most famously the large Spanish dancer Hexabranchus. The nudibranch pictured is an unusual and rather small host for P. imperator (though a very beautiful one). Oddly, the color pattern of this particular shrimp resembles that of individuals living on sea cucumbers rather than those living on the Spanish dancer nudibranch.

colonies are more resistant, probably because they have bleached in their youth, and thus found more suitable partner algae.

THE CHILD OF GLOBAL WARMING

The stress that produced the coral bleaching in Bali in 1998 came from a rise in surface sea temperatures produced by the El Niño Southern Oscillation (ENSO). In a normal year, Indonesia's weather is influenced by the Indonesian Low, a major body of low-pressure air that forms over the archipelago. In combination with the incessant westerly trade winds over the Pacific, the Indonesian Low allows Pacific Ocean water to pile up and flow through Indonesia to the Indian Ocean, with much of this strong surface flow going through the Lombok Strait (see "The Indonesian Throughflow," pg. 130).

During an ENSO year, the Indonesian Low is weak, and develops further east. This disrupts the normal wind-created surface flow, causing western Pacific water to flow eastward, which creates the pocket of unusually warm water off western South America

where El Niño ("The Child" in Spanish) got its name. It also disrupts the normal flow past Bali. For several weeks in the late spring of 1998, the inshore water along north Bali became, in essence, stagnant. This allowed it to heat up to near air temperature, unusually high at the time, which shocked the coral.

The more protected, and shallow, the water, the greater was the damage. For example, the mortality of the coral inside Terima Bay was close to one-hundred percent, with no apparent recovery even a year later. At Tulamben, where perhaps one-third of the shallow coral was bleached at the height of the warm spell, all of the color returned within two weeks after the water temperature dropped, and actual mortality was zero.

Bali got off quite lightly, in fact. The 1982–1983 episode killed fully 97 percent of the coral in the Galapagos. Some scientists now wax apocalyptic, and say that global warming will bring more and more frequent bleaching events, "until coral dominated reefs no longer exist." I don't know if that's true, but it is certainly a chilling thought.

tion this reef will be in when you read this.

Like Menjangan, Jemeluk actually suffered two catastrophes, although in the case of Jemeluk, only the second was natural. The first was what an ecologist would call "anthropogenically-induced environmental stress," i.e., the result of human idiocy.

A few years ago, the fisheries department of Karangasem, the regency—something like a county, in the United States—to which Jemeluk belongs, sent a team to the bay to check its "tourist potential." The result was a farce, as the boat from which this team worked dragged its anchor all across the fields of coral. When we dove Jemeluk at the beginning of our researches for this book, the damage was fresh, and one field of fire coral, in particular, looked like someone had set out purposely to till it.

We tried to have a laugh about it later at Tulamben—"Please, whatever you do, don't tell anybody a place has 'tourist potential'!"—but it was finally too sad. One of Wally's underwater landmarks, a giant barrel sponge on a huge head of *Porites* coral, was completely demolished. The *Porites*, which has probably the toughest and densest skeleton of any coral, was split right down the middle, and the sponge, which had been the size of an easy chair, was nowhere to be seen.

A DESOLATE STRETCH OF COAST

The area from Jemeluk to Gili Selang, which forms Bali's easternmost tip, is still relatively unexplored for diving. The problem is its isolation. The road that rings the Seraya range is rough and unreliable, as the monsoon rains turn its dry rivers into torrents and take out bridges and crossings. A run from Amed around the point to Amlapura makes a nice adventure by dirtbike, but it can take longer than, say,

the entire trip from Kuta to Tulamben. A number of small resorts have been built along the coast here, but they are mostly quiet retreats, and not dive operations. Access to the reefs here, at least in the near future, is most reliable by boat.

Because the Jemeluk dive was always by *jukung* (the local boatmen would run you out to the outer reef, a five-minute trip, and then follow your bubbles) it is easy here to hire a boat to points further east. The problem is the limited power and capacity of a *jukung*, especially when facing such severe current conditions. Future exploration of this area will likely come from operators in Candi Dasa and Padang Bai. Their vessels, sized and powered for the trip across the strait to Nusa Penida, are the right tackle for diving trips to this rough, unpredictable, and little-known stretch of coast.

Lipah Bay, the destination we settled upon when the current thwarted our plans to dive Tanjung Ibus, is the furthest we can recommend going by *jukung* from Jemeluk.

In a way, our plan to dive Ibus was doomed to failure from the beginning. A good spearfishing spot (like a good surfing spot) is almost by definition a bad place for diving. A point that creates the midwater swirl of fish sought by a free-diving spearfisherman, or a point that creates a break that sets up the kind of waves a surfer can exploit, almost always creates a horrible, dangerous mess at diving depths.

When divers look at marine charts they make a common mistake. Their eyes and imaginations are drawn to the rocky points, peninsulas, and exposed islands—the dramatic punctuation marks of coast geography. Probably these sites will be rich, at least in big schools of fish, but they will also almost certainly be plagued by the

Map 2.5 Jemeluk 1:10K

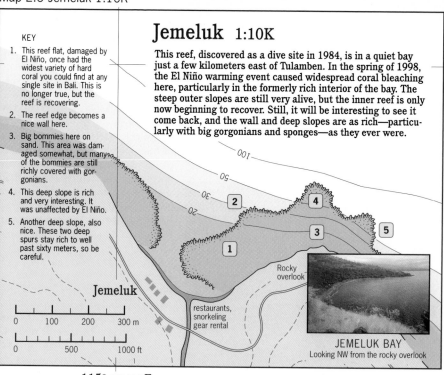

Jemeluk 1:10K

This reef, discovered as a dive site in 1984, is in a quiet bay just a few kilometers east of Tulamben. In the spring of 1998, the El Niño warming event caused widespread coral bleaching here, particularly in the formerly rich interior of the bay. The steep outer slopes are still very alive, but the inner reef is only now beginning to recover. Still, it will be interesting to see it come back, and the wall and deep slopes are as rich—particularly with big gorgonians and sponges—as they ever were.

KEY

1. This reef flat, damaged by El Niño, once had the widest variety of hard coral you could find at any single site in Bali. This is no longer true, but the reef is recovering.

2. The reef edge becomes a nice wall here.

3. Big bommies here on sand. This area was damaged somewhat, but many of the bommies are still richly covered with gorgonians.

4. This deep slope is rich and very interesting. It was unaffected by El Niño.

5. Another deep slope, also nice. These two deep spurs stay rich to well past sixty meters, so be careful.

Jemeluk

| 0 | 100 | 200 | 300 m |

| 0 | 500 | 1000 ft |

Rocky overlook

restaurants, snorkeling gear rental

JEMELUK BAY
Looking NW from the rocky overlook

115° 39' 30" E

kinds of currents that can rip off your face mask, suddenly suck you ten meters downslope, or whisk you two kilometers offshore in the course of a panic-filled twenty-minute dive.

Let me put it this way: it is very nice to see a hammerhead shark while diving, but it is not so nice if it is the *last* thing you ever see. What you need to look for in a dive site is the opposite of an exposed point. You need a bay, a quiet lee, some sort of geographic feature that will generate ameliorating eddies and protect you from the full force of the current and swell. In short, although it may sound unflattering, you need to think like a gorgonian, not like a jack.

Lipah Bay

Lipah (sometimes rendered "Nipah") is a quiet, black sand bay about three kilometers along the coast from Jemeluk, just past Banjar Bunutan. It is protected by Tanjung Puri in the east, and an unnamed rocky point in the west. The good stretch of reef lines the western edge of the bay, from the rocky point—clearly marked by three small temples—to the mouth of Tukad Bantul. (See Map 2.5 pg. 113.) Although we didn't explore this area thoroughly, a quick look revealed that west of and at the three-temple point, the reef was beaten and rough, as it is exposed to the full brunt of the current and swell. East of the river the bottom goes to sand, and coral growth here seems to be hampered by siltation from the seasonal outflow from the river.

The highlight of this dive site is a charming little wreck that sits at six to twelve meters or so, well inside the bay and right where the reef goes to sand. The ship was a small steel freighter, about twenty meters long, and is now beautifully encrusted with gorgonians, sponges, and black coral bushes. It looks like an easy wreck to penetrate, but there is no way to do it without breaking up all of the encrusting life. Wally tried the main chamber, but quickly gave up for this reason. Also, he later told me, he was afraid I would follow him, and wouldn't see the scorpionfish he had found buried nearly

©BURT JONES/MAURINE SHIMLOCK   Trichonotus elegans

The sand divers are a small family of nervous, skinny fishes that hover in groups just off the bottom. It takes a calm and practiced diver to see them, because at the least sign of danger, they dive into the soft sand. The larger and more strongly marked individual above is the male. The others are members of his harem. A male has three long dorsal fin spines—nearly the length of his body—that he can manipulate as a form of display.

up to its eyes in the silt. This was *Inimicus didactylus,* a very interesting scorpionfish that, when not buried, walks around on four little "legs" formed by the rays of its pectoral fins. It is not an aggressive creature, but its generic name honors the virulence of its sting, which is second only to the stonefish in potency. Another reason, perhaps, not to penetrate this wreck.

The slope down away from the wreck is extremely rich in gorgonians, including some very beautiful and unusual species, such as *Semperina,* a deep red and white animal with peculiar furrowed branches, and an odd, bright yellow *Echinogorgia.* I call this latter one "odd" because not only does it have such thick branches that I almost thought it was a kind of sponge, but it also vibrates constantly, even in a very light current. I dubbed this animal the "quaking gorgonian" because its habit reminded me of the quaking aspen, whose leaves flutter

in even the tiniest wind. The gorgonians and whips are full of commensals as well: on a single specimen of the whip gorgonian *Ctenocella,* Wally found three different species of spindle ovulids.

The fish life here is quite good as well, and this is the kind of place where you will have a good chance to find unusual animals. In some places the water was thick with mysid shrimp, which means that shrimpfish, ghost pipefish, seahorses, and the dragonfish *Eurypegasus* might find the right conditions here. Once, about ten years ago, Wally dove here with a group of ichthyologists, and author and photographer Rudie Kuiter found a pure white *Rhinopias,* surely the most beautiful of the scorpionfish.

The reef slopes down to fine black sand at about twenty meters, and continues from there as little outcrops of life to forty meters or more. If you look landward from the deep at the edge of the reef, you can see great bommies in the shallows, looming in the distance like a faraway mountain range. We ended our dive in the shallows around these bommies, and there we encountered our greatest surprise: huge beds of acroporid corals in spikey clumps, giant whorls, and tables, all absolutely pristine.

This may now be the only place on Bali that can offer such a scene. The *Chromis* damsels and anthias gathered in huge swarms, and great schools of fusiliers cut circles in the mid-water. Although it covers a relatively small area, maybe sixty meters across, the Lipah Bay reef flat is as rich as was the top reef of Menjangan a decade ago, and would make a wonderful snorkeling site.

A FINICKY SITE

In late May of 1999, just after the wind had switched for good to a steady southeasterly, we had wonderful diving at this site. But then

Map 2.6 Lipah Bay 1:5K

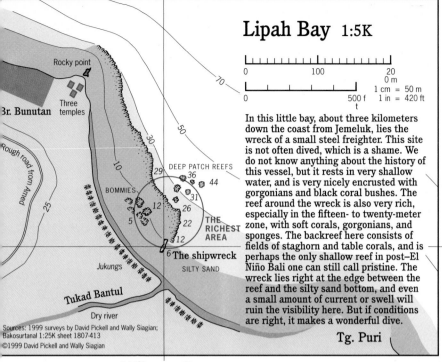

Lipah Bay 1:5K

Rocky point

Three temples

Gr. Bunutan

Rough road from Amed

DEEP PATCH REEFS

BOMMIES

THE RICHEST AREA

The shipwreck

SILTY SAND

Jukungs

Tukad Bantul

Dry river

In this little bay, about three kilometers down the coast from Jemeluk, lies the wreck of a small steel freighter. This site is not often dived, which is a shame. We do not know anything about the history of this vessel, but it rests in very shallow water, and is very nicely encrusted with gorgonians and black coral bushes. The reef around the wreck is also very rich, especially in the fifteen- to twenty-meter zone, with soft corals, gorgonians, and sponges. The backreef here consists of fields of staghorn and table corals, and is perhaps the only shallow reef in post–El Niño Bali one can still call pristine. The wreck lies right at the edge between the reef and the silty sand bottom, and even a small amount of current or swell will ruin the visibility here. But if conditions are right, it makes a wonderful dive.

Tg. Puri

Sources: 1999 surveys by David Pickell and Wally Siagian;
Bakosurtanal 1:25K sheet 1807-413
©1999 David Pickell and Wally Siagian

115° 40' 50" E (approx.)

again, at the time we dove, the water was gemstone blue all along this stretch of coast, which is not always (in fact, not often) the case. Also, because we were planning to dive the difficult Tanjung Ibus, we were picky about our timing, and scheduled our dive for when the tide was at slack high, and thus the most manageable. Under these conditions Lipah Bay was magic.

However, even moderate current or surge will spoil this site, stirring up the fine substrate, and causing visibility to drop dramatically. The site is basically protected from both sides, but even though we had textbook conditions, we could still feel the current going a bit shifty. A little gust east, then west, then downslope. Enough to let you know that in other conditions this site could be a problem. In particular, this is the kind of site that could

produce a downcurrent, so pay attention to the signs. Basically, if you want to have a good dive here, make sure there is no swell, and check the color of the water. If it is blue, you'll be fine. If it's green, you probably shouldn't even bother.

Lipah is not a common dive, but the Jemeluk operators have been taking the occasional client here for some time. After Jemeluk itself, it is probably the most protected site along this stretch, and maybe the only reliable dive here. The *jukung* ride is relatively short—it took us forty minutes out, against the current, and twenty-five back—and the scenery is beautiful, a series of great ridges leading down to the ocean from the Seraya range, forming cleft valleys and points. Don't forget your cigarettes, though, because there is nowhere along this stretch to get any.

Bali's east coast, with its cold water, is a trove of unusual species, like this spotted wobbegong shark, which belongs in temperate Australian waters. This fish grows to three meters, and can get ornery if pestered.

MIKE SEVERNS Crab: Quadrella sp.; Soft coral: Dendronephthya sp.; unidentified crinoid

The soft coral crab is always ready to defend its territory, even against relatively harmless Peeping Toms like our photograp
Crabs of the related genus Trapezia, which live in hard corals, have been known to chase off marauding crown-of-thorns
starfish, intent on eating their homes, by nipping painfully and relentlessly on the starfish's sensitive tube feet.

Fed by the South Bali upwelling, these undomesticated sites are rich, cold, and exciting. They are also wracked by current and pounded by swell, and demand experience and good judgement (and a thick wetsuit) to enjoy.

The East Coast

WALLY HAS A QUICK WIT AND A GENerally boisterous sense of humor, but in the diving community his most lasting verbal contribution might be his simple, admirably compact, and quite accurate description of conditions at the underwater canyon off Tepekong Island when the swell is up. At times like this, he said, this site becomes a giant toilet.

Although all of Bali's dive operators list Tepekong, the most famous of the East Coast sites, in their brochures, I am quite sure if you polled them, most would vote this island their least favorite place to take clients (and nearby Mimpang might come in a close second). The owner of one operation even asked us not to mention Tepekong in our book. When we told him what we thought of this suggestion, he pleaded with us to at least not give it a glowing review. The fact of the matter was, he said, the place gave

his guides the willies, and since he was on the subject, it gave him the willies, too.

Sea conditions are a minor concern at the protected sites in Bali's Northwest, nor do they really mean much at Tulamben or Batu Kelebit, other than creating a bit of current or causing a marginal drop in visibility. But on the rocky little outcrops of Amuk Bay—Tepekong, Mimpang, Biaha—and Gili Selang to the north, conditions mean everything. Bali's east coast offers some absolutely stunning diving, with sharks, big schools of sweetlips, beautiful rocky walls and canyons, and crystal-clear water, but the current and swell can be treacherous.

Study the maps in this section carefully, and the descriptions of current behavior in the text and figures. Be patient. Wait until full slack tide, or even until the next day to dive the trickier points. Amuk—the

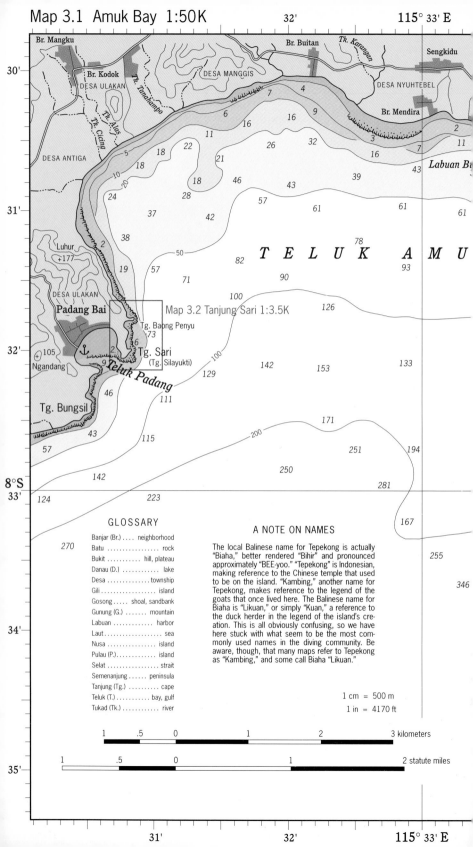

Map 3.1 Amuk Bay 1:50K

115° 33' E · 32'

Br. Mangku · Br. Buitan · Tk. Karangan · Sengkidu

Br. Kodok · DESA MANGGIS · DESA NYUHTEBEL

DESA ULAKAN

Tk. Tanahampo · Br. Mendira

30'

Tk. Atas

Tk. Cicing · DESA ANTIGA · Labuan B

Luhur +177

Padang Bai · Map 3.2 Tanjung Sari 1:3.5K

DESA ULAKAN

Tg. Baong Penyu

Ngandang +105 · Tg. Sari (Tg. Silayukti)

Teluk Padang

Tg. Bungsil

T E L U K   A M U

31'

32'

8°S 33'

GLOSSARY

Banjar (Br.) . . . . . neighborhood
Batu . . . . rock
Bukit . . . . hill, plateau
Danau (D.) . . . . lake
Desa . . . . township
Gili . . . . island
Gosong . . . . . shoal, sandbank
Gunung (G.) . . . . mountain
Labuan . . . . harbor
Laut . . . . sea
Nusa . . . . island
Pulau (P.) . . . . island
Selat . . . . strait
Semenanjung . . . . . . peninsula
Tanjung (Tg.) . . . . cape
Teluk (T.) . . . . bay, gulf
Tukad (Tk.) . . . . river

A NOTE ON NAMES

The local Balinese name for Tepekong is actually "Biaha," better rendered "Bihir" and pronounced approximately "BEE-yoo." "Tepekong" is Indonesian, making reference to the Chinese temple that used to be on the island. "Kambing," another name for Tepekong, makes reference to the legend of the goats that once lived here. The Balinese name for Biaha is "Likuan," or simply "Kuan," a reference to the duck herder in the legend of the island's creation. This is all obviously confusing, so we have here stuck with what seem to be the most commonly used names in the diving community. Be aware, though, that many maps refer to Tepekong as "Kambing," and some call Biaha "Likuan."

1 cm = 500 m
1 in = 4170 ft

1 .5 0 1 2 3 kilometers

1 .5 0 1 2 statute miles

34'

35'

31' · 32' · 115° 33' E

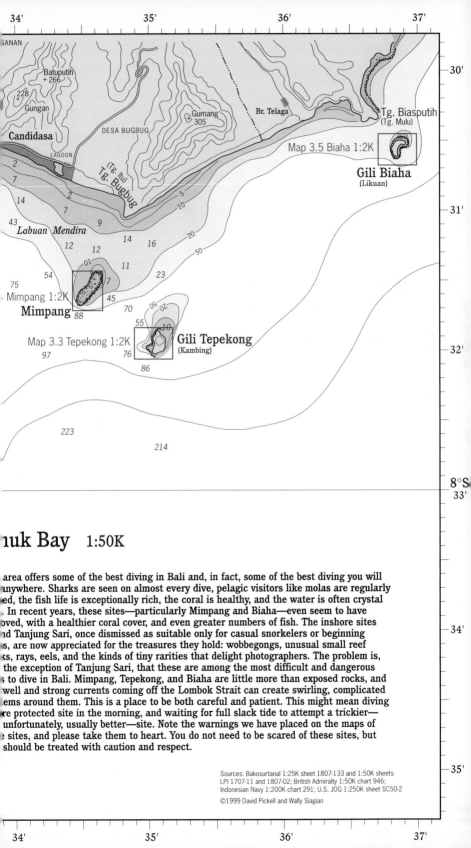

...uk Bay 1:50K

...area offers some of the best diving in Bali and, in fact, some of the best diving you will
...anywhere. Sharks are seen on almost every dive, pelagic visitors like molas are regularly
...ed, the fish life is exceptionally rich, the coral is healthy, and the water is often crystal
.... In recent years, these sites—particularly Mimpang and Biaha—even seem to have
...oved, with a healthier coral cover, and even greater numbers of fish. The inshore sites
...nd Tanjung Sari, once dismissed as suitable only for casual snorkelers or beginning
...s, are now appreciated for the treasures they hold: wobbegongs, unusual small reef
...ks, rays, eels, and the kinds of tiny rarities that delight photographers. The problem is,
...the exception of Tanjung Sari, that these are among the most difficult and dangerous
...s to dive in Bali. Mimpang, Tepekong, and Biaha are little more than exposed rocks, and
...well and strong currents coming off the Lombok Strait can create swirling, complicated
...ems around them. This is a place to be both careful and patient. This might mean diving
...re protected site in the morning, and waiting for full slack tide to attempt a trickier—
...unfortunately, usually better—site. Note the warnings we have placed on the maps of
...e sites, and please take them to heart. You do not need to be scared of these sites, but
...should be treated with caution and respect.

Sources: Bakosurtanal 1:25K sheet 1807-133 and 1:50K sheets
LPI 1707-11 and 1807-02; British Admiralty 1:50K chart 946;
Indonesian Navy 1:200K chart 291; U.S. JOG 1:250K sheet SC50-2

©1999 David Pickell and Wally Siagian

word was corrupted by the English into "amok"—is an aptly named body of water.

A DRYSUIT, ANYONE?

The water here is also very cold. I live in California, where the current brings us water from Alaska, and I have experience with cold water, but we dive in thick Farmer

KAL MULLER Tepekong

Tepekong's rocky canyon, one of the East Coast's premier sites, has a stark, mysterious feel, quite unlike most of Bali's reefs.

John's (and the professionals and smart folk use drysuits). Wally and I happen to own the same make of cheap computer, and ours never read lower than 22°C, which made us feel like crybabies until we noticed that our diving companions, with more sophisticated instruments, were consistently getting readings in the teens. Water temperatures of 20°C or even 19°C (that's 66 American degrees) are not unknown beneath the thermocline at any of these sites. Do not wear a Lycra suit here—I don't care how much magic titanium it has in it. You need a thick neoprene suit, and if you are wise, a hood. You'll still be hugging yourself the entire second half of the dive, but at least your brain won't shut down.

You might derive some comfort from remembering that it is this cold water that makes East Bali so special. The ocean off South Bali is the site of one of Indonesia's five major seasonal upwellings. (The others are West Sumatra, the Makassar Strait,

South Java, and the Banda Sea.) Upwellings bring rich, frigid water from the deep basins to the surface. In Bali's case, this takes place during the southeast monsoon, when easterly winds generate the strong Java Current flowing westward along the south coast of Bali's neighboring island. The only water available to replace the surface water borne away by the Java Current at this time lies in a deep basin one hundred kilometers south of Bali.

The South Bali upwelling is one of the strongest in the archipelago, and depending on the winds in a particular season, brings the cold, abyssal water to a depth of anywhere from ninety meters to the surface. In our experience, the marked thermocline at the East Bali sites is usually around twenty meters.

A TASTE OF SOUTH AUSTRALIA

I was very excited when I received the slide of the wobbegong shark that opens this section. This interesting animal has been living at Silayukti Point for a while now, and it was nice to get a good picture of it. But when I looked at it carefully to make an identification, I became quite puzzled. This was not the fish I thought it was. According to Last and Stevens, which I consider the most reliable chondrichthyan reference, this fish had to be *Orectolobus maculatus,* a relatively common wobbegong—common, that is, if you live in South Australia.

And it is not just the temperate water oddballs that make this area so interesting. Overall, the fish and invertebrate life in East Bali is simply excellent. There are sites where you will always find sharks. Molas are seasonally common. Bali's endemic surgeonfish lives here, as do seahorses, unusual scorpionfish, and a diverse assemblage of corals and gorgonians that is reminiscent of the famous reefs of Komodo and the Banda Sea.

THE EAST COAST
Tanjung Sari

THE FIRST TIME I EVER SAW BALI through a face mask was in 1987, and the place was the rather cinematically named "Blue Lagoon." I was staying at Candi Dasa at the time, and had booked a snorkeling excursion for myself and a companion. Blue Lagoon, we soon learned, was neither blue nor a lagoon, and in fact on the day we visited it might more accurately have been named "Greenish Washbucket." The wind had been blowing steadily for a few days, and this "lagoon," really a tiny bay, had collected a froth of sargassum, seagrass leaves, candy wrappers, plastic bottles, and bits of pink string.

This wasn't our problem, though. Our problem was that the bay had also become a soup pot of plankton. This hurt visibility, of course, but it also hurt *us*. A great pestilential smack of some species of box jelly had gathered here, and these vile creatures immediately began stinging us about the face and lips, and, since we were fashionably dressed for our swim in a tropical lagoon (surfer shorts and bikini, respectively), just about everywhere else, as well. We lasted, I think, about three minutes before clambering back into the boat.

Blue Lagoon is just north of Tanjung Silayukti (see MAP 3.2, pp. 122–123) and it is still a destination for snorkeling jaunts out of Candi Dasa. Given better conditions than we had thirteen years ago, it might be just fine for this purpose, but more importantly, this reef—from the Turtle's Neck Peninsula that marks the northern limit of Blue La-

goon all the way south around Tanjung Sari—is one of the most interesting places to dive in all of Bali.

MAKE MINE VANILLA

Tanjung Sari is the brown tweed blazer of the East Coast sites. Or, if you prefer, the Ford station wagon. At first glance it seems, somehow, *ordinary*. You can basically swim to

> This rocky, unassuming stretch of reef is the sleeper of the East Coast sites. A photographer—or a diver interested in unusual marine life—could spend a week here without getting bored.

it from the beach at Padang Bai. How can this place possibly be as good as those dangerous-looking, current-swept rocks out in the middle of Amuk Bay? Tepekong, now that's an Armani suit—in a Ferrari Daytona.

It is true that the structure of the Tanjung Sari reef is relatively unexciting. The substrate is drab or white sand, with scattered rocks and boulders. Extending out from Silayukti point is a long rocky formation, but the roll-off is basically gentle. The reef forms short sections of wall at the very end of the Turtle's Neck point and just where the channel begins off Tanjung Sari, but most of this area is a sloping reef that thins out and goes to sand at

Map 3.2 Tanjung Sari 1:3.5K

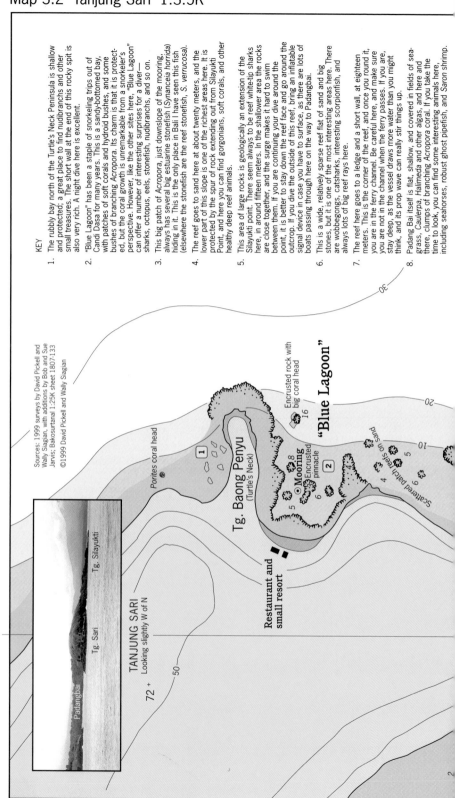

115° 30' 45" E

Sources: 1999 surveys by David Pickell and Wally Siagian, with additions by Bob and Sue Jarvis; Bakosurtanal 1:25K sheet 1807-133
©1999 David Pickell and Wally Siagian

Padangbai   Tg. Sari   Tg. Silayukti

TANJUNG SARI
Looking slightly W of N

72 +

50

Porites coral head

1

Tg. Baong Penyu
(Turtle's Neck)

Encrusted rock with big coral head

16

"Blue Lagoon"

Mooring
Encrusted pinnacle

8

2

6

5

Scattered patch reefs to 10 m

4

3   9   5

20   10

Restaurant and small resort

30

KEY

1. The rubbly bay north of the Turtle's Neck Peninsula is shallow and protected, a great place to find nudibranchs and other small treasures. The short wall at the end of this rocky spit is also very rich. A night dive here is excellent.

2. "Blue Lagoon" has been a staple of snorkeling trips out of Candi Dasa for many years. This is a sandy-bottomed bay, with patches of soft corals and hydroid bushes, and some bushes of branching Acropora. Its charm is that it is protected, but the coral growth is unremarkable from a snorkeler's perspective. However, like the other sites here, "Blue Lagoon" can offer a number of interesting surprises for a diver— sharks, octopus, eels, stonefish, nudibranchs, and so on.

3. This big patch of Acropora, just downslope of the mooring, always has several big estuarine stonefish (Synanceia horrida) hiding in it. This is the only place in Bali I have seen this fish (elsewhere the stonefish are the reef stonefish, S. verrucosa).

4. The reef goes to sand here at about twenty meters, and the lower part of this slope is one of the richest areas here. It is protected by the spur of rock extending out from Silayukti Point, and here you can find gorgonians, soft corals, and other healthy deep reef animals.

5. This area of large rocks is geologically an extension of the Silayukti point. There seem always to be reef white-tip sharks here, in around fifteen meters. In the shallower area the rocks are close together, and the surge makes it hard to swim between them. If you are continuing your dive around the point, it is better to stay down the reef face and go around the outcrop. If you dive the outside of this reef, bring an inflatable signal device in case you have to surface, as there are lots of boats passing through here on the way to Padangbai.

6. This is a wide, relatively sparse reef flat of sand and big stones, but it is one of the most interesting areas here. There are wobbegongs, catsharks, interesting scorpionfish, and always lots of big reef rays here.

7. The reef here goes to a ledge and a short wall, at eighteen meters. This is the corner of the reef, and once you round it, you are in the ferry channel. Be careful here, and make sure you are not in the channel when the ferry passes. If you are, stay deep, as the vessel draws more water than you might think, and its prop wave can really stir things up.

8. Padang Bai itself is flat, shallow, and covered in fields of sea-grass, Caulerpa, Halimeda and other algas, and here and there, clumps of branching Acropora coral. If you take the time to look, you can find some interesting animals here, including seahorses, robust ghost pipefish, and Saron shrimp.

Tanjung Sari 1:3.5K

This area is the most different, and most surprising, of the Amuk Bay sites. It is a coastal site, and supports a distinct set of animals from the offshore islands. This is an excellent site for sharks—including unusual cat-sharks, nurse sharks, wobbegong sharks, and reef white-tips—as well many rare and interesting smaller animals, such as nudibranchs, shrimps, crabs, and squids and octopus. It is just around the corner from Padang Bai, and makes a very convenient—and reward-ing—night dive. Historically this site has been under-appreciated by divers, who have instead fixated on Tepekong—do not make this mistake.

about twenty meters. The coral cover is generally thin, and relatively impoverished in number of species, chiefly robust branching *Acropora* and *Porites*.

But the animals here are remarkable. When we first began working this area, the local operator showed us a picture he had taken of a strange bottom shark. It was the catshark *Atelomycterus mamoratus,* a skinny half-meter-long creature that looks remarkably like a tokay gecko. This fish is common here, as are other interesting bamboo sharks, catsharks, nurse sharks, and of course, the wobbegong shark. The rocky reef flat between Silayukti and Sari is also an excellent place to find rays of several species, including some that are never seen elsewhere in Bali.

Unusual nudibranchs and other gastropods, strange, walking scorpionfish, flying gurnards, stargazers, and many other oddities that you would have a hard time finding anywhere else on the island—or any other island, for that matter—are almost common here. And even those whose taste in marine life is less rarefied will enjoy Tanjung Sari—we have never dived here without encountering at least two reef white-tip sharks, and there is a big Napoleon wrasse that always keeps an eye on visitors to what it considers its domain.

This site has a continental, rather than insular, character. You somehow know you are diving on the edge of Sundaland. Whereas at Tepekong and Mimpang, despite their proximity, you already can believe you are diving a tiny island in the Banda Sea.

THE MONSTER

Tanjung Sari is one of the best places to see Bali's only endemic fish, a strange, still unnamed surgeonfish in the genus *Prionurus* (see photograph, pg. 137). The members of this genus—the sawtails—are among the larger of the Acanthurids, and the species found in Bali appears to reach close to three-quarters of a meter in length. They do not school. You see single specimens, pairs, or sometimes trios, either on their own, or tagging along with a school of unicornfish.

Prionurus is very shy, and for a long time Wally and I could not even reach a consensus on what color they were. I would say dark blue, and he would say, no, they're brown. Then the next time we saw one, I would agree they were brown, or grayish, and he would say no, you were right, they're blue. We have only ever seen the fish in East Bali—Tanjung Sari, Mimpang, Tepekong, Biaha, Gili Selang—and only once at Nusa Penida, in Gamat Bay. In the sunny, crystal-clear water of Gamat, this fish appeared a solid, rich blue, with a yellow tail. Elsewhere, I still don't know. It could all be a matter of lighting and reflectivity, or the fish could be variable in color.

Toward the end of our researches, Wally finally cornered *Prionurus* at Tepekong, and got a close look. "That thing is an ugly monster!" he said, as soon as he reached the boat. As you can see from Jack Randall's photo, it is a coarse, spiky creature. One reason Wally was able to approach the specimen he saw was that it was encumbered by a remora, which gives you a sense of the size of this fish. He also speculated that it was sick because it was eating crinoids, surely a foodstuff of last resort. (Wally has since seen others eating crinoids, however, so perhaps they actually like these crunchy, seemingly nutritionless animals.)

DON'T FORGET THE BAY

Water conditions at Tanjung Sari are not generally a problem. The visibility is quite good, around fifteen meters, and the rocky point

Cheilinus undulatus

A large Napoleon wrasse is often seen at Tanjung Sari. These fish, among the largest fishes on Indo-Pacific reefs, can reach more than two meters, and almost two hundred kilograms. Their strong jaws allow them to eat mollusks and spiky echinoderms such as sea urchins.

rovides protection from the worst f the current. Surge can be an annoyance in the shallows and up round the rocks off Silayukti oint, but it is not enough to be a azard. The only thing to be careful f is the channel. The ferry runs ere several times a day, and many maller boats come in and out of the ay on an irregular basis. Never surce in the channel, and watch your epth there as well—the ferry raws a lot more water than you night think. Always dive here with signal device, and surface away om the channel and away from the ilayukti rocks.

This area makes an excellent ight dive as well. Some of the most nusual animals—like the cathark—are nocturnal, and the reefs re shallow enough, and close nough to Padang Bai, to be safe for ighttime work.

Also, do not visit here without aving a look at the bay itself. Padang" means "plain" or "field," nd the bay was given this name beause of its flat, even character. Ex-

cept for the channel, it is everywhere just a couple meters deep. There are fields of seagrass, and *Caulerpa* and *Halimeda* algae here, with scattered outcrops of *Acropora* coral. It is an interesting—and different—environment to explore. With sharp eyes and patience you can find interesting seagrass bed–adapted species such as snake eels, razorfish, and wrasses, and invertebrates like box crabs and sea cucumbers.

The bay also used to be a prime spot for pipefish and seahorses, but a few years back seine-netters came in and swept it for the traditional Chinese medicine market (smoothbodied seahorses and the doubleended pipehorse *Syngnathoides biaculeatus* are apparently the most valuable). It has since been nearly impossible to find a seahorse here, but just as I was finishing the manuscript, Wally told me he found one right under the dock (hard to tell from his description, but *Hippocampus spinosissimus* would be my guess), so things might be improving a little bit.

This tiny character, found by the photographer at Tanjung Sari, reminds me somehow of a mouse deer. It has four cirri or 'whiskers' on its chin, and the first ray of each of its pectoral fins is free of webbing and used as a walking leg. It must be a scorpionfish, but otherwise it has me stumped. This dive site has a knack for producing surprises: strange scorpionfish, catsharks, wobbegongs, unusual nudibranchs, and many others.

Amuk Bay
Tepekong, Mimpang, and Biaha

THE FRINGING REEFS SURROUNDING Tepekong, Mimpang, and Biaha have the most untropical appearance of any in Bali. Fierce currents keep the coral and gorgonian growth generally low and coarse, and the chilly water and stark rock structures are startlingly at odds with the warm, quiet lushness one expects in the tropics, whether above water or below. These are very healthy reefs, with an exceptional diversity of invertebrate and fish life. But they do not have the

With sharks, molas, and great schools of fish, these islands—little more than current-swept rocks, really—have a feral beauty unique in Bali. They can bite back, too.

voluptuous beauty one usually associates with coral reefs. Their beauty is jarring, almost harsh, like that of the twisted trees clinging to a windswept mountainside. Their appearance manifests constant struggle—or put another way, constant rebirth—which, if there were yet any precision left in the word, could be called sublime.

The current flowing past East Bali is literally a torrent (see "The Indonesian Throughflow," pg. 130), and carries a constant supply of plankton and larval animals across these reefs, which is the primary

source of both their diversity and health. During the southeast monsoon, the South Bali upwelling pushes cold, rich water to the surface, bringing with it the molas, sharks, and schooling pelagic fish.

Though similar, each of the sites has its own distinct character. Tepekong, the most famous of the group, is also the most difficult to dive, and the living surface of its reef is the most scoured and rough of the three. But Tepekong's Canyon is also the most dramatic underwater structure here, and on a good day is swarming with fish. In the past Mimpang has been considered a lesser site, and conditions here can be almost as difficult as at Tepekong (and even harder to predict). But Mimpang is perhaps the most reliable place in Bali to see sharks, and the southernmost extent of this reef, though small, is now one of the most beautiful reefs in all of Indonesia. Biaha is the most distant but it also has the most developed reef of the three, and unlike the others it is diveable—with both wall and slope, both very rich—for almost its entire circumference.

KNOW YOUR MOON

The northwest monsoon, approximately December through March, is when the winds across Bali tend to be westerly, and in general a west wind produces the best diving conditions at these sites. Southeast winds, which prevail during the rest of the year, can make things difficult, particularly one that blows fresh or better for any appreciable length of time.

Unfortunately, the upwelling occurs during the southeast monsoon,
and this is when these sites seem the
most alive, and when you have the
best chance to see molas and other
big pelagics here. Our best dives in
this area, in fact, have been during
the southeast monsoon. The im-
mediate concerns at these sites are
not so much the wind, but the
strength and direction of the swell
and current.

The southeastern sides of these
islands rise steeply from the ocean
floor, and swell coming in from the
Lombok straight, when it hits the
sudden and complicated bathymetry around them, can wreak havoc.
Swell is generated by mid-ocean
waves, and it can travel great distances. Heavy swell at Tepekong, for
example, can come about because
two days of steady winds have
raised seas a hundred or more kilometers away. Swell is something that
you have to look for, not something
you can predict.

The current through this area
behaves somewhat according to a
pattern set by the monsoon seasons,
tending south overall, but the tides
are a more important factor for diving. In general, the best and safest
diving conditions are created by the
neaps, around first quarter moon
and last quarter moon. Spring
tides, around full and new moon,
cause the most trouble. For some
reason new moon is always worse
than full moon, and frankly, it is better not to dive here during the period spanning a day or two before,
and even longer after, the actual date
of new moon.

Whatever the moon phase, the
calmest conditions are at slack
water, within about an hour of full
high or full low tide. This is true of
any dive site, but particularly at Tepekong's Canyon and at Mimpang,
this should be considered an iron-
clad rule: dive only at slack tide, and
coming up on high tide is best.

In theory then, the best conditions for diving will be during the
northwest monsoon, following a period of light winds throughout the
area (no swell), on an out-of-phase
tide, and at slack water. A quick cal-
culation (four months of west
winds, two neaps a month, etc.) suggests that the combination of these
ideal conditions might pertain for

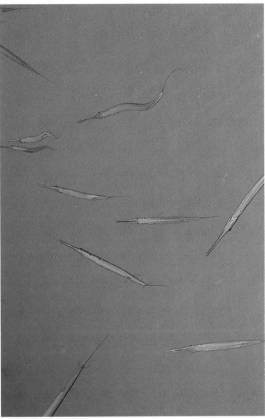

WALLY SIAGIAN Fistularia commersonii

no more than a dozen days a year. In
truth you can have good diving here
more often than this. But you have
to go have a look first, and be willing to change your plan. The local
variability is considerable, and at a
time when Tepekong looks risky,
things at Mimpang might be fine.

The visibility here, as expected
on offshore reefs, is very good, usually twenty meters and sometimes

Very often divers
forget to look up.
These cornetfish,
hunting plankton in a
small school, have
created an interest-
ing pattern against
the surface.

even better. There is never a silt problem, but plankton in the water can cut visibility by five or even ten meters. The upwelling itself can also reduce visibility. The mixing of 28°C surface water and 22°C (or colder) deep water creates a thermally disturbed layer that looks like melted glass, and your visibility in this zone is close to nil.

Tepekong

The first time I dove Tepekong, conditions from the surface were, according to Wally, perfect. Too perfect, maybe, because he couldn't help feeling suspicious. Amuk Bay was a glassy lake. We motored up to the indicator point, a rocky extension of the island's southwest extremity that underwater becomes the Canyon. There was no swell at all, and only the tiniest waves lapped at the black rock. This, Wally said, was very unusual, and he sniffed around the point for a while like a dog that had found a snake that it wasn't quite sure was dead. Then he shrugged and we suited up.

We dropped in tight against the island's western face, and headed down the steep, cobbled slope. Underwater, it was dead calm, just as conditions at the point indicated. Working our way south, we reached a group of large boulders, and then, the Canyon. As soon as we appeared, two reef white-tip sharks reluctantly wandered off, but without even a hint of current to make things interesting to the fish, the Canyon was almost deserted.

It did not even occur to me to be disappointed with this state of affairs. The water was crystal clear, and I looked up to find myself in a stunning, rocky amphitheater that could easily have been carved out of California's Sierra Nevada. Without the distraction of the large schools of fish and swirling current that would later command my attention on visits to this site, my eyes were

drawn immediately to the Canyon's essence: great, black, cornered blocks of basalt, cascading sharply down to forty meters.

I could imagine Ansel Adams here, if he had been a diver and had found an engineer willing to build a housing for an eight-by-ten camera, parking his tripod in the sand, setting the aperture of his trusty old Dagor to F64, and waiting for the sun to sink just enough for the light to settle seductively on the Canyon walls.

Still, cavernous, and with an alpine beauty made surreal by its underwater setting, the indefinable power of this place was immediately apparent. At fifteen meters, halfway down the island side of the Canyon, a flat-topped spur projects straight out. Sit down on the end of this, and look up and out at the dramatic sweep of rock. Then close your eyes for a minute. I am sure you will feel it too.

I am not the kind of person to drive an old Volvo to Red Rock, Arizona and sit on a cactus-covered butte for a week with a crystal in my lap. But I can feel something at Tepekong, and I am sure it has to do with the spiritual magnetism of the place. Wally, less burdened, perhaps, by the Yankee pragmatist tradition (and not ever having had to contend with the "New Age" movement) can be more frank, and simply says: "Tepekong has power, and you have to respect it."

THE LESSON OF THE GOATS

A long time ago, maybe fifty years, maybe two hundred and fifty years, this rocky, steep-sided island was home to a small herd of goats. Tepekong has the approximate profile of a bowler hat, and most hoofed animals would take one look at the thorny scrub and vertical rocks and give up. But goats are very resourceful and their foot work is deft, and to them this kind

L MULLER Plectorhinchus polytaenia (mostly) and P. lineatus Tepekong

f place is more than satisfactory. Nobody knows how they got there.

Tepekong has always been venerated by the Balinese as a place of great, and perhaps even dangerous, power. Bali's small Chinese community also recognizes this (the word "tepekong" means Chinese temple in Indonesian). Although the Balinese are quite fond of satay kambing, they considered the island's goats sacred as well, and did not molest them.

But one day, a Bugis ship—the Bugis are from South Sulawesi—stopped at the island. The sailors had seen the goats, and decided to round them up and slaughter them for a feast. This they did, with little trouble, and then proceeded to gorge themselves in a party that lasted most of the night. The next morning, they set sail.

The Bugis are the archipelago's great sailors, far more famous for this than the Balinese, for example. And this crew was very familiar with these waters, having passed through them many times on their way

home. Still, within minutes of leaving Tepekong, the great wooden *pinisi* hit the reef, split open, and sank like a stone to the bottom. Every single man on the ship died. Since then, no goats have been seen on the island.

THE CANYON

Although reef surrounds the entire island, the Canyon is by far the most interesting site on Tepekong. The best dive plan is to drop in next to the rock wall on the island's western face, and head south and downslope. Explore the Canyon, and, if conditions allow, continue to the offshore pinnacles, and finish up on the northern, protected side. (See MAP 3.3, pp. 134–135.) This is not a lot of area to cover, but that isn't the point of Tepekong. The best thing to do, particularly if the current is up, is to simply crouch in among the rocks of the Canyon and watch the swirling show.

Although there are a few gorgonians in the protected area of the slope just before the Canyon, for the

Schools of sweetlips, often forming great, jagged columns, are one of the most colorful features of Tepekong's canyon. Some half-dozen species of sweetlips can be found in Bali, and at different times, different species dominate at Tepekong. When this photo was taken— maybe six years ago— the ribbon sweetlips were most common, and this was the case in 1999 as well. But a few years back there were more lined sweetlips (formerly called Goldmann's) here than any other species.

Ten Thousand Rivers Run Through It

IF INDONESIA DID NOT EXIST, THE EARTH'S day would be significantly shorter than the approximately twenty-four hours to which we have become accustomed. This would have a dramatic impact on the clock industry, of course, and familiar phrases like "twenty-four/seven" would have to be modified. But Indonesia does exist, and its seventeen thousand islands, together with a complicated multitude of underwater trenches, basins, channels, ridges, shelfs, and sills, continue their daily work of diverting, trapping, and otherwise disrupting the most voluminous flow of water on earth, a task that consumes so much energy that it slows the very spinning of the globe.

The flow that passes through Indonesia is called the Arus Lintas Indonesia, the Indonesian Throughflow. Its source is the Philippine Sea and the West Caroline Basin, where the incessant blowing of the Trade Winds, and the currents they generate, have entrapped water from the great expanse of the Pacific. In the Pacific Ocean northwest of the Indonesian archipelago, the sea level is fifteen centimeters above average; in the Indian Ocean south of Indonesia, because of similar forces acting in an opposite direction, the sea level is fifteen centimeters below average. This thirty centimeter differential—an American foot—sets off the biggest water movement on earth.

The volume of this flow is so great that familiar units like cubic meters and gallons quickly become unwieldy, so oceanographers have invented a unit they call the "Sverdrup," named after Norwegian scientist Harald Sverdrup of the Scripps Institution of Oceanography. One Sverdrup is a flow of one million cubic meters per second, which is a lot of moving water. Think of a river one hundred meters wide, ten meters deep, and flowing at four knots, and then imagine *five hundred* of these rivers—that's one Sverdrup of flow. The Indonesian Throughflow, scientists estimate, represents 20–22 Sv, or *ten thousand* of these rivers.

Three quarters of this flow is carried in the upper few hundred meters, and the rest moves through Indonesia's network of deep basins. The seasons affect the rate of the Indonesian Throughflow, and it is strongest during the southeast monsoon, particularly June, July, and August. An El Niño year disrupts this pattern by diverting the Equatorial Tradewinds, pushing the water east, away from Indonesia.

STYMIED BY GEOGRAPHY

As it tries to cross Indonesia, the Throughflow finds itself blocked and shunted aside by the archipelago's complex geography. The deep flow immediately hits a barrier at the Sarangani Sill, a berm that connects Sulawesi and the Philippines below about fifteen hundred meters. The Sarangani forces the flow down the western flank of Sulawesi, entering the Banda Sea through the Lifamatola Strait, between the Sula archipelago and Obi. From the Banda Sea the deepwater flow reaches the Indian Ocean in a complicated mix with the shallow flow.

The shallow flow is able to cross the Sarangani Sill. It heads south through the Makassar Strait east of Sulawesi and enters the Bali Sea, and from there, the Flores and Banda Seas. At this point the water, still trying the reach the Indian Ocean, meets a barrier: the Lesser Sunda Islands, sweeping in a tight chain from Bali to Timor. There are only a few significant breaks in this chain: the Lombok Strait, the Sape Strait (between Sumbawa and Komodo), the Ombai Strait (between Alor and Timor), and the perforations between the little islands of Leti, Sermata, and Babar northeast of Timor.

Of these, the Lombok Strait offers the most direct path, and an estimated twenty percent of the shallow water flow through Indonesia passes here, or a flow volume of 3–3.3 Sv. This means that the net flow south past East Bali equals more than fifteen hundred of our hundred-meter-wide rivers running at four knots.

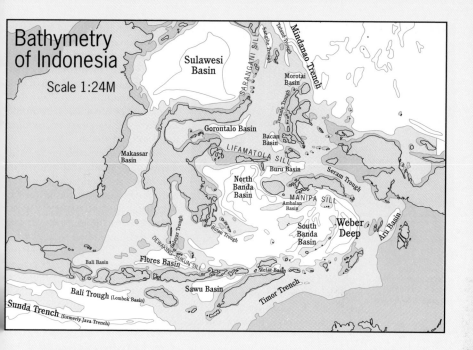

Bali and Lombok are about thirty-five kilometers apart at the narrowest point, between Gili Selang and Gili Trawangan, Lombok. The net south-tending flow through here, then, is equivalent to the entire top forty meters of water running at four knots. Since this is an average over the year, and the direction of flow through the strait shifts with the tides, one can easily see how things get very, very wild at the East Bali (and Nusa Penida) dive sites.

STIRRING THE POT

The reefs of Bali, particularly in the northeast and east, are in an ideal position to benefit from this flow. Water pulled from all over the Pacific Ocean, then swept through the rich nooks and crannies created by the Indonesian archipelago, carries with it the planktonic eggs and larvae of just about every species of fish and invertebrate known in the entire Pacific region. This, to a large degree, is why the reefs of Bali are so incredibly diverse, and why, with enough time, you could probably find just about any animal here that you want to see.

And Bali, unlike most of eastern Indonesia, is positioned to receive Indian Ocean in-

fluences as well. Because of the strong net throughflow from the Pacific, little Indian Ocean water reaches, say, the famous reefs of the Banda Sea. But Indian Ocean water—and Indian Ocean plankton—cycles through Bali and the other Lesser Sunda islands on a seasonal basis.

The Indonesian Throughflow also performs another very important function. Because it is so strong, and the bathymetry of the islands is so complex, the force of the throughflow churns together deep and surface water. Tropical seas are typically unproductive, and in many cases this is because nutrients like phosphorus and nitrogen are trapped in solution in deepwater basins. This is not the case in Indonesia, because the force of the throughflow keeps the waters mixed.

In some areas this mixing occurs as a seasonal upwelling of deep, nutrient-rich water. Bali is one of the most important of these, and every southeast monsoon draws to the surface cold, fertile water from the Bali Trough, a three-and-a-half-kilometer-deep basin just south of the island. The upwelling fuels an explosion of phytoplankton growth, bringing new vitality to the reefs of East Bali and Nusa Penida.

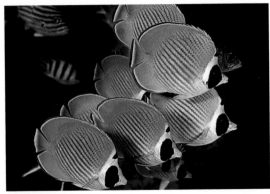

MIKE SEVERNS *Chaetodon adiergastos*

The eye-patch butterflyfish—sometimes, the "Panda" butterflyfish—prefers coastal reefs, where it travels in small groups or pairs.

it down in right front of him. Perhaps this was a kind of threat, or parrotfish braggadocio, a way of saying, "Let's see you do that, Wimpy." Or it could have been a form of stotting, to communicate to Wally that, should he be a predator, he would be better off looking for a weaker and less bold victim.

Sharks are relatively common at Tepekong, usually reef white-tips, although they tend to be more shy and not as numerous as at nearby Mimpang. Molas have been seen as well. Perhaps the most interesting shark sighting in Bali took place at Tepekong. The species was the large mackerel shark *Carcharodon carcharias,* the famous villain of "Jaws." The sighting took place a long time ago, but the observer is very reliable.

When he saw the shark, this normally bold diver attempted to become one with the Canyon wall, and stayed that way until the graceful animal vanished into the inky black. I seriously doubt if great whites are often in the area, but those tempted to regard this report with skepticism should bear in mind that a great white in East Bali would be no further outside its typical range than the wobbegong photographed for this book at Tanjung Sari.

most part the cover here is a modest growth of *Dendronephthya* and other soft corals, small gorgonians, pale yellow cup coral trees, and fist-sized heads and colonies of branching coral. In many areas crinoids provide the dominant cover. On the shallow tops of the offshore pinnacles, polished by the surge, only leather corals, pink coralline algae, and sparkling clumps of the iridescent alga *Galaxaura marginata,* are durable enough to survive.

But rich, coral-covered surfaces and macro-scale treasures are not what Tepekong is about. It is the great scale of its structure, and of the huge schools of fish, that make this site exciting. My most enduring picture of this site is staring up into the canyon, with great jagged lines of sweetlips—like striped lightning bolts—stacked up before me. Sweetlips, batfish, jacks, snappers, rainbow runners—when the conditions are right, these fish can nearly fill the Canyon. A big Napoleon wrasse lives here, and bumphead parrotfish patrol the tops of the mounds west of the Canyon proper.

The oldest and largest of the bumphead parrotfish at Tepekong is the one, Wally said, that once behaved in one of the most peculiar ways he has ever seen a fish behave. Seeing Wally in its territory, the animal grabbed a big rock in its mouth, carried it over, and plopped

Figure 1

Figure 2

WHEN YOUR BUBBLES SINK

The same dramatic structure that makes the Canyon so beautiful also makes it dangerous. The prevailing current past Tepekong usually runs southwest, at times with great strength. When this current combines with swell from the east or northeast, a strong, spiraling down-current develops, which turns the Canyon into the infamous Toilet. The best place to check for swell is at the southeast point of the island. Even if the surface is smooth, if there is breaking water here, you should not dive. Even one-meter waves crashing over this point indicate very dangerous conditions below. The surface water, off the point, will look like it is boiling.

Another problem at Tepekong comes from a shift in the angle of the main current. The usual southwest current blows straight past the island, making the southeast undiveable, but leaving the north and west in the lee (see FIGURE 1, at left). At times the angle shifts, however, and an eddy develops that can become a kind of branch current that swings around the northern point of Tepekong, rejoining the main current at the canyon (see FIGURE 2). Look for the existence of this condition by reading the current against the west side of the island. There should be no noticeable south-running current here. If there is, wait for conditions to change, or pick another site.

Either of these conditions can create problems underwater. If you do end up facing a rude downcurrent in the world's biggest toilet, try not to panic. Stay very tight to the wall, or if you are outside of the Canyon, to the bottom, and seek protection behind or between the boulders if you can. Rest for a minute until you've regained your composure. Then, slowly and methodically, work your way back up into the shallows of the Canyon, and eventually, the relatively protected slope north of the Canyon. If the conditions were created by the eddy running south along the island's western face, this flow will try to thwart your progress the whole way, but remember: though annoying, this eddy is still weaker than the main current. Crawl if you have to, but don't rush, and don't panic.

If that sounds bad, understand that things can get quite a bit worse. The downcurrent can be so intense that it sucks your bubbles down, and most divers become rather concerned in such a situation. Seek protection, but realize that a current

that can pull bubbles down can probably pull you down, too, and there comes a point when you can't fight it. What you need to do in this case is dump the air in your B.C. and calmly start swimming west. The current will immediately drag you down and away from the Canyon (south), but by about forty or forty-five meters it runs out of

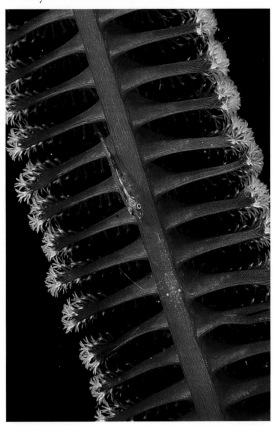

©BURT JONES/MAURINE SHIMLOCK Pleurosicya mossambica; Periclimenes sp.; Virgularia sp.

steam. Continue west—you probably will have no choice, since this is the direction of the prevailing current—so your boat has a better chance of seeing you, and surface carefully in open water.

Mimpang

As we were wrapping up work on The East Coast section of this book in the summer of 1999, we

Sea pens, anemones, and soft corals are always worth checking for commensals, especially if they are growing in an isolated area. Porcelain crabs and, as shown here, gobies and shrimp, are known associates of sea pens.

Map 3.3 Tepekong 1:2K

115° 35' 00" E

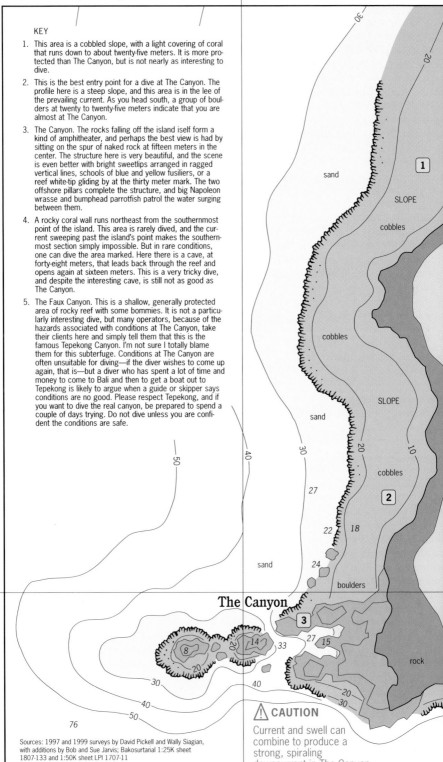

KEY

1. This area is a cobbled slope, with a light covering of coral that runs down to about twenty-five meters. It is more protected than The Canyon, but is not nearly as interesting to dive.

2. This is the best entry point for a dive at The Canyon. The profile here is a steep slope, and this area is in the lee of the prevailing current. As you head south, a group of boulders at twenty to twenty-five meters indicate that you are almost at The Canyon.

3. The Canyon. The rocks falling off the island iself form a kind of amphitheater, and perhaps the best view is had by sitting on the spur of naked rock at fifteen meters in the center. The structure here is very beautiful, and the scene is even better with bright sweetlips arranged in ragged vertical lines, schools of blue and yellow fusiliers, or a reef white-tip gliding by at the thirty meter mark. The two offshore pillars complete the structure, and big Napoleon wrasse and bumphead parrotfish patrol the water surging between them.

4. A rocky coral wall runs northeast from the southernmost point of the island. This area is rarely dived, and the current sweeping past the island's point makes the southernmost section simply impossible. But in rare conditions, one can dive the area marked. Here there is a cave, at forty-eight meters, that leads back through the reef and opens again at sixteen meters. This is a very tricky dive, and despite the interesting cave, is still not as good as The Canyon.

5. The Faux Canyon. This is a shallow, generally protected area of rocky reef with some bommies. It is not a particularly interesting dive, but many operators, because of the hazards associated with conditions at The Canyon, take their clients here and simply tell them that this is the famous Tepekong Canyon. I'm not sure I totally blame them for this subterfuge. Conditions at The Canyon are often unsuitable for diving—if the diver wishes to come up again, that is—but a diver who has spent a lot of time and money to come to Bali and then to get a boat out to Tepekong is likely to argue when a guide or skipper says conditions are no good. Please respect Tepekong, and if you want to dive the real canyon, be prepared to spend a couple of days trying. Do not dive unless you are confident the conditions are safe.

sand

SLOPE

cobbles

cobbles

SLOPE

sand

cobbles

27

22   18

24

sand

boulders

The Canyon

3

14

33

8

20

27 15

rock

30

20

40

40

50

20   30

76

⚠ **CAUTION**

Current and swell can combine to produce a strong, spiraling downcurrent in The Canyon.

8° 32' 00" S

Sources: 1997 and 1999 surveys by David Pickell and Wally Siagian, with additions by Bob and Sue Jarvis; Bakosurtanal 1:25K sheet 1807-133 and 1:50K sheet LPI 1707-11

©1999 David Pickell and Wally Siagian

Tepekong 1:2K

This little island is the most famous of the Amuk Bay sites. "The Canyon," a striking structure of angular black boulders, is by far the best site here, attracting big schools of sweetlips and jacks, big groupers, sharks, and pelagics like molas. Because of the strong currents that swirl through it, the coral cover is minimal, and The Canyon has a stark, un-tropical look, like a rocky outcrop somehow transplanted from the Bering Strait. The water temperatures here—which can dip below 20°C—can give the same impression. Tepekong's Canyon is also, unfortunately, probably the single most dangerous site in Bali. With the prevailing strong south-west-running current, even moderate swell can produce a swirling downcurrent here, a condition that makes divers' bubbles go down, and turns The Canyon into, in Wally's memorable words, "The Toilet."

SHALLOW SLOPE

boulders

coral bommies

5

Lighted beacon ✦ +23

20

Tepekong

Also Kambing, and occasionally, Bir

10

scrub

10

16

20

30

50

4

WALL

WALL

Very strong current along this reef edge

100

0 — 50 — 100 m

0 — 100 — 200 — 300 ft

1 cm = 20 m
1 in = 167 ft

8° 32' 00" S

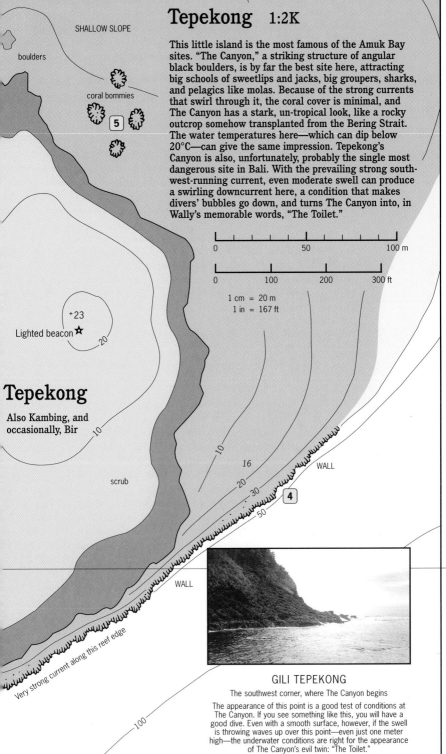

GILI TEPEKONG

The southwest corner, where The Canyon begins

The appearance of this point is a good test of conditions at The Canyon. If you see something like this, you will have a good dive. Even with a smooth surface, however, if the swell is throwing waves up over this point—even just one meter high—the underwater conditions are right for the appearance of The Canyon's evil twin: "The Toilet."

spent our afternoons reviewing the day's dives at a beachside restaurant in Padangbai. From this vantage we could watch the fishermen drag their *jukung*s ashore, and when they did we always went over to have a look at their catch. At first the men were bringing in small tuna and the occasional dorado (mahi-mahi). But a couple weeks after the east winds began to blow steadily—signaling the start of the southwest monsoon—their catch improved, and we began to see marlin and sailfish. Finally, by late summer, the *jukung*s were returning every day with four or five thresher sharks each.

The run on the sharks, Wally told me after I left, lasted into September. The men, he said, had their best luck at a site in the open waters of the Badung Strait they call Pentutupan, literally "the closing," as in the closing of a window. To find Pentutupan they leave Padangbai harbor and sail straight toward a fixed point on Nusa Penida until they can no longer see through to the end of the channel between Lembongan and Penida (the closing window). There they set their lines.

The run on the threshers coincided with a run of more interest to divers. Very nearly every day during this entire period, divers at Mimpang saw molas. These strange and still poorly understood fish have a circumglobal range, in both tropical and temperate seas. They are true pelagics, and follow the plankton. It is thought that their favored food is jellyfish, but even this is not known for sure. The scientific name of the species seen in Bali is *Mola mola*, and many divers double the name as well; "mola," from the Latin for millstone, refers to the flat, roundish body of the fish.

The appearance of the molas and the thresher sharks was doubtless connected to the period of upwelling. This is a regular event in South Bali, but with all of the disruptions produced by El Niño and the subsequent phenomenon La Niña, it is impossible to predict whether this will become a regular occurrence.

TARGET PRACTICE

Mimpang is a small archipelago of four big rocks, and another half-dozen smaller ones, just over a kilometer northwest of Tepekong (see MAP 3.4, pp. 138–139). Only the center two of the rocks have any vegetation, and even this is only a rough covering of grass. A sea eagle has nested on a tower adorning the second rock (working from south to north) for many years.

The rocks follow an underwater ridge that runs north by northeast. Mimpang's southern extent drops off sharply to deep water, but the north becomes a shallow, rubbly reef that continues much of the way to mainland Bali, though it does leave a boat passage. Tepekong is more of a true offshore island, with some eighty meters of water in the channel between it and Mimpang.

According to the skippers in the area, these rocks were used as target practice by the Indonesian airforce in 1961 and 1962. I have always been skeptical of this story, as there are so many islands in Indonesia much further from population centers to use for this purpose, if such is required, but it has been confirmed by so many people that I now have to believe it. The southernmost rock in particular is quite broken up, and it is easy to imagine it having been ripped apart by explosives. Unlike the others, the water around this rock is full of sharp-edged boulders, plausibly the result of it having been shelled.

Mimpang is often considered a kind of poor relation to Tepekong, and serves chiefly as a back-up location if conditions at nearby Tepekong are too frightening. This does a disservice to Mimpang,

'Tidal streams are sometimes so strong in the passages between [Mimpang] and Gili Tepekong, and [Mimpang] and Tanjung Bugbug, that it is difficult to keep a vessel on her course, and should only be made at slack water.'

Indonesia Pilot, Vol. II
The Hydrographer of the British Navy

JOHN E. RANDALL   *Prionurus* sp.   Padang Bai

which in our opinion is a very fine site. And this reef can serve as a fall-back dive for Tepekong only because conditions at the two locations are not often in sync. Taken on its own, Mimpang can be just as demanding to dive as is Tepekong.

The standard dive at Mimpang starts just west of the middle point of this miniature island chain and runs down the western flank to end up a bit northwest of the southernmost rock. Operators like this, because it is a reliable way to show their clients sharks, and the current—although it can be strong—is for the most part predictable. The eastern side, however, is usually ignored.

A FRESH COAT OF PAINT

When we dropped in on the eastern side of the southernmost rocks in 1999, we were both flabbergasted. We dove Mimpang together early in the course of our fieldwork for this book, and Wally has dived it many, many times. But even Wally hadn't taken a look at the eastern side in more than a year.

The place we found can only be called magic. The scenery was crisp and alive, and glowed with the freshness of a new coat of paint. We drifted among the boulders, in about fifteen meters of water, and let the swaying surge carry us gently into great clouds of anthias and among ragged schools of striped sweetlips. Reef white-tip sharks broke path calmly to wind around us. Small colonies of hard coral clung to the rocks, their tips pink and blue with new growth. Clumps of bright yellow sea cucumbers were everywhere. We have never seen this animal—*Colochirus robustus,* a lumpy filter-feeding cucumariid about the length of two joints of your little finger and related to the sea apples—anywhere else in Bali. We wound downslope to a protected area, where we found big gorgonians and barrel sponges growing on a terrace.

The beauty of this area was intoxicating. In fact, when we re-

This is the 'monster,' East Bali's endemic tang. The only place this strange, spiky fish has been seen is at Padang Bai, Tepekong, Mimpang, Biaha, and Selang, although on one occasion we saw a single individual at Gamat. This fish is never very numerous—just one or two, often mixing with a school of more common surgeonfish—and is frustratingly difficult to approach. Ichthyologist Jack Randall had to corner this one in a crevice to get the picture above. Unfortunately, Jack has been too busy to prepare the monograph, so it still lacks a species name. The genus prefers more temperate waters, and he speculates that this species is a relic, once more widely distributed but now restricted to the area of cold upwelling in East Bali.

Map 3.4 Mimpang 1:2K

115° 34' 30" E

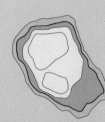

rubble

Mimpang 1:2K

Mimpang, which is sometimes inaccurately called Batu Tiga ("Three Rocks"), is a group of four rocky outcrops about a kilometer northwest of Tepekong. The local fishermen say that in 1961 and 1962, the Indonesian air force used Mimpang for target practice, which might be one reason the outcrops are so broken up, particularly in the southern extent of the group. Mimpang, unlike Tepekong, is connected to the Bali shelf, and the back part of the group is flat and shallow. Though it covers a rather small area, the southern end of this reef is one of the richest in all of Bali, and reminds us of the famous sites of southern Komodo and Rinca. It is remarkably varied, combining wall and sloping reefs, jagged rocks and boulders, and hard corals, soft corals, and big gorgonians. The fish life is exceptional, including schooling fish, unusual small reef fish, lots of sharks, and even molas. This site, particularly in the southeast, has improved dramatically in the last five years, and now has the glow of extreme health.
Current conditions can be tricky here, like the rest of Anuk Bay. Choose your entry and exit points with care. In some cases you will be limited to diving either the east or the west end of the southern point. These are small irritations for such a fine diving area, however.

KEY

1. These rocks, off the second island, are covered with tables of robust *Acropora* coral. This is an area of strong surge, and the current can sometimes penetrate here as well. Best to stay back unless conditions are perfect.

2. This is a beautiful, rich area. The bottom is white sand, and you are surrounded by rocks and boulders, everything covered with a fresh growth of coral and swirling with fish. This area, at around fifteen meters, is protected from the brunt of the current, and is one of the few places here where you can stay put, with maybe a bit of surge, and simply watch the passing fish and the bright scene.

3. The slope down away from area #2 continues to be rich, and there is a very large gorgonian (*Muricella*) at twenty-four meters on a terrace.

4. A huge barrel sponge (with lots of Siagian's squat lobsters) marks the reef corner. This is a good area to glimpse pelagic fish as well, including molas.

5. The southernmost extent of the Mimpang reef is a wall, which is nicely encrusted, but because of the current, one usually does not get to spend much time here. Off the point here is where most of the molas are sighted at Mimpang. People differ as to their favorite sections of the Mimpang reef: my personal favorite area is #2; while others like #7, because of the sharks.

6. There is an overhang here at thirty meters, and from here north the wall becomes more rugged.

7. This area of slope and wall is also very beautiful. Just before the corner (and where the current picks up the reef is a steep wall, completely covered with beautiful *Dendronephthya* soft corals. Just a bit further north, and out of the current, just as the profile goes to a slope, you can always find sharks. Reef white-tips are the most commonly seen, but grays are not unknown, and even a bull shark showed up on one occasion. The marked area on the other side of the reef is also a reliable place to see sharks.

8. Here there is a big *Porites* coral head, with an opening encrusted with gorgonians, soft corals, and other growth. A diver could almost fit through, but please do not try—you would certainly break up all of the beautiful growth, particularly as this is a very surgey area.

9. The back reef at Mimpang is a flat area of rubble and sand, with low coral ridges extending back toward the Bugbug Peninsula. The bottom is dominated by tough leather corals and *Acropora*, and is relatively barren and often current-swept. I accidentally had an interesting dive here once, but it is not really worth exploring.

9

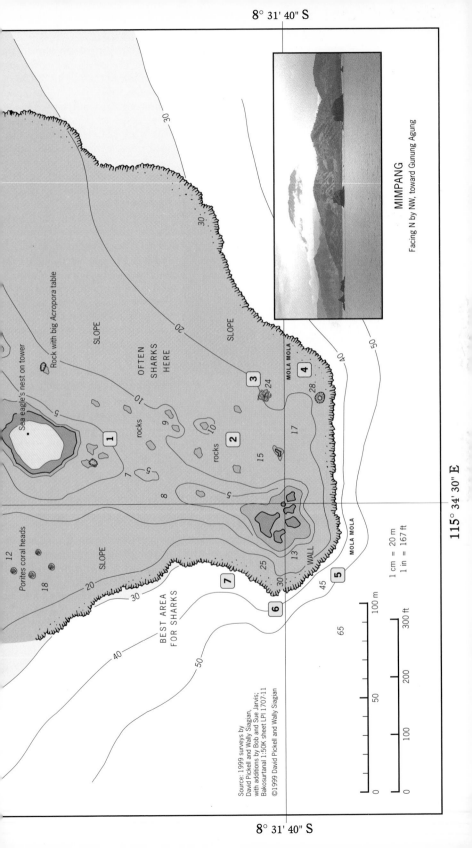

8° 31' 40" S

30

MIMPANG

Facing N by NW, toward Gunung Agung

Sea eagle's nest on tower

Rock with big Acropora table

SLOPE

OFTEN SHARKS HERE

SLOPE

rocks

10

5

7

8

5

5

rocks

15

17

MOLA MOLA

3

24

4

28

40

50

30

30

20

10

9

Porites coral heads

12

18

SLOPE

20

30

BEST AREA FOR SHARKS

40

50

25

30

13

WALL

MOLA MOLA

45

65

5

7

6

1 cm = 20 m
1 in = 167 ft

100 m

300 ft

50

200

100

50

100

0

0

Source: 1999 surveys by
David Pickell and Wally Siagian,
with additions by Bob and Sue Jarvis;
Bakosurtanal 1:50K sheet LPI 1707-11
©1999 David Pickell and Wally Siagian

115° 34' 30" E

8° 31' 40" S

turned to the boat, both Wally and I had the same sense: this place is now like South Komodo, which is a high compliment indeed. The unusual sea cucumbers (common in Komodo), the vibrance of the colors, the fish life, the almost casual fecundity of this site put it in the same category as Gili Motang or South Rinca or Tala in the Komodo area.

WALLY SIAGIAN Pomacanthus semicirculatus

The semicircle angelfish is not uncommon around Bali's reefs. The fluorescent blue markings around its gill plates are very visible underwater and advertise the fish's sharp gill spine.

The whole southern extent of the Mimpang reef—in both the west and the east—is now excellent, whether your interest is small animals or large.

And of course there are the sharks. After we had been in Padangbai for a few days, the operator there told us he had a some video footage he would like us to see. It was of a group of sharks at Mimpang, he said, and there was one he was having trouble identifying. Wally and I sat down with our beers and had a look. The camera was following a group of big reef white-tips, and now and then smaller reef black-tips would dart in and out of view. Then another specimen, fat and vaguely thuggish-looking, joined the group. "That one," our host said, pointing to the screen. "What kind of shark is that?"

The shark had some of the aspect and movements of a gray reef shark, but it was too blunt and heavy for this species, and lacked the crescent of black on the trailing edge of

its tail. It never got very close to the camera (or was it the other way around?), but we both, rather reluctantly, told our host that in our opinion it was a bull shark. This aggressive species is not one that many divers are keen to encounter. *Carcharhinus leucas* has been implicated in more attacks on humans than any other shark, even the more commonly feared species like tigers and great whites.

But the more I think about it, the more Mimpang's environment seems wrong for this species. The bull shark is associated with murky habitats like estuaries and harbors, and it is the criminal, for example, that occasionally takes a leg or an arm from a workman cleaning barnacles from a moored boat, or from a kid playing in the water around a dock. I am no shark expert, but in retrospect I think it is more likely that the animal on the Mimpang tape was the Java shark, *Carcharhinus amboinensis*, a species that is physically similar, but behaviorally much more benign than the bull shark. In any case, I'd really *like* to believe this.

Biaha

Gili Biaha, strangely enough, was not always an island. A long time ago, for reasons that remain occult even to this day, the tip of Cape Biasputih shook and rattled and finally pulled itself free of the mainland. This rebellious piece of Bali's terra firma then began creeping south, toward Nusa Penida. Normally, an event like this wouldn't be cause for alarm. But Nusa Penida is a strange, and even evil place. Not evil in the blunt Christian sense of the word, but evil in the Hindu-Balinese sense, a kind of counterweight to good. Both good and evil are necessary, in equal measures, for the maintenance of Bali's spiritual equilibrium, and this equilibrium is where the problem lay. If a piece of the mainland were to somehow come into contact with Nusa Penida, it would throw off the balance of things, creating a very dangerous situation for everyone on the island.

As it turned out, nobody needed to have worried. Seeing the island moving, a quick-thinking Balinese duckherd took his flag—the ducks are trained from birth to follow this device—and thrust it out over the disobedient island, commanding it to stop. It did, and the people of Bali breathed a collective sigh of relief.

Biaha has never moved since, although the Balinese still like to call the island Likuan, from *ikuan*, the tail of the duck.

HAWAI'I—WITH A DIFFERENCE

Biaha is a rocky outcrop with the approximate shape of an inverted comma, lying about four kilometers northeast of Tepekong (see MAP 3.5, pp. 142–143). A rounded, grassy knoll caps the the thick end of the island, and if the swell is substantial, a blowhole appears in the rocky northern curve. A very healthy reef surrounds the entire island, approximately half of it a wall, and the other half a cobbled slope.

Tepekong and Mimpang are dived far more often than Biaha, which is a shame because this island has what is probably the most developed reef of any of the East Coast sites. The best part of the Biaha wall, the heavily split and terraced section in the southeast, is one of the richest and most unusual stretches of reef in Bali.

The wall is black, basaltic rock, which in sections displays a striking cleavage pattern, like brickwork. In many ways the scenery reminds me very much of the backside of Molokini, off Maui (except that unlike the barren underwater world of Hawai'i, this one is covered with life). I was so struck by this similarity the first time I dove here that I was not even surprised to see the gilded triggerfish *Xanthichthys au-romarginatus*, which is common in Hawai'i and other offshore islands. It does not belong so near to a continental shelf, however, and we have never seen it elsewhere in Bali.

A CURIOUS MIX

The set of fishes at Biaha, and to a lesser extent at Tepekong and Mimpang, are quite different from

©BURT JONES/MAURINE SHIMLOCK   *Tozeuma armatum* on *Antipathes* sp.

the rest of Bali. You can find the endemic *Prionurus* tang here. The beautiful Meyer's butterflyfish (*Chaetodon meyeri*), rare throughout its range, is common here. Even common families are present here in different groupings. For example, among the fusiliers, unfamiliar-looking members of the genus *Pterocaesio* seem to dominate.

Sharks are not uncommon, but

With its banded coloration and long, stick-like shape, only the most sharp-eyed predator could detect the black coral shrimp. Note also the tiny goby, similarly banded, hiding just off the tip of the shrimp's pointed rostrum.

Map 3.5 Gili Biaha 1:2K

115°

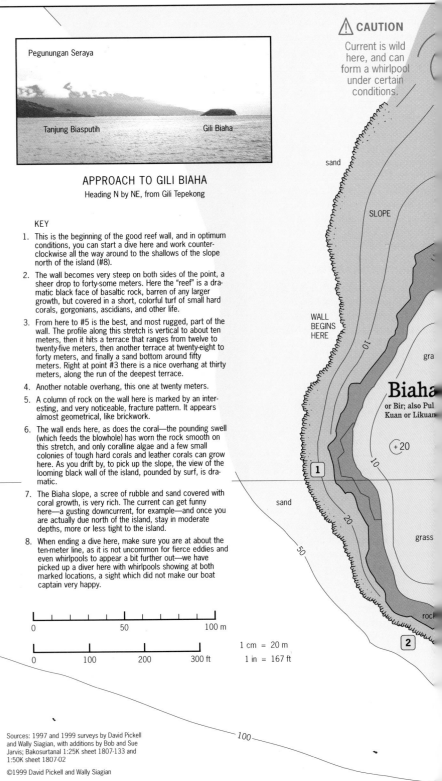

Pegunungan Seraya

Tanjung Biasputih

Gili Biaha

APPROACH TO GILI BIAHA

Heading N by NE, from Gili Tepekong

KEY

1. This is the beginning of the good reef wall, and in optimum conditions, you can start a dive here and work counter-clockwise all the way around to the shallows of the slope north of the island (#8).

2. The wall becomes very steep on both sides of the point, a sheer drop to forty-some meters. Here the "reef" is a dra-matic black face of basaltic rock, barren of any larger growth, but covered in a short, colorful turf of small hard corals, gorgonians, ascidians, and other life.

3. From here to #5 is the best, and most rugged, part of the wall. The profile along this stretch is vertical to about ten meters, then it hits a terrace that ranges from twelve to twenty-five meters, then another terrace at twenty-eight to forty meters, and finally a sand bottom around fifty meters. Right at point #3 there is a nice overhang at thirty meters, along the run of the deepest terrace.

4. Another notable overhang, this one at twenty meters.

5. A column of rock on the wall here is marked by an inter-esting, and very noticeable, fracture pattern. It appears almost geometrical, like brickwork.

6. The wall ends here, as does the coral—the pounding swell (which feeds the blowhole) has worn the rock smooth on this stretch, and only coralline algae and a few small colonies of tough hard corals and leather corals can grow here. As you drift by, to pick up the slope, the view of the looming black wall of the island, pounded by surf, is dra-matic.

7. The Biaha slope, a scree of rubble and sand covered with coral growth, is very rich. The current can get funny here—a gusting downcurrent, for example—and once you are actually due north of the island, stay in moderate depths, more or less tight to the island.

8. When ending a dive here, make sure you are at about the ten-meter line, as it is not uncommon for fierce eddies and even whirlpools to appear a bit further out—we have picked up a diver here with whirlpools showing at both marked locations, a sight which did not make our boat captain very happy.

⚠ CAUTION

Current is wild here, and can form a whirlpool under certain conditions.

sand

SLOPE

WALL BEGINS HERE

gra

Biaha

or Bir; also Pul Kuan or Likuan

+20

sand

grass

roc

8° 30' 35" S

0   50   100 m

0   100   200   300 ft

1 cm = 20 m

1 in = 167 ft

Sources: 1997 and 1999 surveys by David Pickell and Wally Siagian, with additions by Bob and Sue Jarvis; Bakosurtanal 1:25K sheet 1807-133 and 1:50K sheet 1807-02

Gili Biaha 1:2K

This island—really a rock, with a rounded cap of grass—is the most remote of the Amuk Bay sites, but also one of the most beautiful. A steep drop-off reef, nicely fissured and terraced in places, rings most of the island, going to a slope in the north. The inside of the island's curve is always protected from the current, but heavy swell can make things dicey up near the rock face, particularly for your boat pilot. If the blowhole is active, it is a good indication that your dive will be limited to the lower portion of the east-facing wall, and you will be entering and exiting in open water.

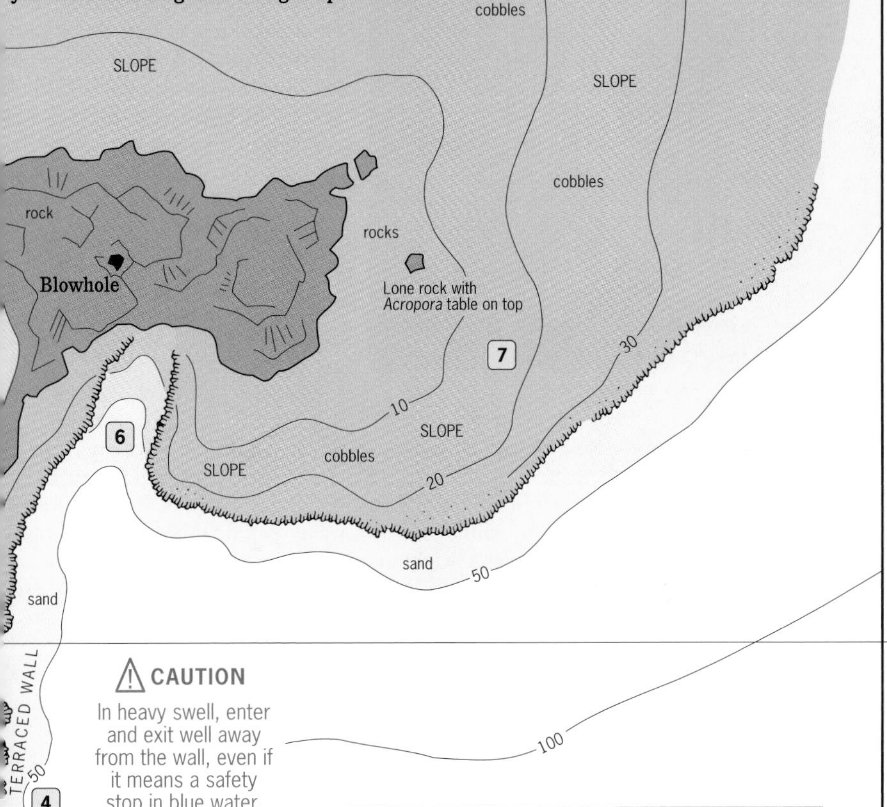

sand

⚠ CAUTION

Current is wild here, and can form a whirlpool under certain conditions.

cobbles

SLOPE

SLOPE

cobbles

rock

rocks

Blowhole

Lone rock with *Acropora* table on top

7

6

10

SLOPE

30

SLOPE

cobbles

20

sand

50

sand

8° 30' 35" S

TERRACED WALL

50

⚠ CAUTION

In heavy swell, enter and exit well away from the wall, even if it means a safety stop in blue water.

100

4

3

GILI BIAHA

Southernmost tip, looking just E of N

This photograph was taken on a day when conditions for diving were excellent. This view of the island always makes me think of a storybook whale, although the blowhole is at the wrong end.

Mimpang and Tepekong are more reliable places to see them. Molas have not yet been reported from Biaha, but that may be because it is not dived as often as the other sites. What makes Biaha special is its trove of fascinating smaller species, such as cuttlefish, octopus, interesting nudibranchs, and the rich soft corals, gorgonians, and black

MIKE SEVERNS   Chromodoris sp. (bullocki complex)

These beautiful nudibranchs are similar to the familiar Bullock's chromodoris, but are much larger (to ten centimters), and have stronger coloration in the body, rhinophores, and gills. They are common around Bali.

corals, many with commensals.

On one dive I found a pycnogonid or "sea spider," a very strange animal that has eight long legs with seemingly too many joints and no proper body at all. It was bright orange, and of a size that would alarm any arachnophobe on land. These creatures have a peculiar way of walking, as if each leg goes about its business without communicating with the others. Wally was photographing on the wall above me, just five meters away, but this section was devoid of landmarks, and so well encrusted I knew if I even looked away, I would not find this animal again.

In any case, Wally was finding plenty to shoot: nudibranchs, odd shells, and commensal shrimps and crabs. Nudibranchs in particular are very common here. A diving partner showed me a huge and lumpy nudibranch she found in the shallow slope north of the island. It had the size, and general appearance, of a slipper lobster, which from a distance is what I thought she was calling me over to see. I don't have any idea what this animal was—maybe a Dendrodorid?—but a nudibranch lover would find more interesting puzzles than just this one here.

A MODICUM OF PROTECTION

Like the other Amuk Bay sites, heavy swell at Biaha can create problems, generating strong currents across (and down) the slope to the north, and making it dangerous for a boat to get close to the island to drop off or pick up divers. Biaha is in almost the same category as Tepekong when it comes to diving accidents and near accidents, mostly when divers find themselves in the current-swept northern area.

Although the map makes it look like Biaha is almost a tombolo, as if the mainland were somehow reaching out to retrieve its prodigal child, in fact the channel is deep and the tidal current sets strongly through it. This, combined with the curved shape of the Biasputih Peninsula, directs the current in unfortunate ways, making things very squirrelly indeed north of Biaha.

The island does offer one area that seems always to be protected, and unlike the north side of Tepekong, for example, this area is also rich: the section of wall from the southernmost point up the southeastern flank of the island. Several years ago we dove this area on a rough, rainy day that represented anything but ideal conditions. Starting in the south, we were not bothered by current at all until we began to approach the area that feeds the blowhole.

Once you cross the "gorge" that feeds the blowhole and reach the slope, however, things can turn strange. Even on a good day, this area warns you—with brief, unpredictable gusts of current—that the water here is not to be trifled with. Always be careful and conservative.

THE EAST COAST
Gili Selang

WITH THE WARM MORNING SUN AT starboard, good company, a cup of hot coffee in hand, and twin eighty-fives singing out back, the ride from Padangbai up the East Coast of Bali to Gili Selang is a delightful way to spend forty-five minutes. The Seraya Range dips its long green fingers into the sea here, creating a dramatic coastline of sheer cliffs and steep valleys. The valleys end in tiny pocket beaches, where *jukung*s glow blue and white against the black sand.

By the time you get to the bottom of your second cup of coffee, the vegetation begins to thin to scrub and grass, and along the cliff faces, just cactus. The coconut palms that crowded the edge of the coastal forest at the beginning of the journey are gone, leaving only tall, brush-topped *lontar* palms standing like sentinals along the ridgetops. Finally, just off the sharp point of Bali's eastern tip, the odd-looking island of Gili Selang appears, steep-sided, flat-topped, and round, like a thick green coin.

Selang is actually closer to Tulamben than to Padangbai, and closer yet to Jemeluk. But the boats out of Padangbai, designed to survive Amuk Bay and runs across the Badung Strait to Nusa Penida, will get you there faster and more safely than the *jukung*s or small outboards you can find in the north. A road loops around the Seraya Peninsula as well, and Selang is just offshore. But this road is very rough, washes out frequently, and although tolerable by motorcycle, even one time around in a truck will subtract years from the serviceable life of your kidneys.

Gili Selang currently has a reputation for being a secret, undiscovered insider's spot—the best, wildest, and last pristine reef on the island. It is the kind of place a group of expatriate dive guides might go if they can get a day off together. In fact, this island has been dived—albeit not very frequently—for many years, and its reputation for unspoiled, frontier diving, although few realize it, is something that has come and gone more than once in

This remote and demanding site, with an interesting mix of both north and east coast reefs, suffers most from its exaggerated reputation as Bali's great, unspoiled frontier.

the last decade.

It is Selang's position on the map that makes it so tantalizing. That tiny, faraway dot, thrust right out into the Lombok Strait, just *has* to be good. And if a couple of divers do head out there, they usually experience a very wild ride, which leads to the kind of word-of-mouth advertising that only makes the site more attractive.

WHERE NORTH BECOMES EAST

The scenery around Selang gives a clue to its exposed position. The beaches at Tulamben and other sites to the northeast are made up of volcanic pebbles and cobbles, rounded stones roughly up to the size of a human fist. But the steep, two-hundred-meter-long beach fronting the little village of Kutumanak, just north of Selang, is made up of rounded stones roughly the size of a human *head,* and some are even bigger. The rocky points on the mainland here are sharp, and the wave bench is deep, in one place even forming a cave (where swiftlets nest). Underwater, things are not much different.

The area between the island and the point marking the southernmost extension of Kutumanak Bay is the most protected section of the Selang reef (see MAP 3.6, opposite). The shallows here have some bommies, and the cover is dominated by the leather corals *Sinularia* and *Sarcophyton,* with some healthy stands of robust branching *Acropora* and *Porites* heads. This assemblage is typical of a healthy but current-swept reef. A few gorgonians grow in the protection between the bommies, but it is further downslope, where the hard coral thins and goes to sand, that the black coral bushes and gorgonians grow big and lush.

This deep slope, just north of the island, is the most protected and richest area here, and it has much of the same character as the deep slope at Tulamben. Further south, once you start to round the island itself, the scenery abruptly changes. Here is where, in a sense, North turns to East, and you enter a current-swept rubble slope reminiscent of the northern extension of Gili Biaha.

TAKE THE TRAIN SOUTH

The slope is a scree of cobbles and small boulders leading at a steep angle down and away from the island. The rocks are nicely encrusted, but because of the constant current, everything growing here can be measured in centimeters. This south-tending current can make for a nice ride at about the twenty meter level, with bright, clear water and a dramatic view of the waves crashing against Selang's sheer edge, which continues underwater down to ten meters or so.

The main problem comes after you've rounded the midpoint of the island, by which time you might be moving south with the help of a two- or three-knot current. The bathymetry follows Selang's rounded outline, but the current sets basically due south. In other words, you want to go east, but the train is still running south. We've come around this island, and reaching this point, seen our bubbles head casually downslope. We've also seen a diver here drift from eighteen meters to thirty before he realized what was happening. The slope is very even and the bottom is monotonous, so it is easy to get disoriented. Watch yourself, and check your depth.

South of the island you reach another lee, an area of bommies and healthy reef. Again, the cover is dominated by leather corals and tough stony corals, and though the structure is relatively interesting, it is not as diverse as some other sites. You will appreciate the protection from the current, though.

OVERSOLD?

Reef white-tip sharks are common at this site, and we have seen bumphead parrotfish, schooling reef fish, and in and among the rocks, lots of moray eels and other interesting animals. When Wally whooped through his regulator to call the jacks at Selang, he immediately drew a large school of them, along with a big white-tip shark. The shark acted as if it had been tricked (which of course it had) and left immediately. The jacks didn't stay much longer, and when they whirled and snapped their tails in unison, they created the strange

Map 3.6 Gili Selang 1:5K

115° 42' 42" E

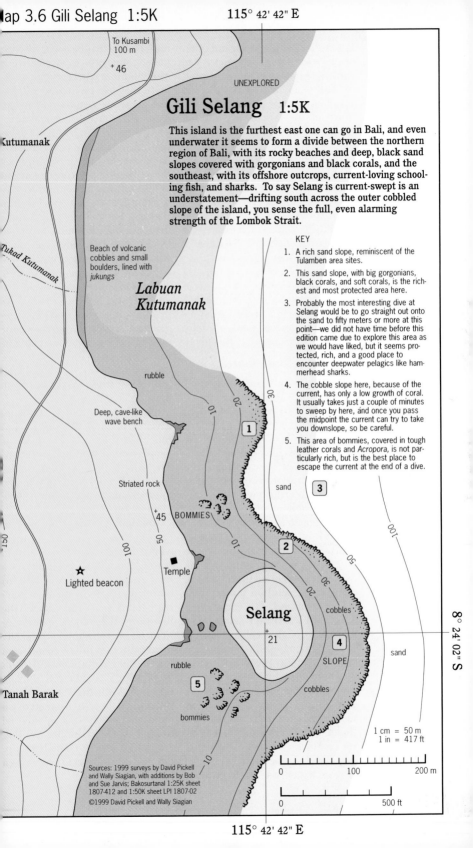

UNEXPLORED

Gili Selang 1:5K

This island is the furthest east one can go in Bali, and even underwater it seems to form a divide between the northern region of Bali, with its rocky beaches and deep, black sand slopes covered with gorgonians and black corals, and the southeast, with its offshore outcrops, current-loving schooling fish, and sharks. To say Selang is current-swept is an understatement—drifting south across the outer cobbled slope of the island, you sense the full, even alarming strength of the Lombok Strait.

KEY

1. A rich sand slope, reminiscent of the Tulamben area sites.

2. This sand slope, with big gorgonians, black corals, and soft corals, is the richest and most protected area here.

3. Probably the most interesting dive at Selang would be to go straight out onto the sand to fifty meters or more at this point—we did not have time before this edition came due to explore this area as we would have liked, but it seems protected, rich, and a good place to encounter deepwater pelagics like hammerhead sharks.

4. The cobble slope here, because of the current, has only a low growth of coral. It usually takes just a couple of minutes to sweep by here, and once you pass the midpoint the current can try to take you downslope, so be careful.

5. This area of bommies, covered in tough leather corals and *Acropora*, is not particularly rich, but is the best place to escape the current at the end of a dive.

To Kusambi 100 m

+ 46

Kutumanak

Tukad Kutumanak

Beach of volcanic cobbles and small boulders, lined with *jukungs*

Labuan Kutumanak

rubble

Deep, cave-like wave bench

Striated rock

+ 45

BOMMIES

Temple

☆ Lighted beacon

Selang

+ 21

cobbles

SLOPE

sand

rubble

+ 5

bommies

Tanah Barak

sand

cobbles

cobbles

sand

1 cm = 50 m
1 in = 417 ft

0   100   200 m

0   500 ft

Sources: 1999 surveys by David Pickell and Wally Siagian, with additions by Bob and Sue Jarvis; Bakosurtanal 1:25K sheet 1807-412 and 1:50K sheet LPI 1807-02

©1999 David Pickell and Wally Siagian

8° 24' 02" S

115° 42' 42" E

boom that jacks, sharks, and other strong-swimming species can sometimes manage.

The area here that we think has the most promise is the deep slope north of the island. We did not spend as much time on this steep, black-sand slope as we would have liked, but here is where there are the big host gorgonians for Bargibant's seahorse (see "Hippocampus bargibanti," pg. 149), barrel sponges, and black corals. And this is the safest place to go deep, which means you may have a chance to see unusual sharks and other pelagics here.

Overall, however, we're not sure Selang deserves the hype it occasionally receives. It is certainly a good site, but it is not, in our opinion, better than the islands of Amuk Bay, for example, or even Tulamben.

TRY THE BATHROOM INSTEAD

A couple years back Wally and I were in Tulamben doing mapping and research for this book, mostly at Batu Kelebit and the other sites just east of Tulamben. After dinner one night we were talking about Gili Selang. I had not dived Selang at the time, and it had been years since Wally had been there. He was telling me about one of his early dives there, in the late 1980s.

Wally was diving with a competent German diver with whom he often worked at the time, and the two somehow ended up very deep, out over the sand on the exposed side of the island. The current had been mild when they started, but midway through their dive it grew strong, stirring up the bottom and causing visibility problems, even at the more than fifty meter depths where they found themselves. As they drifted along, a shipwreck suddenly appeared out of the gloom. This wreck is not marked on any charts, and neither of them had ever heard of it before.

The wreck was an interesting find, but since it began at fifty-five meters, and lay on a current-swept, sandy bottom with very poor visibility, they had no interest whatever in exploring it. At the time, in fact, it was taking all of their attention and self-control just to figure out a way of surfacing safely—and within two nautical miles of their waiting boat. It was, Wally said in conclusion, one of the scariest dives of his life.

It turned out that our conversation had been overheard, and the next morning we were confronted by an expatriate dive instructor who begged us to accompany him to Selang to find this wreck again. Wally was patient, explaining that not only was he discussing a dive that took place ten years ago, but that his story, if anything, should be understood as a cautionary tale. The wreck starts in *fifty-five meters*. The vis was maybe *eight*. The current was *three knots*. What are you thinking, man?

Still, his enthusiastic entreaties never stopped until he left for Europe three days later. I know some people routinely dive in conditions like this, and with even colder water. Wally could certainly handle this dive, and I guess I could, too, if I had to. But *why?*

For some reason Gili Selang continues to attract the kind of diver whose biggest thrill comes from scaring himself (and it is always a him) to a point just shy of where his bowels evacuate of their own accord. If this is you, our advice is the following: Tell your skipper to position his boat one hundred and fifty meters due east of the island. Suit up, put on eight kilos of lead, dump your B.C., and roll off. The wreck is down there somewhere. But do have the good manners to tell the skipper what you are up to, so he doesn't have to bother waiting around for you to come back up. Oh, and don't forget to take along a magazine.

Searching for a Seahorse

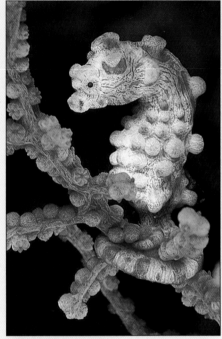

MIKE SEVERNS Hippocampus bargibanti Bunaken Island

KAL MULLER Gili Selang

IN JULY 1969, GEORGES BARGIBANT, A COLlector for the Nouméa aquarium in New Caledonia, placed a routine catch of invertebrates into the holding tanks. Only then did he notice, clinging to a gorgonian he had hauled up live from thirty meters, a tiny, cryptic seahorse. This little animal, which could sit on a signet ring, matches its host with such precision that even an experienced diver like Bargibant missed it underwater. It was duly described in 1970, and named in his honor.

This is a good story (and a true one), but almost as interesting as the seahorse is the fact that Bargibant was collecting live gorgonians for a public aquarium in 1969. The Nouméa aquarium, founded by René Catala in 1956, pioneered the captive keeping of invertebrates with open system water circulation and natural sunlight. The facility is famous, for example, for being the first to keep and breed nautilus.

Hippocampus bargibanti is currently in vogue with underwater photographers, and its known range has expanded rapidly over the last few years to include the Great Barrier Reef; Milne Bay, Papua New Guinea; Lembeh Strait and the Bunaken Group in Sulawesi; and several sites in the Komodo Region.

We contend that it is in Bali, too, particularly East Bali. Work on this book has gotten in the way of a concerted search, but the proper host gorgonians exist at every East Bali site except Tepekong, and the current stream is so direct from Sulawesi to Bali that it is inconceivable that they are not here, too.

The host species are: *Muricella paraplectana* (which is yellow) and *M. plectana* (which has red polyps, although the branches appear purple-gray under water). These gorgonians are large, noticeably cupped, and their holdfasts are gnarled like an old tree root. They favor depths of greater than twenty meters (we have seen a couple at eighteen) and, oddly, seem more often closed than open, even when other species are fully expanded. Typically of invertebrates, which have second-class status in marine science,

actual size

The above photograph makes it clear what the fuss is about. This is a remarkable fish. At left, we briefly, and fruitlessly, search yet another large Muricella plectana for our tiny and elusive quarry.

the gorgonians weren't named until 1996.

Find the gorgonian and start looking. It is not easy, by the way. Remember, these animals are tiny and match their host perfectly. We've both found them in Komodo, and although Wally is much better at it than me, even my computer-burned eyes can do it.

By the way, if you want another challenge, there is a second species of cryptic seahorse now showing up in photographs from the area, sometimes misidentified as *H. bargibanti*. This one has a longer nose, is not as chubby, is only slightly bumpy, and lives on the gorgonian *Subergorgia*. I (and photographer Mike Severns) vote for *H. lichtensteinii,* but the scientific jury is still out.

Silhouette from: Seahorses, An Identification Guide to the World's Species and their Conservation, by Sara A. Lourie, Amanda C.J. Vincent, and Heather J. Hall. This excellent work, published by Project Seahorse (www.seahorse.mcgill.ca), is highly recommended for anyone interested in these fascinating animals.

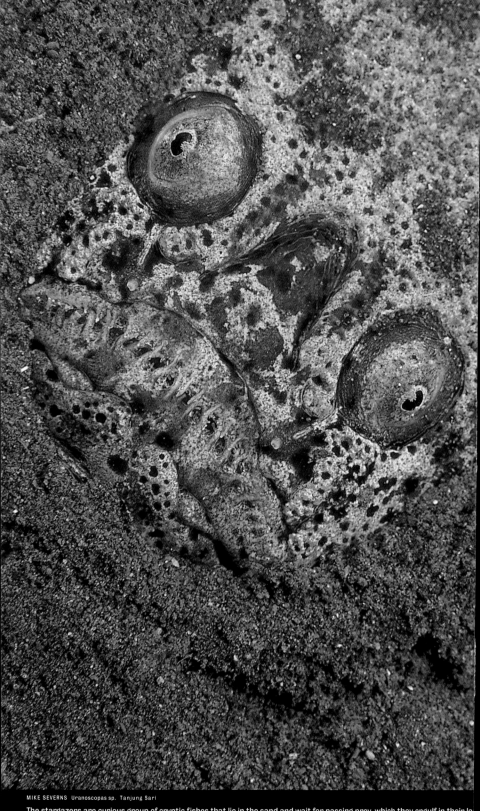

MIKE SEVERNS Uranoscopas sp. Tanjung Sari

The stargazers are curious group of cryptic fishes that lie in the sand and wait for passing prey, which they engulf in their la
mouths. Some improve their luck by wiggling a tentacle in their lower jaw, which serves as a lure. They have two sharp, venomous spines on their backs, behind their gill plates, and should never be handled. Stargazers seem to prefer colder water.

Mainland Balinese consider this low, dry limestone island to be almost haunted, but divers have long flocked to its clear, current-swept reefs. Molas, big sharks, and healthy coral are here, but so are four-knot currents and monster swell.

Nusa Penida

ABOUT FIVE YEARS AGO, AN OLD Japanese photographer came up from his dive only to find himself alone in the water, with no boat in sight. He had been diving Ental Point, the northeast extremity of Nusa Lembongan, one of Nusa Penida's sister islands. Since he was a photographer, he spent his dive pretty much in one place, patiently setting up shot after shot of the macro subjects that were his stock in trade. The rest of the group, including the guide, were swept by the current in a drift west and south around the point.

As the photographer floated, waiting for some sign of his boat, the guide and skipper were frantically searching for him—south of the point. Finally, afternoon began to yield to dark, and since he was running low on fuel and did not want to risk his other clients in a night crossing, the guide reluctantly gave up

and headed back to Sanur, whence the dive charter had begun that morning.

The photographer, still floating north of Lembongan, was getting tired of waiting, and decided to take matters into his own hands. With the setting sun and his compass to guide him, he leaned back, camera in his lap, and started steadily paddling to Bali. Night fell, and he kept paddling, now and then turning around to check his bearing against the lights of the Sanur strip. At ten o'clock the next morning he found himself in front of his hotel—eighteen hours and twenty kilometers of open sea later.

He crawled up onto the beach, walked straight to the bar, and ordered a drink. The bartender called the diving desk and soon a hubbub of activity surrounded the tough old soldier. His equipment lay in a damp heap next to the bar. When he

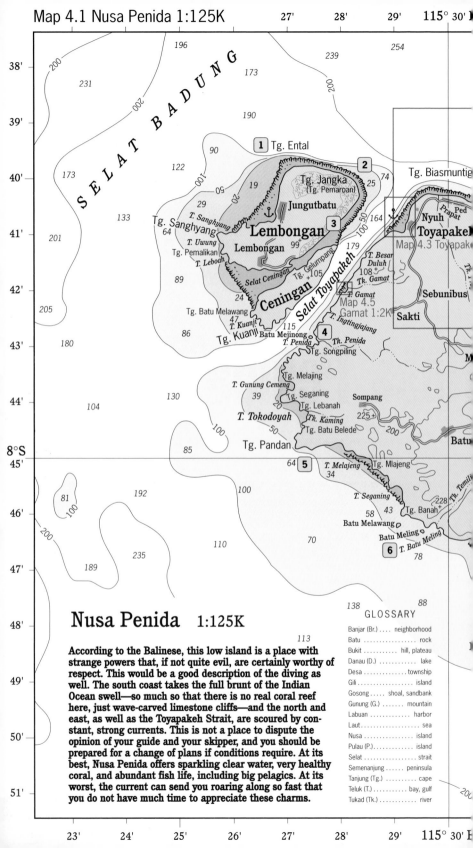

Map 4.1 Nusa Penida 1:125K

Nusa Penida 1:125K

According to the Balinese, this low island is a place with strange powers that, if not quite evil, are certainly worthy of respect. This would be a good description of the diving as well. The south coast takes the full brunt of the Indian Ocean swell—so much so that there is no real coral reef here, just wave-carved limestone cliffs—and the north and east, as well as the Toyapakeh Strait, are scoured by constant, strong currents. This is not a place to dispute the opinion of your guide and your skipper, and you should be prepared for a change of plans if conditions require. At its best, Nusa Penida offers sparkling clear water, very healthy coral, and abundant fish life, including big pelagics. At its worst, the current can send you roaring along so fast that you do not have much time to appreciate these charms.

GLOSSARY

Banjar (Br.) .... neighborhood
Batu .... rock
Bukit .... hill, plateau
Danau (D.) .... lake
Desa .... township
Gili .... island
Gosong ..... shoal, sandbank
Gunung (G.) .... mountain
Labuan .... harbor
Laut .... sea
Nusa .... island
Pulau (P.) .... island
Selat .... strait
Semenanjung ...... peninsula
Tanjung (Tg.) .... cape
Teluk (T.) .... bay, gulf
Tukad (Tk.) .... river

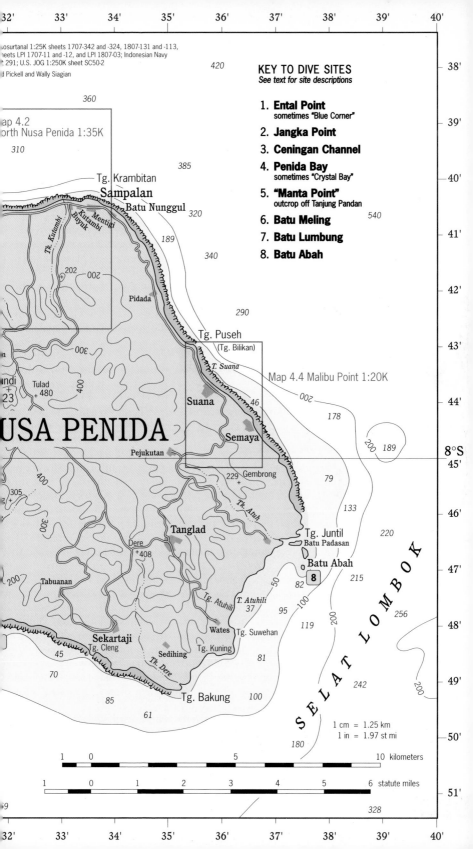

KEY TO DIVE SITES
See text for site descriptions

1. **Ental Point**
   sometimes "Blue Corner"

2. **Jangka Point**

3. **Ceningan Channel**

4. **Penida Bay**
   sometimes "Crystal Bay"

5. **"Manta Point"**
   outcrop off Tanjung Pandan

6. **Batu Meling**

7. **Batu Lumbung**

8. **Batu Abah**

osurtanal 1:25K sheets 1707-342 and -324, 1807-131 and -113,
eets LPI 1707-11 and -12, and LPI 1807-03; Indonesian Navy
t 291; U.S. JOG 1:250K sheet SC50-2
d Pickell and Wally Siagian

ap 4.2
orth Nusa Penida 1:35K

Tg. Krambitan
Sampalan
Batu Nunggul

Mentigi
Kutambi
BΛyŋk
Tk. Kutambi

Pidada

Tulad
+480

USA PENIDA

Pejukutan

Tg. Puseh
(Tg. Bilikan)
T. Suana

Map 4.4 Malibu Point 1:20K

Suana

Semaya

8°S

Gembrong
Tk. Atuh

Tanglad

Dere
+408

Tabuanan

Tg. Juntil
Batu Padasan

Batu Abah
8

Tg. Atuhili
T. Atuhili

Wates
Tg. Suwehan

Sekartaji
Tg. Cleng
Sedihing
Tg. Kuning
Tk. Dere

Tg. Bakung

SELAT LOMBOK

1 cm = 1.25 km
1 in = 1.97 st mi

1   0   5   10 kilometers

1   0   1   2   3   4   5   6 statute miles

saw that a weight belt was still there, the operator was flabbergasted. "My god, why didn't you ditch your belt?" The photographer quietly replied, "Because it isn't mine."

The photographer finished his drink, and before heading upstairs to his room to get some rest, asked the operator to please put his name down for the dive boat the next

KAL MULLER Plectorhinchus polytaenia Nusa Penida

Although often rich in fish life, in the more current-swept areas of Nusa Penida the reef surface is a relatively low growth of sponges and tough hard and soft corals.

morning. He also asked for a pair of rental fins. Unfortunately, he said, I lost one of mine in the crossing.

FAST AND FURIOUS

Nusa Penida diving offers all the superlatives that make a diver's mouth water, including sharks (even gray reefs, silver-tips, and oceanic white-tips), sea turtles, molas, pristine hard coral reefs, deepwater wire corals five meters long, bright, healthy fishes, and the kind of stunningly clear visibility that refuses to quit until the whole ocean glows a deep, rich blue. As they would say in Los Angeles, Nusa Penida gives good brochure.

But—and there is always a "but"—it can be a very wild ride. The current sweeping past Penida means that just about every dive here turns into a drift. Many divers enjoy this, but a two-knot current can make it a bit difficult to take a good macro shot of a nudibranch, for example, unless you don't mind that its gills are blown flat as a floor

mop. On a drift dive around Penida, which is to say on any dive around Penida, it is worth bearing in mind the following points.

¶ Always stick close to the reef. This will allow you to periodically seek protection behind coral heads and bommies, and the current flow right up against the reef is always less fierce than the flow even a few meters away in the open water. Many divers stay too far away from the coral, and shoot along helplessly like rag dolls in the current.

¶ Overall, Nusa Penida is not the most rewarding place for still photography. For conditions that will allow you to properly set up still shots, you have to look for protected areas, such as Gamat, or among the bommies at Toyapakeh. Underwater video is more suited to drift conditions, however, and since the water is quite clear, videographers will find these sites more satisfactory to their needs.

¶ Penida is a place to be conservative. Because of the strong currents, which often change in both intensity and set during the course of a dive, groups can easily get separated, and divers can end up far from their planned ascent point. Stay with your group, and always bring an inflatable signal device so that if you do get separated your skipper will be able to see you.

We have concentrated our coverage on Nusa Penida's north and northeast coast, and on the two finest sites in Toyapakeh Strait. This is the best diving Nusa Penida offers, combining healthy reefs and lots of marine life with conditions that are, if not easy, at least manageable. Most of the rest of the island is rough, even dangerously so, with reefs that are too barren to make the effort worthwhile. Listen to the advice of your dive operator and skipper, and always stay with your group. Unless, that is, you want to swim back to Bali.

The North Coast
From Toyapakeh to Malibu Point

MY FIRST DIVE OFF NUSA PENIDA was at Toyapakeh, a small Muslim village at the northern opening of the strait that separates Nusa Ceningan and Penida. Wally and I dropped onto the shallows around the middle of the bay, and headed out to the reef edge.

At first, I admit, I was underwhelmed. The bottom was a bit rubbly, and covered with the healthy but somehow boring growth that typifies a relatively current-swept reef—robust *Acropora* colonies, *Porites* boulders, and big leather corals. There were plenty of reef fish darting about, but I couldn't help thinking that this site was somehow, well, ordinary. We soon hit the deeper area, where, at about twenty-five meters, the reef ran to a slope of sand and rubble. There we encountered a current, which carried us in a steady drift north along the reef edge.

It was then that I began to change my mind. Gazing east, I looked up into a region of towering bommies. I don't know if it was because at the time I had recently moved from New York City, but when I saw those great, squared-off pillars of coral, swarming with huge schools of unicornfish and batfish and a veritable snowstorm of orange and pink anthias, I imagined a kind of underwater city. In scale and drama, it reminded me of the Manhattan skyline.

The view did not last long, however, and we probably made a tactical error by staying deep and not heading in immediately to finish our dive in this area. As it was, the current freshened quickly and within minutes we were carried past the "skyline" and hurtling across a relatively barren slope at a rate of well over two knots—and we were still accelerating.

We began finning upslope with purpose, and when we crossed the big submerged rock that marks the end of the Toyapakeh pier at the north end of the bay, the current was like a river. We surfaced, and finned like mad, making for the lee just behind the pier. Our effort was successful—too successful, in fact—and we ended up in shallow, calm water

The heartland of Nusa Penida diving offers stunning visibility, healthy reefs, and pelagics. And you won't even have to swim here, as every dive is a drift.

just a couple of dozen meters north of the pier. We were also completely entangled in fishing lines. Neither of us had a knife on him, which was foolish, but we are known to be a bit lax when it comes to this kind of thing (since then I have tried to remember to carry a small knife in my B.C. pocket).

With no other choice, we took turns biting off the lines that had become tightly wrapped around our tank valves, spare second stages, gauges, and every other bit of equipment. Getting rid of these

The Current Meter

ALTHOUGH MANY DIVERS COME UP FROM A DIVE AND talk about "a three-knot current," the true rate of current flow is something difficult to judge with precision and, like size and distance underwater, most guesses tend to be on the inflated side. A physical oceanographer would use a current meter, but this would be a ridiculous thing for a diver to carry.

And it would be unnecessary. The best judges of current are the fishes, who after all have had millennia to contend with it. By carefully observing their behavior, a diver can make a very accurate assessment of the rate of current. Schooling small species are the most sensitive indicators. The anthias or fairy basslets, common at all of the Nusa Penida sites, are probably the best. The following scale was developed by Wally over many years of observation.

NO CURRENT The small fish are swimming happily in every direction, in large schools distributed both vertically and horizontally.

LIGHT CURRENT (to 1 knot). The small fish are aligned, all facing up-current. If they are still in large, spread out schools, the current is around a half-knot. If the schools are low and wide, close to the coral, the current is closer to one-knot.

MEDIUM CURRENT (1–2 knots). The small fish are now hovering in a school spread out like a mat just above the coral, and finning madly. A current of this strength begins to show in the behavior of the larger fish as well, as they face the current and tend to concentrate behind bommies or in other lee areas.

STRONG CURRENT (2–3 knots). In a current of this power, the small fish are all hiding among the branches of the coral. The big fish are gathered in lee areas, or very close to the bottom. By the time the current approaches three knots, you won't need the fish as an indicator. Hang onto the edge of a bommie and swing around and face the current full on. If your mask is fluttering and threatening to fly off, and your regulator begins to free-flow, you are there.

When you are being blown across the reef by a strong current, most of the fish will be hiding, but not all of them. Look behind bommies, or in natural hollows in the reef surface. If the fish here are swimming around, you have found a lee, where the current is locally light or absent. Sometimes the fish are all up in the water column in an area physically identical to the rest of the reef. This is a place where the current shifts or an ameliorating eddy has formed. And, like the fish, this is where you want to be.

pesky lines was not as easy as you might think. The Balinese are not sport fishermen, and despite that they are only pulling up rainbow runners and the like, their monofilament was the diameter of a chopstick. We had to gnaw through it like animals.

Our efforts were not helped by the angry chorus of curses that showered down on us from the pier. As soon as my white face became evident, we even got an occasional, perfectly intoned, "[BLEEP] YOU!" We know fishing gear is relatively expensive for a Penida villager, but considering the obviousness of our predicament, this behavior seemed to us to be a bit heartless.

RICH, CLEAR, AND FAST

This first dive lasted maybe fifteen minutes. I have since had much longer dives here, of course, but in a way this first experience nicely sums up North Penida diving. Healthy, and in places, very beautiful reefs, and fast and unpredictable conditions. And sparkling clear water. Twenty meters might be a typical visibility around the island, and in good conditions it might be double that. When a skipper follows the divers, this usually means that he follows the divers' bubbles. But at Nusa Penida, it can mean he literally follows the *divers*.

Once I was on the boat while Wally and a client were diving, again at Toyapakeh. I put on a mask and leaned over the edge of the boat. The two were looking closely at a wire coral near a large barrel sponge, on the slope just past the area of bommies. My guess was that Wally was showing him a commensal shrimp on the coral. This would be unremarkable except that they were at twenty-five meters and well downslope of the boat, which put at least forty meters of water between us. My only limitation in seeing what was going on came from my

eyes. The water may as well have been air.

A DRY, MYSTERIOUS ISLAND

Nusa Penida is a dry, limestone plateau covering about two hundred square kilometers. There is no volcanic rock here at all, and the soil is weathered limestone. Bukit Mundi, the highest point on the island, rises to 523 meters. From the north coast, the slope up to Mundi, in the island's center, is gradual, but along the south coast the plateau ends abruptly in sheer, chalky cliffs, some of them two hundred meters high.

About fifty thousand people live on Nusa Penida, and most of the villages are concentrated along the coast. The small city of Sampalan, on the island's northeast point, is the island's largest populated area. Batu Nunggul, one of several villages that together make up Sampalan, is the political capital or *ibu kota*—literally "mother city"—of Nusa Penida.

Unlike south-central Bali, with its wet, fertile, volcanic soil, Nusa Penida is a difficult place to make a living as a farmer. It is much too dry to grow rice, and even drinking water must come from cisterns. The islanders grow manioc (tapioca), corn, sweet potatoes, and beans. Fishing, on a small scale, supports some fifteen hundred families, and in Lembongan and along the north coast of Penida, an estimated nine hundred families earn their living growing seaweed (see "Seaweed Farming," pg. 163).

For most Balinese, Nusa Penida is a mysterious, and even dangerous place. They would call it *angker*, that is, possessed of fearsome and occult powers (*angker* is sometimes translated as "haunted"). Until the early twentieth century, this bleak island was used as a penal colony by the Rajah of Klungkung, and not many Balinese are anxious to visit even today.

The one time mainland Balinese do come to Nusa Penida is on Buda Cemeng Kelawu of the Pawukon anniversary cycle. This is the day of the temple festival for Pura Dalem

The lizardfish is an ambush predator of small fish, a lifestyle to which it is very well adapted. Lizardfish sit motionless, often in pairs, until a damsel or cardinalfish or some other unlucky fish wanders too close, upon which with lightning speed the lizardfish seizes its victim. The teeth, visible here, are extremely effective, and the mouth is huge, allowing them to capture and swallow prey of very unlikely size. This species is the only common coral reef lizardfish in Bali; the others prefer sandy bays, and stay partially buried while they wait for a passing meal.

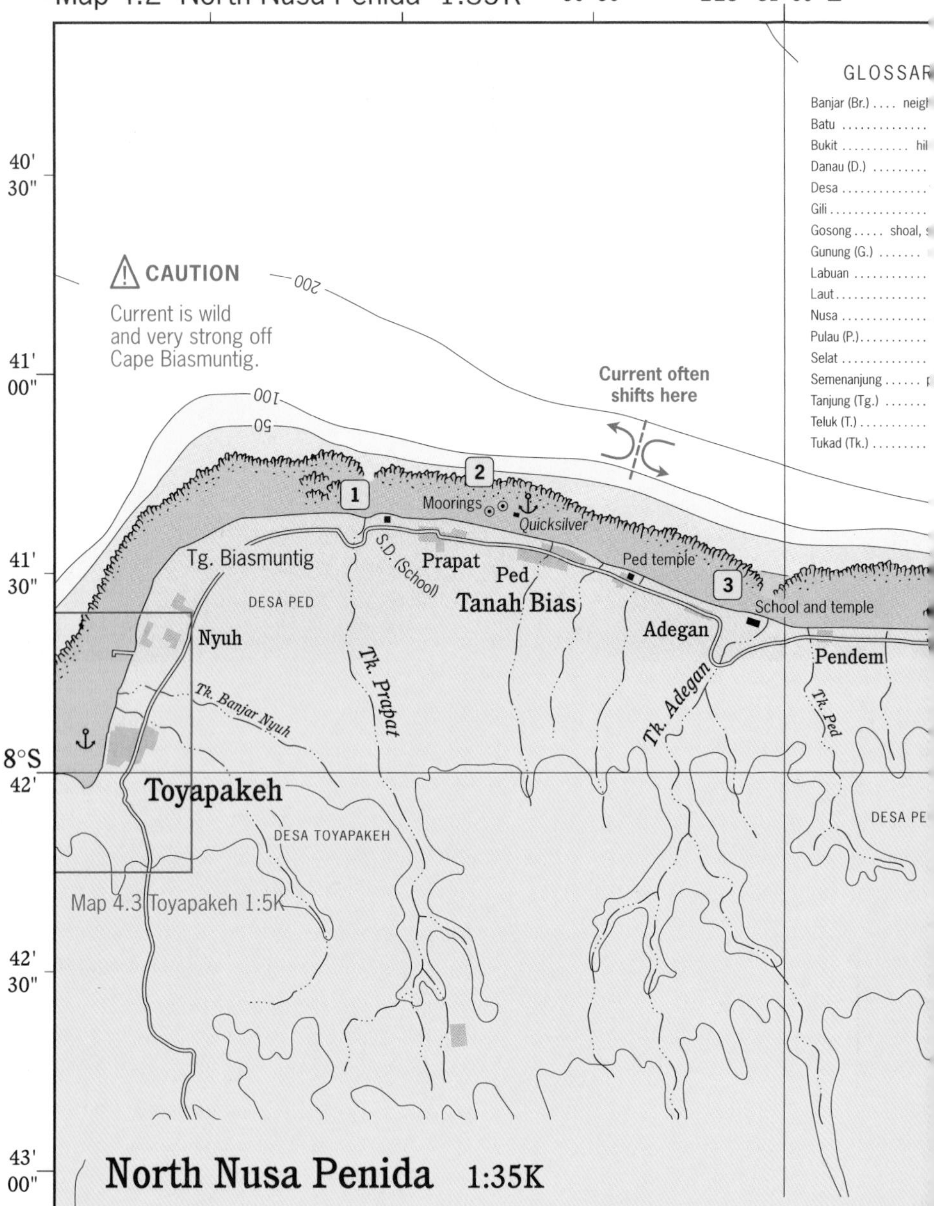

Map 4.2 North Nusa Penida 1:35K

30' 30"   115° 31' 00" E

40'
30"

41'
00"

⚠ **CAUTION**

Current is wild
and very strong off
Cape Biasmuntig.

002

Current often
shifts here

41'
30"

Tg. Biasmuntig

DESA PED

Nyuh

100

50

Moorings

Quicksilver

Prapat

Ped

Tanah Bias

Ped temple

1

2

3

School and temple

Adegan

Pendem

S.D. (School)

Tk. Prapat

Tk. Banjar Nyuh

Tk. Adegan

Tk. Ped

8°S
42'

⚓ **Toyapakeh**

DESA TOYAPAKEH

Map 4.3 Toyapakeh 1:5K

DESA PE

42'
30"

43'
00"

43'
30"

44'
00"

GLOSSAR

Banjar (Br.) . . . . neigh
Batu . . . .
Bukit . . . . hil
Danau (D.) . . . .
Desa . . . .
Gili . . . .
Gosong . . . . . shoal, s
Gunung (G.) . . . .
Labuan . . . .
Laut . . . .
Nusa . . . .
Pulau (P.) . . . .
Selat . . . .
Semenanjung . . . . . . p
Tanjung (Tg.) . . . .
Teluk (T.) . . . .
Tukad (Tk.) . . . .

North Nusa Penida 1:35K

The coast of northern Nusa Penida from the Biasmuntig Peninsula to the Krambitan Peninsul.
is, after Toyapakeh, the most frequently dived area on the island. The reef is quite healthy, an
of a similar structure all along this stretch: a slope of low hard corals, with patches of bommies, that runs to fifty meters or so. There is always current here, from a pleasant knot-and-a-
half to a roaring four knots, which keeps the water clear, but also insures that the coral growt
is generally low and tough. There are no big gorgonians here, for example. Because of the pro:
imity of deep water and the strong current, this is a good area to see molas, big requiem
sharks, and other pelagics, but as always, this is not guaranteed. Just about every dive here
becomes a drift, and you can cover a surprising amount of territory. For example, you might
start at Buyuk, and find yourself at the mouth of the Adegan River by the end of your dive.

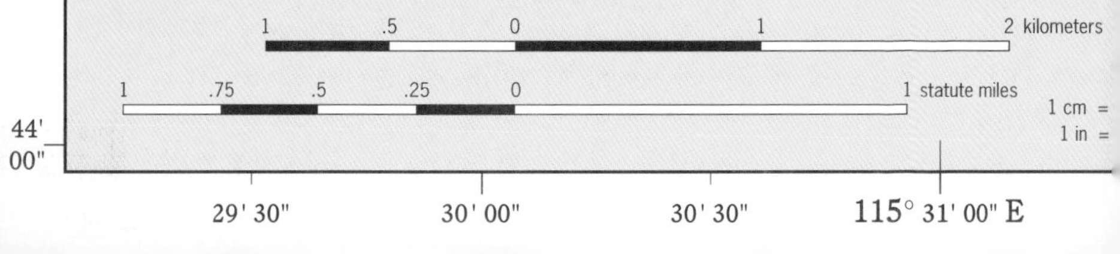

1   .5   0   1   2 kilometers

1   .75   .5   .25   0   1 statute miles

1 cm =
1 in =

29' 30"   30' 00"   30' 30"   115° 31' 00" E

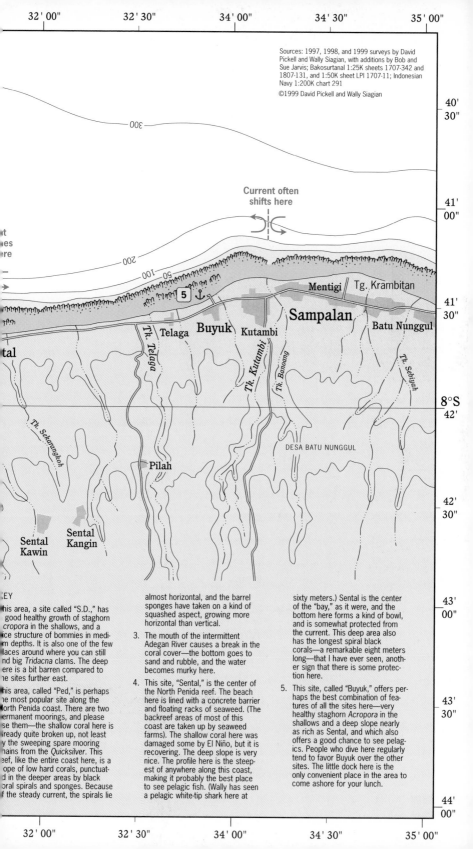

Sources: 1997, 1998, and 1999 surveys by David Pickell and Wally Siagian, with additions by Bob and Sue Jarvis; Bakosurtanal 1:25K sheets 1707-342 and 1807-131, and 1:50K sheet LPI 1707-11; Indonesian Navy 1:200K chart 291

©1999 David Pickell and Wally Siagian

Current often shifts here

Mentigi Tg. Krambitan

5 ⚓

Tk. Telaga Telaga **Buyuk** Kutambi **Sampalan** Batu Nunggul

Tk. Kutambi Tk. Banang Tk. Sebiyh

al

Tk. Sekorongkoh

8°S

DESA BATU NUNGGUL

Pilah

Sental Kawin Sental Kangin

KEY

his area, a site called "S.D.," has good healthy growth of staghorn *cropora* in the shallows, and a ice structure of bommies in medi- m depths. It is also one of the few laces around where you can still nd big *Tridacna* clams. The deep ere is a bit barren compared to e sites further east.

his area, called "Ped," is perhaps e most popular site along the orth Penida coast. There are two ermanent moorings, and please se them—the shallow coral here is lready quite broken up, not least y the sweeping spare mooring hains from the *Quicksilver*. This eef, like the entire coast here, is a ope of low hard corals, punctuat- d in the deeper areas by black oral spirals and sponges. Because f the steady current, the spirals lie almost horizontal, and the barrel sponges have taken on a kind of squashed aspect, growing more horizontal than vertical.

3. The mouth of the intermittent Adegan River causes a break in the coral cover—the bottom goes to sand and rubble, and the water becomes murky here.

4. This site, "Sental," is the center of the North Penida reef. The beach here is lined with a concrete barrier and floating racks of seaweed. (The backreef areas of most of this coast are taken up by seaweed farms). The shallow coral here was damaged some by El Niño, but it is recovering. The deep slope is very nice. The profile here is the steep- est of anywhere along this coast, making it probably the best place to see pelagic fish. (Wally has seen a pelagic white-tip shark here at sixty meters.) Sental is the center of the "bay," as it were, and the bottom here forms a kind of bowl, and is somewhat protected from the current. This deep area also has the longest spiral black corals—a remarkable eight meters long—that I have ever seen, anoth- er sign that there is some protec- tion here.

5. This site, called "Buyuk," offers per- haps the best combination of fea- tures of all the sites here—very healthy staghorn *Acropora* in the shallows and a deep slope nearly as rich as Sental, and which also offers a good chance to see pelag- ics. People who dive here regularly tend to favor Buyuk over the other sites. The little dock here is the only convenient place in the area to come ashore for your lunch.

Penataran Ped (or Peed), the most powerful temple on the island—and one of the most respected in all of Bali. The Ped temple is not particularly beautiful ("outstandingly ugly," is how one guidebook describes it) or large. But it is nevertheless a very important site.

The significance of the Ped temple comes from a small shrine to I

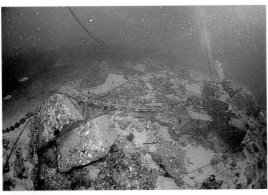

The Quicksilver floating barge, a platform for day-tripping revelers—snorkeling, being towed on inflatable hot-dogs, etc.—looks like this underneath. This is the one at Ped; the one at Toyapakeh is not much better. The worst is not the concrete mooring blocks, dumped here like so much trash, but the untended anchoring chains, which have swept a large area of formerly rich reef here down to a barren desert of rubble and sand.

Macaling, a dread figure who is known for sowing sickness and evil all over the island. This is the spot where a practitioner of black magic would come, and I Macaling has been called "the patron saint" of Bali's witches. But the Balinese treat evil and good with equal respect, and I Macaling is a powerful protector as well.

The histories of I Macaling are complicated and various, but the most common suggests that he was the head of a group of *wong gamang*—powerful and invisible supernatural beings—and an advisor to the 16th-century ruler of Nusa Penida, Dalem Dukut. (In this capacity he helped oppose two invasions by the East Java–based Majapahit empire, and since the Majapahit wrote the history, this may be sufficient explanation of his bad reputation.)

THE PENIDA SILL

The flow through the Lombok Strait is, overall, south-tending, although the strength and direction of the tidal streams are influenced by the monsoon seasons. During the southeast monsoon, the tidal flow tends south; during the northeast monsoon, the tidal flow tends north. In the area of the strait north of Nusa Penida, the pattern is relatively simple, with a flow, at peak tide, of about three-and-one-half knots. But when you reach the area around Nusa Penida, things get very messy indeed.

Nusa Penida is essentially the exposed portion of a submarine sill that connects Bali and Lombok. Water flowing either north or south through the Lombok Strait has a nice, thousand-meter-deep channel to pass through until it reaches a point fifteen kilometers south, or twenty-five kilometers north of Penida. There the bathymetry pushes it upward, and it is thwarted by a bewildering set of rises and channels (see the Nusa Penida area of MAP 0.1 on the front endpaper).

Off the eastern tip of Penida, in the Lombok Strait narrows, the tidal currents can reach six knots, and the seas south of this area are often turbulent and wild. On the other side, in the Badung Strait and through Toyapakeh Strait, things are even more convoluted.

"Tidal streams in Selat Badung are semi-diurnal, but owing to the fact that its direction runs obliquely to the general S to N direction of Selat Lombok, and the curved shape of the channel, the character of the stream is very complicated," states the Hydrographer of the Navy's *Indonesia Pilot Vol. II*.

This "very complicated" is almost droll, and the volume follows with nearly a full page of text attempting to describe the tidal current behavior in this area. I would love to distill from this a few simple rules to help predict the current at the Nusa Penida dive sites, but this is unfortunately impossible. Th

A Long Way from Carragheen

LAND PLANTS LIVING IN A HARSH, WIND-blown environment have evolved to become tough, squat, and woody. The power of the ocean is far greater than even the strongest winds, however, and marine algas, instead of trying to stand up to the forces of their environment, approach it in the manner of a Zen Buddhist. They do not break in the surge and waves because they have become as fluid and flexible as the water itself.

Cooks across Southeast Asia have long exploited this property in agar, from algae in the genus *Gelidium,* which they use to make a variety of sweet, gummy, desserts. Agar is Asia's (vegetarian) version of Jell-O. The Balinese use agar in a popular snack called *jaja bulung* ("bulung" is Balinese for seaweed) and the relatively small international agar market is chiefly supplied by Japan.

But the most valuable substance from seaweed is carrageenan, a thickening and stabilizing agent with an infinity of uses in manufacturing prepared foods and cosmetics. The strange name comes from the Irish coastal town of Carragheen, near which the alga *Chondrus cripus,* or "Irish Moss"—the first source of carrageenan—grew in great profusion. Today most carrageenan comes from the tropical brown algas *Eucheuma denticulatum* (still called "spinosum" in the trade), and *Kappaphycus* spp. (called "cottoni" in the trade). The latter yield more and firmer-setting carrageenan, and are almost twice as valuable.

MACHINE AGE FOOD

Carrageenan, in itself, has no taste or color or other inherent value as a food item. What it does have is a property that allows a combination of substances to be squeezed, mixed, and otherwise processed through a battery of machines with a result—after microwaving or reconstituting—that at least approximates real food. When you cut the top off a can of prepared soup and the contents plop out in a wet cylinder that matches the shape of the can exactly, you are probably witnessing the wonder of carrageenan. In the 1960s, as time-strapped American families learned to accept Cheez-Wiz and other "food products," the carrageenan supply grew tight and prices for the dried algae reached a historic high of $630 pre-inflation dollars per ton. The processed food industry began scouring the world, particularly the Third World, for additional (and cheaper) sources.

Farming experiments began in earnest in the mid-seventies. In Indonesia, the first attempts in Java, North Sulawesi, and the Riau Islands failed. Then, in 1978, the Copenhagen Pectin Factory, Ltd. (a subsidiary of U.S. Hercules, Inc.) established experimental farms near Tanjung Geger in South Bali. This experiment, which lasted until 1984, was a qualified success, but the tourism department feared the farms were too close to Nusa Dua, and the company found that the algae, if anything, grew too quickly at Geger, producing a product with little carrageenan content. Thus, after considerable study, the farms were moved to Nusas Lembongan, Ceningan, and Penida.

Today, "fields" of seaweed line almost every protected coastline in this area. Farmers tie sprigs of the algae to lines they have staked out in the shallows in waist-high water, and when the crop grows out, they gather and dry it for sale.

A VOLATILE MARKET

In the 1980s prices hovered around $50 a ton for the dried algae, producing a decent living for the farmers, but in 1990 Balinese seaweed farmers suddenly found that the market for their product had collapsed. This came about because of changing market demands (e.g, the shift to *Kappaphycus*) that were not properly communicated to the farmers, adulteration of the dried alga by crooked middlemen to cheat up its weight, and simple fluctuations in the world supply.

The situation has improved, but prices are still not back to 1980s levels, and Bali's seaweed farmers remain vulnerable to the vagaries of an international market over which they have little control.

best summary I can offer is: The entire Badung Strait area from Amuk Bay down the coast of Bali and across to Nusa Penida is a rat's nest of shifting current streams and eddies that are, individually, local in influence, brief in duration, and fierce in effect.

What you need to do here is time your dive for slack water, look closely at the conditions pertaining locally at the various sites, and listen to the advice of your skipper. (And always, always bring an inflatable signal device.)

Toyapakeh

Toyapakeh is probably the most commonly dived site on Nusa Penida. It is also, in many people's opinion, the best. The "skyline" that impressed me so much on my first dive is a very beautiful stretch of reef, and in the southern part of the bay there is a similar area of rugged bommies, rich with color and fish, that is, if anything, even better (see MAP 4.3, pp. 166–167).

Big schools of fish, sea turtles, and occasionally, molas are highlights of Toyapakeh diving, but these can be found at the other sites on Nusa Penida as well. What makes Toyapakeh special is its structure; those great pillars of coral. Wally and I are very partial to Gamat, and "Malibu Point" off Suana holds a very special place in Wally's heart in particular. And we have had excellent dives at most of the sites along the north coast. But if you could make only one dive on Nusa Penida, Toyapakeh is where you should go.

JUDGING THE CURRENT

If you mention Toyapakeh to me, the first image that forms in my mind is not of the reef itself. It is of Wally and I standing on the bow of a boat, half suited up, staring at the water just off the southernmost corner of the bay. Usually we have a couple of cigarettes going, and always we are scratching our heads.

Offshore south of the bay is the best place to try to get a sense of where the current is heading, which makes all the difference when diving here. Toyapakeh is not really much of a bay, and offers little natural protection. And the current can be frustratingly difficult to decipher. The key is less the strength of the current than its direction.

If the current sets southwest, directly through the channel, it will form an eddy along the Toyapakeh reef face that curls off and runs north–northeast (see FIGURE 1 at left). This eddy generally produces a nice, manageable drift dive northward along the northern half of the reef. The southern half can still be tricky in conditions like this, however, as it is very hard to tell exactly where the influence of the eddy begins. If you miss it, you will feel the main current, which can carry you southwest into the channel. In conditions like this, it is best to start your dive near the middle section of the reef.

If the current sets at an angle oblique to the lie of the channel, be very careful. Anything significantly south of southwest is a problem, with due south being the worst (see FIGURE 2). If this condition pertains, the current does not really eddy. What happens is that the full force of the main current hits the bay and turns, heading north with great force. This is not a diveable condition, and a current like this will quickly spit a diver north and out of the channel altogether.

If the current sets northeast, you can actually follow the main current along the reef edge (FIGURE 3). When this condition is active, you can make a dive that takes in the whole length of the reef, from the *kepeng* tree to the pier. For northeast-running water, Toyapakeh is at the end of the strait, where the cha-

Figure 1

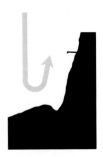

Figure 2

Figure 3

el widens and the water can finally settle down. But for southwest-
running water, it is the funnel at the
beginning of the strait, where the
water speeds up and sends frus-
trated eddies curling off. You can
never follow the main current run-
ing southwest.

THE DUCK AND THE DOG

It is relatively easy to tell the difference between a northeast-run-
ing current and a southeast-run-
ing one, and if it is not obvious

combine with the direction and rate
of the current to land the bird at the
desired spot. A dog, in contrast,
does not possess this sophistication.
A dog swimming across a current always heads directly toward its destination. This is a mistake, and by
the end of the journey the dog will
find itself swimming against the full
force of the current. And at the end
the duck's path—"the duck curve"—
is always shorter than the dog's
path—"the dog curve."

The *jukung* pilots think like the

om the water, look at the *jukung*s
aving Toyapakeh. These boats are
eaded west to East Bali, and the
ap says that the shortest way to get
ere is to head west–northwest past
ntal Point. But on many occasions
e *jukung*s head south. This puz-
ed me the first time I saw it, and
ked Wally what was up. "They are
llowing the duck curve," he said.

If a duck needs to swim across a
urrent, it knows to lead the current,
tting off at a heading upstream of
s desired destination. The direc-
on and rate of the duck's paddling

duck, and if they head south
through the strait, it means the current is running northeast. If they
head north, it means the current is
running southwest. They are never
wrong.

It is considerably more difficult
to determine the exact angle of a
generally southwest-tending current. And here, all we can suggest is
to look at the lines of disturbance on
the surface of the water out toward
the channel, smoke a couple of cigarettes, and try to reach a consensus.
Eventually, the safe move is to drop

The actinodendrid
anemones, which tend
to bury their columns
in sand, have a very
powerful sting. For
this reason a number
of commensal
shrimps seek refuge
in their tentacles,
such as this unidenti-
fied Periclimenes.

Map 4.3 Toyapakeh 1:5K

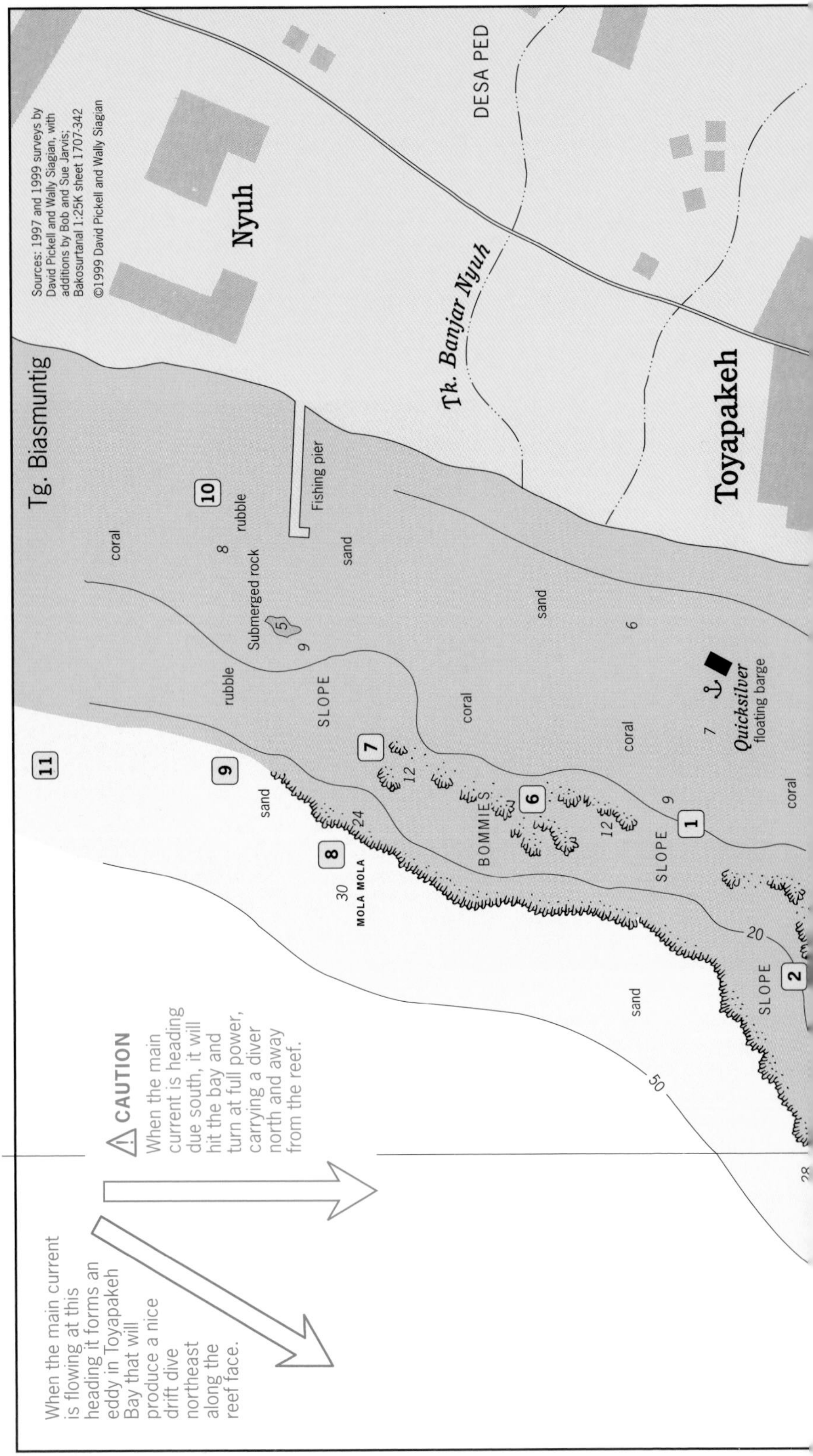

115° 29' 00" E

Sources: 1997 and 1999 surveys by
David Pickell and Wally Siagian, with
additions by Bob and Sue Jarvis;
Bakosurtanal 1:25K sheet 1707-342
©1999 David Pickell and Wally Siagian

Nyuh

DESA PED

Tg. Biasmuntig

Tk. Banjar Nyuh

Toyapakeh

Fishing pier

10

rubble

8

coral

Submerged rock

5

9

sand

sand

6

11

9

rubble

SLOPE

coral

7

Quicksilver
floating barge

7

sand

7

12

coral

9

6

SLOPE

12

BOMMIES

1

8

24

24

coral

30

MOLA MOLA

20

SLOPE

2

sand

50

28

⚠ CAUTION

When the main
current is heading
due south, it will
hit the bay and
turn at full power,
carrying a diver
north and away
from the reef.

When the main current
is flowing at this
heading it forms an
eddy in Toyapakeh
Bay that will
produce a nice
drift dive
northeast
along the
reef face.

DESA TOYAPAKEH

MOLA MOLA

12

5

sand

sand and coral

Toyapakeh 1:5K

```
0        100      200      300 m
|----|----|----|----|----|----|
0      500        1000 ft
```

1 cm = 50 m
1 in = 417 ft.

This is probably the single most popular dive on Nusa Penida, and deservedly so. The water is clear, the coral is rich, and the bay, although it is quite exposed, does offer some protection from the strong current flowing through the strait. The underwater topography here is very nice, with the ten- to fifteen-meter area in particular being made up of great coral boulders and pillars. Drifting along at twenty meters, and looking upslope, these appear as a kind of coral city, which makes a nice change from the basically flat structure of the North Coast. The protection these bommies provide makes Toyapakeh (together with Gamat) one of the few places on Nusa Penida where you can see big gorgonians and soft coral bushes. The fish life here is also excellent, and the deeper areas offer chance encounters with molas and other pelagics. The current, unfortunately, can be frustratingly difficult to read at Toyapakeh, and if you judge it poorly, you can drift past the good reef and into the rubble out past the pier in a mere fifteen minutes, so it is definitely worth taking some time to evaluate the conditions.

KEY

1. Unless you are absolutely certain of the current direction, this is the best place to drop, as you can then head either north or south as conditions permit. Make sure someone watches your bubbles and the boat follows. Also pay attention to the schedule of the annoying *Quicksilver*, which blasts into the bay at 9 am and out at 3 pm. You do not want to be in the water when this takes place.

2. This area, protected by bommies, has big gorgonians and soft coral bushes.

3. This is probably the single best area of the Toyapakeh reef. The bommies create a beautiful structure, and it is very rich: huge schools of *Anthias*, soft corals, healthy hard corals—everything you could ask for.

4. Although the nice structure begins to level off, the deep area off the south end of the reef always has huge schools of batfish, sweetlips, fusiliers, and jacks. It is also one of the best places here to see mola-mola.

5. Here the reef narrows, and the profile becomes steeper. There is a cave, and some unusual long bommies here. The shoreline is a limestone wall, and clinging to it, literally growing sideways, is a tough old tree. People have tossed antique coins—*kepeng*—into the water here as a kind of offering. If you find one, do not take it, as it will certainly bring the worst kind of misfortune.

6. This is another very rich area, second only to area #3. The structure is beautiful, and the fish life and coral are exuberant.

7. This protected area is another place with big gorgonian fans and soft coral bushes.

8. The deep area here is another good place to find mola-mola, if luck happens to be on your side.

9. Just off the pier, the bottom becomes a steep rubble slope. It is a dead and barren area, and the current usually begins to pick up here, sometimes dramatically. If you are in around ten meters, you will pass a large coral rock. At this point in your dive, you should swim in to the area behind the pier, which is always protected from the main force of the current.

10. If your drift takes you past the pier, this is where you want to finish up (although do not come in so close that you end up in the bramble of fishing lines coming off the pier). It is a bit rubbly, but safe. The reef just north of here is actually quite rich, but because of the eddy—which is what protects this area—the visibility is low.

11. Here is where you do not want to end up, because if you do you will not be here for long. The typical current at this point will be blowing you north—usually powerfully—into the middle of the Lombok Strait. Divers who have made this mistake have been recovered *two miles away*! (And they are the lucky ones.)

115° 29' 00" E

WALLY SIAGIAN   Unidentified ovulid (perhaps Dentiovula) on Dendronephthya sp.   14m

The texture and color of this ovulid's mantle is a remarkable match with the surface of its soft coral host.

into the middle—that way if the eddy is pushing north, you can dive the north half of the reef, and if you have missed the eddy, you can dive the south half.

If you head north, always pull in behind the jetty, as the water further north is rough and the current can spit you north. Similarly, if you head south, do not go past the *kepeng* tree—beyond here you are in the Toyapakeh Strait.

The North Coast

A healthy reef lines the entire north coast of Nusa Penida, from the Biasmuntig Peninsula, just north of Toyapakeh, to Tanjung Krambitan at Sampalan (see MAP 4.2, pp. 160–161). There are at least five named dive sites along this eight-kilometer stretch, although the profile and zonation of the reef is similar at each.

Almost the entire length of the calm, sandy back reef area here is used for seaweed farming, and in some areas the shoreline has been stabilized by low concrete retaining walls. The coral begins in earnest at three to five meters. In some areas this is very healthy—dominated by glowing thickets of lettuce corals and fine, bristly *Acropora*—and in others it is a rubbly mix of low fire corals and algae. This is the part of Nusa Penida that felt the effects of the 1998 El Niño warming, but its impact was spotty, which is strange for a reef with such a consistent structure. The best shallow areas were unaffected, and remain very healthy. These—particularly S.D and Buyuk—make excellent snorkeling sites if the current is willing to cooperate.

From five meters on, the reef is a slope, with a generally good growth of hard coral down to about fifteen or twenty meters. Here and there throughout this stretch, there are bommies, but no formations as large or dramatic as those at Toyapakeh. Except for a few deep, relatively quiet areas, there are no big gorgonians here—the current is too strong. This slope is narrow, but quite healthy. At twenty meters or s the coral runs out, leaving a rubble slope covered by barrel sponges and, a little deeper, long wire corals.

This deep slope is our favorite part of this reef. In most areas the steady current has shaped the barrel sponges into strange, squat lumps, far wider than they are tall. The wire corals have a similar wind-blown look. They grow upward for a mere half-meter or so, then make a ninety-degree turn and head off in a loose spiral parallel to the bottom.

In the quieter areas, some of these remarkable corals grow to five meters or more in length. In the deepest part of Sental and Buyuk, in particular, the wire corals form thick forests. On one dive at Buyuk, at forty meters, we hit a thermocline that turned the water to syrup. The wire coral forest, seen through the glass onion of mixing water, appeared like an hallucination.

The most popular sites here are "S.D."—the name comes from the initials for grade school in Indonesian, and the site is just offshore from such a school—and Ped. These are the closest to mainland Bali, and the most familiar to dive operators, but not, in our opinion, the best. We prefer Sental and Buyuk, at the eastern end of the reef, and overall a dive starting at Buyuk is probably the most rewarding.

THE TRAIN RIDE

On a typical dive, our group dropped in just a bit west of the Buyuk pier, and Wally and I headed straight downslope to the deep. The shallows were lively, with bright little firefish hovering above the sand, and here and there an occasional *Chaetodontoplus* angelfish, a rare sight anywhere but Nusa Penida and East Bali. We had timed our dive well, it seemed, and there was little current.

As we wandered the deep slope, at thirty to forty meters, we encountered a few big gorgonians, and everywhere those mysterious spirals. Molas had been sighted here several times in the past few days, so we constantly scanned the deep horizon. I saw what looked like two big silvery shapes downslope at about fifty meters depth, but the edge of the cold water lay between us, making everything behind it appear as through a pebbled bathroom window. And in any case, our attention was soon occupied by a gusty current that had appeared from nowhere.

The current started buffeting us around, and our bubbles, instead of surfacing, swirled around us and hung strangely in the water. We were not really keen on this, particularly since we were at close to forty meters and completely exposed. We decided it would be prudent to head up to the edge of the coral, at about twenty meters.

There we caught the train west, and twenty minutes later, surfaced fully three kilometers from where we entered the water. The key to enjoying Nusa Penida is to find a way not to panic if you get tossed around, or sent hurtling along the reef. Because this will happen. Remember: the current always shifts. We have never been on a dive at Penida where the current was consistent through the entire dive. Stay close to the reef, and if you want a break, look at the fish and find a place to hide (see "The Current Meter," pg. 158). A drift, after all, can be a lot of fun. Don't fight it, just enjoy the ride.

Malibu Point

It was a rainy, off-season day when I first dove Malibu Point (see Map 4.4, pg. 171). Our boat was underpowered, and the ride from the mainland had been long and wet. Wally had been telling me about this site for years, and I was anxious to dive it. Actually, with the brooding clouds making early afternoon look like dusk, and great swirls of current showing off Semaya, I was just plain *anxious,* period.

Malibu Point is the best place to see sharks off Nusa Penida. Not just reef white-tips, but gray reefs, silvertips, oddballs like the little Port Jackson shark, and even big open water requiem sharks. I don't get particularly nervous around sharks, and I like to see them while diving as much as the next person. But the day was so dark, and the water so cold, that I didn't really mind when a strong eddy thwarted our efforts to reach the rocky slope where the sharks congregate. An oceanic white-tip would be an exhilarating sight (I've never seen one underwater) but it's a different kind of exhilaration if your visibility is a mere five meters of gloom.

On a good day, Malibu Point is one of the nicest sites on the island. The reef has a lot of the character of the north coast, except that the structure is much more interesting, with big, rich bommies entending down to twenty-five meters. It is a bit like Toyapakeh in this regard, but it is also somehow wilder, with great schools of jacks and rainbow runners, and dogtooth tuna. And, of course, the sharks. There are more giant reef rays (*Taeniura meyeni*) here than anywhere else we've dived, although they are not uncommon along the north coast either. Visibility is always good at Malibu, at least twenty meters (if, that is, it isn't pouring rain).

Wally pioneered this site in 1987, and named it after the dive shop in Rockingham, south of Perth, Australia, where he worked for a while and took his advanced divemaster training. For many years the members of this outfit made an annual pilgrimage to this site.

The heart of the Malibu reef, and the "point" itself, is off the village of Suana. Because of the bommies, this area is almost always diveable, since you can seek shelter within the structure. In fact, a one- or two-knot current is probably ideal here, with enough movement to keep the fish interested, but not enough to cause a diver problems.

TRICKY, BUT WORTH IT

The difficulty arises when you head southeast to where the sharks can be found. Sharks seem to prefer rough, exposed areas, and Malibu is no exception. The bottom becomes barren and rubbly here. The sharks are found in a reasonable depth, fifteen to thirty meters, and you do not want to go deeper. Nor, in fact, do you want to go as far as the second point under any circumstances.

The point past the shark area is so current-swept that the bottom will not even hold sand. Be very, very careful here, and if the current is strong, stay in the bommies and don't bother looking for the sharks. The current at the point is always four or even five knots, and it will catapult you off the point and into the strait itself. Currents through the narrows, a mere five kilometers away, are known to reach six knots, a speed not every boat can keep up with. Do not end up there.

Few people dive Malibu Point. Most operators will tell you that it is no better than Buyuk or the other North Coast sites, but this statement needs a little translation. What they are really saying is: "It takes a lot more fuel to get to Malibu Point, we don't know this reef at all, and frankly, the place scares our guides."

We think this site is worth the effort and extra distance. The structure alone makes this area more interesting than the north coast, and the almost guaranteed opportunity to see sharks is an added bonus. On the other hand, conditions can bring even a very experienced diver up blanched and shaking.

The Port Jackson shark (Heterodontus sp.) is an unusual horn shark that feeds on echinoderms and other bottom-dwelling invertebrates. It grows to a bit over a meter long. Port Jacksons have been seen at Malibu Point.

Map 4.4 Malibu Point 1:20K

Tg. Puseh
(Tg. Bilikan)

1

Br. Celagilandan

Teluk Suana
rubble

**Current often
shifts here**

2

Notable bridge

sand

Tk. Merani

Notable
trees

Small temple

Suana

Tk. Tanjung Kiri

Biggest
temple

DESA SUANA

Tk. Kentugan

64

Malibu Point
CARCHARHINUS ALBIMARGINATUS

54

4

*TAENIURA
MEYENI* 32

sand

3

THE RICHEST AREA

CARCHARHINUS SPP.

5

sand

rubble

6

⚠ **CAUTION**
See note #6

Big temple

Tk. Batu Kuning

Tk. Dibus

Temple

Semaya

Temple

+ 144

KEY

1. This area is barren and relatively uninteresting.

2. This is where the current usually breaks. The shifting current drops the visibility here, compared to further south along this reef, but the steep profile and swirling current make this the best place to see mola-mola and manta rays.

3. This is the heart of the Malibu Point reef. There are numerous bommies here, and particularly big table corals. In the deeper areas, past twenty meters, great schools of jacks and rainbow runners gather.

4. The reef goes to sand at about forty meters, where there are always big reef rays (*Taeniura meyeni*).

Once, on a dive out on this sand slope to fifty-four meters, Wally encountered a pelagic white-tip shark.

5. This area, in fifteen to thirty meters, is the best place to encounter sharks. The reef also gets a bit rough and rubbly here, and the current usually picks up, so be wary.

6. You do not want to find yourself out on this point. Past the shark area, the bottom goes to rubble, and soon you reach an area where even the sand disappears, and the bottom is scoured stone. The reason for this is the fierce current, which will blow you out and *away from the reef!* If you dive Malibu Point, do not go south of the big temple.

8° 44' 00" S

Malibu Point 1:20K

This site, on Penida's east coast, is much like the north coast sites, except that visibility is generally a bit better, the bommies are richer and extend to deeper water, and there are more schooling fish, more big reef rays, and particularly, more sharks. Unfortunately, the current is even fiercer and trickier than the north. This is a nice dive in a one- or even two-knot current— you can hide a bit in the bommies—but anything more and it turns scary. On the other hand, if you are up for it, in the south end of this reef you always find sharks: reef white-tips, gray reefs, silvertips, nurses, and rarely, although they have been sighted here, blues, oceanic white-tips, and Port Jacksons.

Sources: 1997 and 1998 surveys by
David Pickell and Wally Siagian;
Bakosurtanal 1:25K sheet 1807-131
©1999 David Pickell and Wally Siagian

500	0	500 meters
1000	0	1000	2000 feet

1 cm = 200 m
1 in = 1670 ft

115° 36' 00" E

NUSA PENIDA

The South Coast
(and Lembongan)

"Shipwreck is a fun hotdogging right that gives you a great barrel section to boot. It breaks during dry season trades and can even work during the wet season as long as there is no wind. [...] Best at mid tide because it floods out with too much tidal surge."

—Leonard and Lorca Lueras,
Surfing Indonesia

"SHIPWRECK" IS THE SURFER'S NAME FOR the break off Ental Point, the northwest corner of Lembongan, the biggest of Nusa Penida's sister islands. The name comes from the

'If surfers are there, divers beware.' Some sites are better left to surface breathers, particularly those where the Indian Ocean swell romps in unmitigated glory.

rusting hulk of a freighter that lies partially exposed on the tidal flat south of the point. Oddly enough, Ental Point is also a dive site, which operators call "Blue Corner," presumably after the famous site of the same name in Palau.

A surfer's map of mainland Bali begins at Medewi, on the southwest coast near the mouth of the Pulukan River. The good surfing spots continue counter-clockwise from there down around Bukit Badung and up the southeast coast almost to Padangbai. A diving map of the island covers precisely the other half of the island—from Padangbai counterclockwise around the island to Menjangan.

This pattern is not accidental, nor does it derive from some kind of détente between surfers and divers. It is, if you will, a matter of physics—they are on top of the water, we are *in* the water. Good surfing sites are found in areas that receive deep ocean swell, particularly areas where a rocky point, a reef, or a sandbar is able to shape that swell into big, smooth, consistent waves. A place that receives swell of this energy will have battered or non-existent coral, and the conditions underwater will fall somewhere between dangerous and suicidal.

This is the problem with most of the sites off Nusa Penida's south coast and Lembongan. They are exposed to the full brunt of the Indian Ocean swell, and are thus both frightening, and for the most part, barren. Below we offer our comments on the sites here that occasionally lure divers (the locations are keyed to MAP 4.1, pp. 154–155).

Ental Point ("Blue Corner")

This site is a sparse, sloping reef with a terrace at twenty-four meters. The dive starts east of the point, and you are swept in a drift west to the corner, whence you head south inside the bay—toward the shipwreck—to seek some protection. The fish and coral life here is not particularly rich, and the current starts out strong and gets worse as you approach the point. Even very experienced divers have been known to panic here.

The reason Ental is a dive site at all is because, in season, molas are seen here. A mola is a very nice animal to encounter, but we don't consider this sufficient rationale for diving here. Molas are also seen at other sites—Toyapakeh, North Penida, and Mimpang, for example—and these areas have far richer reefs and more enjoyable conditions.

Lembongan is a fine place for surfing, however, with three highly regarded breaks. "Shipwreck," while good, is not the island's best. That distinction falls to the "bowling righthander" that forms a bit further south, closer to Jungutbatu. This wave, in the arch manner of the surfing community, has been named "Lacerations," a reference to the shallow coral flat there that bites the bounders and weaklings who aren't up to the wave's challenge.

Jangka Point

This site, in front of some seaweed farms off northeast Lembongan, is probably a better bet than the three- or four-knot drift at "Blue Corner." Eddies form here, as they do across the strait at Toyapakeh, and these give you some protection from the full strength of the current. The profile is a very gradual slope, and again, it is not as rich as the sites on Nusa Penida proper. In the past the big table corals in the shallows here were full of lobsters.

Ceningan Channel

This is a very nice spot for an overnight anchorage, as it is protected from the swell and current. It also makes a safe and enjoyable night dive. The bottom is sand and mud, with a limestone slope as you get further out toward Toyapakeh Strait. It is not really rich enough to recommend as a daytime dive, however.

A few people have tried Ceningan Point (Tanjung Gelumpang),

which has a very different character. The swell and current at the point combine to produce a strange, shifting current that blows north and then, with a frequency of maybe ten minutes, blows south— and then repeats itself. It can be quite unsettling. The coral here is very rich and healthy, and the pulsing current attracts big schools of

MIKE SEVERNS   Cyclichthys sp.

fish. It is a very uncommon dive, but if you feel you can handle the peculiar water behavior (and can find an operator willing to take you here) it is worth trying.

Penida Bay ("Crystal Bay")

This is another nice anchorage, and the rocky islands have an interesting form; something like an old, resting elephant. The bay is very vulnerable to swell, creating up- and down-currents. It is much worse here than at Gamat, and the current doesn't shift or switch, it just gets stronger. The reef is not particularly rich, either, and overall Gamat is a much better site.

"Manta Point"

This is a limestone rock off Pandan Cape. The above-water scenery is dramatic, with sheer limestone cliffs cut out by the monstrous swell that pounds this coast year-round. The swell is so strong that even being on a boat here is very uncomfortable.

The burrfishes are quite secretive by day, coming out at night to hunt hard-shelled invertebrates, of which their hard, fused teeth make short work. When threatened, they gulp water, and no predator can contend with the hard, spiky ball that results. Burrfish spines, which are modified scales, are immovable, and always erect. On the related porcupine fish (genus Diodon) the spines lie flat until they are called into action by the fish.

The profile is a slope down to fifty meters, and there is no coral at all, just bare limestone rock. At eighteen to thirty meters there are huge boulders that have fallen from the cliff above. The only reason to dive this site is to see mantas, tiger mackerel, tuna, and other pelagics. They are here, of course, but bear in mind that their abilities underwater

MIKE SEVERNS Chaetodon adiergastos and Plectorhinchus orientalis

Fish generally school for protection, and bright, contrasting colors make it very difficult for a would-be predator to single out a victim. Sweet-lips shelter in schools during the day, and forage at night. This species of butterfly-fish may do the same.

are considerably better than yours.

There is no real current here, just swell, but if it is heavy this becomes a very dangerous site. You can be tossed around like a plastic bag underwater, or even shot to the surface. One diver, who has literally hundreds of dives at tricky places like Tepekong, Gili Selang, and other sites on Nusa Penida, considers her one dive at Manta Point to be the

scariest of her life. Do not get in the water here if the swell is strong (which is most of the time). If you can't tell, look at the cliffs. If spumes of water are shooting up through blowholes, the swell is strong.

Batu Meling, Batu Lumbung, and Batu Abah

These sites, all of which are mere exposed rocks—hence "batu"—are similar to Manta Point. They are rough, always have strong swell, and have no real reef to speak of, just tough leather corals and blank, white, limestone. The dull white rock gives these sites the visual interest of a quarry dive, but at least in a quarry you aren't being tossed around.

Of the lot, Batu Abah is probably the best, as the structure of the rocks gives you a lee to hide in. Still, this is not really a reef, and if you are going to go all the way to the far side of Penida, you'd be better off diving Malibu Point.

Truthfully, the South Penida sites are only interesting to pelagic chasers and spearfishermen. Even surfers have no use for this coast, chiefly because there is no access.

The biggest problem with these sites is that clients book the dives, and the operators make the long trip out there only to find when they reach this coast that the swell is pounding so hard, it looks like it is going to split the island in half.

With the boat tossing around so much that everyone is having trouble keeping their breakfast down, the dive obviously should be scrubbed. But the guide may be reluctant to waste the gasoline and time he has already invested or to disappoint his client. And the client, for his or her part, may be drunk with overconfidence. More often than you'd think in a case like this, people just suit up and get in, which is very, very dumb.

Gamat Bay

WALLY AND I HAD BEEN TAGGING along with a Padangbai-based operator for a week, mostly diving various sites on Nusa Penida's North Coast, when we learned that neither of our hosts had ever been to Gamat. This little bay, about halfway down Toyapakeh Strait, is one of our favorite sites, so we suggested a dive there for the next day.

When we arrived, at about ten o'clock on a bright morning, our hosts—and their skipper, and their clients—looked very skeptical. The surface of the water was scarred by ragged swirls of foam, and a visibly strong current spiraled ominously around the bay.

"What do you think, Wally, is *that* diveable?" the dive leader asked. Wally, looking again at the faces on the boat, said, "No, it seems a bit rough today. Maybe we should try Toyapakeh." As the boat sliced out into the strait and headed north, Wally said to me, sotto voce, "It would have been fine, you know."

This, really, is the problem with Gamat Bay. Underwater it is a beautiful place, but what you can see from the surface is often just plain ugly. It's easy to say our hosts were just being a couple of girl's blouses, but Gamat really did look like a washing machine.

LIKE A PAINTING

It was several years ago when Wally first took me to dive this odd little square-sided bay (see MAP 4.5, pp. 176–177). We anchored in a sandy section of the back reef, over about six meters of water, and dropped in. I was immediately charmed by this place. Every surface here is covered with a colorful layer of soft corals, hard corals, antipatharians, and patches of glowing algae. The sides of the bommies, in particular, are wonderful, covered with fluffy growths of a very delicate kind of *Dendronephthya* in unusual pastel hues: pinkish, a light yellow

This underrated site is one of the few places on Penida that you can actually stay put. It is a jewel of a site, and—quite literally, in fact—pulsates with color and life.

bordering on green, pale orange. The diversity of species—both invertebrates and fish—is as good here as at any site on Bali.

The bottom in the shallows is mixed sand and bommies, and the reef becomes a steep, rugged slope—almost a wall—at the mouth of the bay. The water is always crystal clear.

This bay is a perfect place for a still photographer. Shallow reefs can sometimes be rather colorless, as the cover is usually dominated by the cream or tan or brown hues characteristic of photosynthetic corals. But Gamat's shallows are filled with encrusting growth more typical of deep water—gorgonians, *Dendronephthya,* black corals— and their colors simply glow.

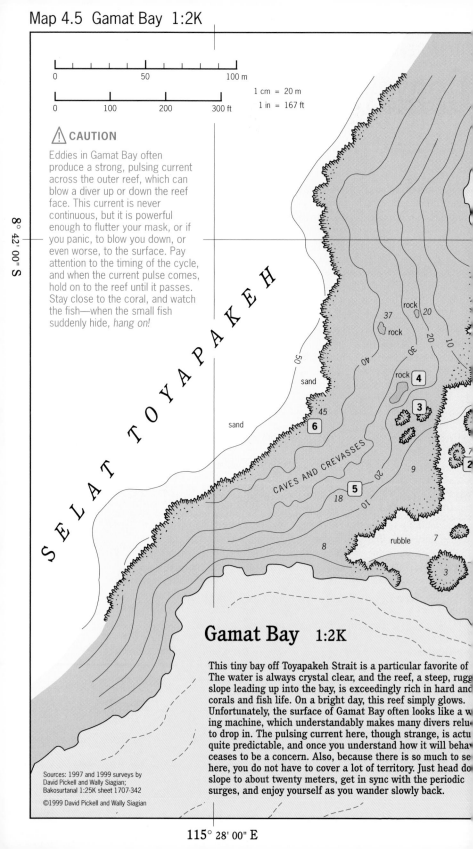

Map 4.5 Gamat Bay 1:2K

0 — 50 — 100 m

0 — 100 — 200 — 300 ft

1 cm = 20 m
1 in = 167 ft

8° 42' 00" S

⚠ **CAUTION**

Eddies in Gamat Bay often produce a strong, pulsing current across the outer reef, which can blow a diver up or down the reef face. This current is never continuous, but it is powerful enough to flutter your mask, or if you panic, to blow you down, or even worse, to the surface. Pay attention to the timing of the cycle, and when the current pulse comes, hold on to the reef until it passes. Stay close to the coral, and watch the fish—when the small fish suddenly hide, *hang on!*

S E L A T   T O Y A P A K E H

37
rock
rock
20
20
30
10
rock **4**
40
50
sand
3
45
sand **6**
CAVES AND CREVASSES
9
5
20
18
10
8
rubble 7
3

Gamat Bay 1:2K

This tiny bay off Toyapakeh Strait is a particular favorite of The water is always crystal clear, and the reef, a steep, rugg slope leading up into the bay, is exceedingly rich in hard and corals and fish life. On a bright day, this reef simply glows. Unfortunately, the surface of Gamat Bay often looks like a w ing machine, which understandably makes many divers relu to drop in. The pulsing current here, though strange, is actu quite predictable, and once you understand how it will beha ceases to be a concern. Also, because there is so much to se here, you do not have to cover a lot of territory. Just head do slope to about twenty meters, get in sync with the periodic surges, and enjoy yourself as you wander slowly back.

Sources: 1997 and 1999 surveys by David Pickell and Wally Siagian; Bakosurtanal 1:25K sheet 1707-342

115° 28' 00" E

GAMAT BAY
Facing E by SE, from Toyapakeh Strait

20

30

10

5

sand

sand

coconut

Tukad Gamat

coconut

sand 6

E L U K

rubble

Shelter

Very large fig tree

G A M A T

coconut

sand

Notable tree

Shelter

coconut

KEY

1. The reef here consists of bommies and patches of coral over sand, and it is the best place to anchor. There are no permanent moorings in Gamat, so make sure your operator is careful, and check the anchor on the way down to see that it is not breaking up the coral.

2. These are big, healthy *Acropora* tables. The shallows here are exceptionally rich, and you should spend some time looking closely at the life clinging to the bommies and the bottom.

3. Here, in ten to twenty meters of water, are a series of big bommies. This area is very rich, and because of the structure, protected from the current pulses. Overall, this is probably the nicest part of the Gamat reef.

4. Under this notable rock is a cave, which almost always has whitetip reef sharks hiding in it.

5. This end of the reef is rough and craggy, full of overhangs and small caves. At eighteen meters there are two caves, and you will often find a green turtle here.

6. The reef stays rich all the way down to fifty meters, by which point you are actually into the channel proper. At forty-five meters here is a very large potato grouper (*Epinephelus tukula*) that is always around.

7. Before you dive, take note if there are fishermen perched on the rock here. If so, pay attention underwater—particularly if your dive takes you to the northern end of the reef. Their lines end in multiple hooks, and you definitely do not want to tangle with one of these.

Early on during this first dive, while I was still soaking up the brilliance of the scenery, I heard Wally grunt through his regulator, and turned. He was pointing at a huge, helmet-shaped coral head, more than three meters high. My first thought was, what happened to that *Porites?* It must have been damaged somehow, because fully three-quarters of its surface was overgrown with coralline algae, turning its normally tan hue to bright pink.

As I approached the coral head, I suddenly realized what had happened. The pink color was not from algae at all. It was from what must have been millions of Sergeant Major eggs. These fierce little striped damselfish surrounded their collective nest in a tight cloud, each defending its own patch. As I moved in for a closer look, the fearless Sergeants charged me, banging repeatedly against my face mask. A ragged band of wrasse and hawkfish wasted no time taking advantage of the distraction I caused, and swooped in to devour the eggs. The damsels, their furious clicks audible underwater, darted back and forth in frustration, and I felt guilty and moved away.

The shallows are excellent, but the best part of this reef is a rugged, terraced slope at the mouth of the bay that stays rich all the way down to fifty meters. It is full of small caves and crevices, and the numbers and variety of reef fish and invertebrates here are exceptional. There are almost always turtles and reef sharks here, and the deep is the territory of a big potato grouper. Gamat is the only place outside of East Bali I have seen the endemic *Prionurus* surgeonfish, and the specimen here was bright blue.

NO, SIZE DOESN'T MATTER

The actual area you can cover in a dive here is not very great, maybe one hundred meters square. This doesn't seem like a lot, but the reef is rich enough to make this more than adequate. Gamat is one of those places that really rewards the diver who is willing to put his or her face mask five centimeters from the bottom and investigate what's visible at a macro level—nudibranchs, unusual shells, commensal crustaceans, and rare little reef fish.

In fact, Gamat is the only good site on Nusa Penida that does not require a drift dive, and this is one of its great charms. Although drifting is fun, after a two- or three-day dive series at Nusa Penida, you get a little weary of never being able to stop and look closely at the surface of the reef. If this is the case, Gamat is your perfect antidote.

Gamat is not dived very often, and there are no permanent moorings here. Make sure your operator takes care where he sets anchor. The back reef area has open patches of sand, easily visible through the clear water, and this is where you should set anchor.

When we dove Gamat in 1999, we were alarmed by an area of broken table coral south of where we normally anchor. We thought at first that it may have been anchor damage, or damage from fish bombing, but closer inspection determined that it could not have been from either of these. The coral was broken up, but still alive, with no gouges or craters. The previous winter had been very rough, and we are convinced this was storm damage. Also, it was not very widespread, and the reef overall was very, very healthy, with lots of new growth already pushing up in and around the broken tables.

THE PULSING CURRENT

But of course, there is that rough-looking surface. Gamat, Wally is wont to say, is always protected. There can be a seven-knot torrent running through the strait and you can still be safe diving Gamat. This is true, but only if you are comfortable with Gamat's strangest feature—a peculiar, pulsing upcurrent. You don't feel this in the back reef area, although it is usually surgy. But out on the reef face, approximately every thirty seconds, you feel a brief updraft. Then the water goes slack, and thirty seconds later, another updraft.

Whether the surface of the bay is rough or calm (and it is usually rough), this phenomenon is always present. Sometimes the gusts are very strong, and other times relatively weak. Usually they are fierce enough to flutter your mask. The trick is to crouch among the coral, and when the force of the updraft comes, find some solid coral and hang on (look for something covered with pink coralline algae so you don't break off any growth). When it stops, continue on your way.

The key is to not panic. If you hold on and wait a few seconds, everything will be fine. If you panic, and get away from the coral, you

may very well be shot upward, which is not a good thing at all. I realize that this is easier to say than to do. Even though Wally told me to expect the pulses, the first time I felt one trying to spit me up to the surface, an involuntary panic brought the taste of copper to my mouth. But I got used to them. Perhaps because of their extreme regularity, you quickly adjust, and simply settle into the pattern—pause, hold on, and then continue swimming; pause, hold on, then continue swimming. If not too strong, the phenomenon is almost relaxing, like drifting in a kind of vertically oriented surge.

This strange current behavior is so mathematical that I'd be tempted to say it comes from a resonance frequency reaction of the bay itself, like a seiche. The eddies that always swirl around on the surface here have something to do with this behavior, but I am at a loss to explain the mechanism. Just try to enjoy it, if possible. As they say in the product liability business, "That's not a defect, it's a *feature*."

Many fish use sponges for shelter. The striking coral grouper is a common member of Bali's reef community. This species has a very wide range, from the Red Sea to Christmas Island.

WALLY SIAGIAN Cephalopholis miniata

The longnose hawkfish is a relatively uncommon deepwater fish that prefers drop-off reefs. It perches on black coral bushes or gorgonians, and snaps small crustaceans from the passing plankton.

WALLY SIAGIAN *Oxycirrhites typus*

KAL MULLER   Unidentified Thaliacean

This strange animal—animals, really—is a salp, a pelagic tunicate (here in its asexual budding, colonial stage). Salps are not common on reefs, but show up occasionally with other ocean borne plankton. Like sessile tunicates, they are chordates, that members of our own phylum, although being acraniate (brainless) they are not famous for their intelligence.

This modest reef's proximity to the luxury hotels of Nusa Dua is the best thing going for it. Though it's not the place to find molas, sharks, or great schools of fish, you can have an après-dive lunch prepared by a three-star chef and accompanied by a fine old Burgundy.

The South

IF THIS WERE ONE OF THOSE GUIDE-books that ranked dive sites with rows of little stars—you know, two stars if the site is underwater, five stars if the writer saw a shark—I guess we'd have to give Tanjung Benoa, the only area of the South that is regularly dived, two-and-a-half stars. Okay, three, but only on an incoming tide.

This doesn't sound very good, and it isn't. But frankly, Tanjung Benoa's reason for being has nothing to do with its merits as a dive site. This reef could be a strip of bombed-out coral with a few sad damselfish fluttering about (and it's not *that* bad) and there would still be dive operators lining the Benoa road, because it has those three magic qualities, in the old real estate bromide, that trump everything: location, location, location.

Menjangan is calm and beautiful. Tulamben has phenomenal diversi-ty. The East Coast is dramatic and rich. Nusa Penida is just plain thrilling. The South is ... ten minutes from the Nusa Dua hotels.

BUILD IT AND THEY WILL COME

In 1973, with United Nations Development Program money, a team of Japanese consultants laid the plans for one of the most perfect velvet-lined cages ever built for tourists anywhere—Nusa Dua. What these consultants understood was that most well-heeled travelers don't want Bali, they want "Bali Hai," and never mind that this densely populated island with its old and sophisticated Indic culture has very little to do with the South Pacific.

They picked a forlorn and ignored little corner of the Bukit, sunk a well, and within a few years, a perfect simulacrum of a Polynesian island emerged, with palm trees, beautiful flowers, and a long stretch

The fang blennies are noxious little creatures who use their eponymous dentition to rip shreds of scale, fin, and flesh from passing larger fishes. The fangs, as this photograph makes clear, extend from the lower jaw, which opens very wide to deploy them to advantage.

The bluestriped fang blenny is not the worst of its genus (probably *P. tapienosoma*, which has been known to bite divers, gets this award), although juveniles mimic juveniles of the cleaner wrasse *Labroides*, which allows them to approach their victims with impunity—a bit like an axe murderer posing as a doctor.

of sandy beach. And, most important of all, a gate, so there are no screeching roosters, motorbikes, and pestering trinket salesmen to interrupt the fantasy.

The formula has been phenomenally successful, and today Nusa Dua can accommodate a quarter of a million visitors a year in four- and five-star luxury.

A South Pacific vacation is all about water, of course, and here is where Benoa Cape diving fits in. It is part of a lengthy program of water sports, including snorkeling, windsurfing, parasailing, Jet Ski–riding, water-skiing, and sportfishing.

A DIVE AND SOME DOM, PLEASE

I ride a seventeen-year-old Kawasaki with a transmission that likes to jump out of second gear at the most inappropriate moments, and Wally's little Honda, if memory serves, is a prototype that Soichiro-san himself bolted together just after the war from an old bicycle frame he found in the alley behind his house. Neither of these vehicles signals a lifestyle that includes spending a lot of time in three-hundred-dollar-a-night hotel rooms.

But we realize that scuba divers come in all sizes, tastes, and net worths, and some might very well find themselves cocooned in a swank Nusa Dua hotel room with a spouse or special friend on a three-day package of pure, hedonistic luxury. If this is you, first off, we're jealous. Second, why are you reading this book? Put it down, order some more oysters and foie gras, and get back to your sweet, musky partner.

It is true, however, that diving can be a great relaxant in its own right. But do you want to sit in a car for four hours to get to Tulamben? Of course not, you do that in Los Angeles every day on your way to the office. Do you want to climb in a speedboat and blast up to Tepekong or across to Nusa Penida? Well, maybe, but if you are a busy executive you might not have been in the water for two years, and let's just say that three-knot currents are not consistent with a program that is, after all, about relaxation.

What you do is this: pick up the room phone and ask for the diving counter. Tell them to get some gear ready and put your name down for a dive at Benoa Cape. You will need your sunglasses and a bathing suit. Everything else will be taken care of, and in little over an hour you'll be right back in the lap of luxury.

A bit of nitrogen in the blood, a bit of time with the corals and fishes, why not? So what it's not Bali's best reef. This is *Bali Hai's* best reef. Call downstairs for a magnum of Dom Perignon and some caviar. You're on vacation.

WALLY SIAGIAN Plagiotremus rhinorhynchus

THE SOUTH
Tanjung Benoa

I HAD BEEN DIVING IN BALI, ON AND off, for more than six years before I ever saw the reefs of the South. And when I was finally suited up and standing on a boat floating over the outer edge of the Tanjung Benoa reef, my dear partner refused to get in the water with me.

"C'mon Wally, let's go."

"It's okay, David, go with the guide, it'll give you a better sense of the full experience of diving here."

"*Wally?*"

"Sorry. I'll see you when you come up."

Wally was still pouting from having recently lost his good Ray-Bans playing on a Jet Ski (karma, perhaps?) but this wasn't the problem. The problem was that diving this reef was, to Wally, a bothersome chore—like taking out the garbage, cleaning the bathroom, or paying the phone bill. I hadn't dived here before, so obviously I had to go down and have a look, but he had been here many times. Why should we both suffer? This logic was unassailable, so I quit protesting and jumped in without him.

I won't say this reef, often called Nusa Dua, is awful. You won't see any pelagics or big schools of fish, but the usual smaller reef fish—damsels, wrasses, parrotfish, butterflyfish, angelfish, and the like—are all here, and the coral growth is good, if not remarkably diverse. You'd be very lucky to see even a small reef white-tip shark, but guides will usually be able to find a moray eel for you and point out some colorful nudibranchs. This is still Bali, after all, and if you have one

of those plastic cards with a dozen or so species on each side, you could surely find them all at Benoa.

But this would not be our first choice of dive sites here. There are beautiful, rich reefs in the Northwest, the Tulamben Area, the East

This classic, spur-and-groove fringing reef makes a convenient dive, but not an exceptional one. And silty effluent from Benoa harbor is making things worse.

Coast, and on Nusa Penida. In this distinguished company, the Tanjung Benoa reef is definitely the runt of the litter. But there will be at least one sympathetic soul out there who will want to take this skinny and weak-looking dog home, give it a bath, and name it Scratchy.

A TEXTBOOK REEF

Although mediocre from a diver's point of view, the Tanjung Benoa reef is one of the most studied reefs in all of Bali. It is part of a fringing reef complex that extends from Nusa Dua—the two small attached islands at the far eastern tip of Bukit Badung—five kilometers north to the tip of Tanjung Benoa (see MAP 5.1, pp. 186–187). In fact, after the natural break leading to Benoa Harbor and Serangan Island, where the reef has been spoiled by construction, the reef complex

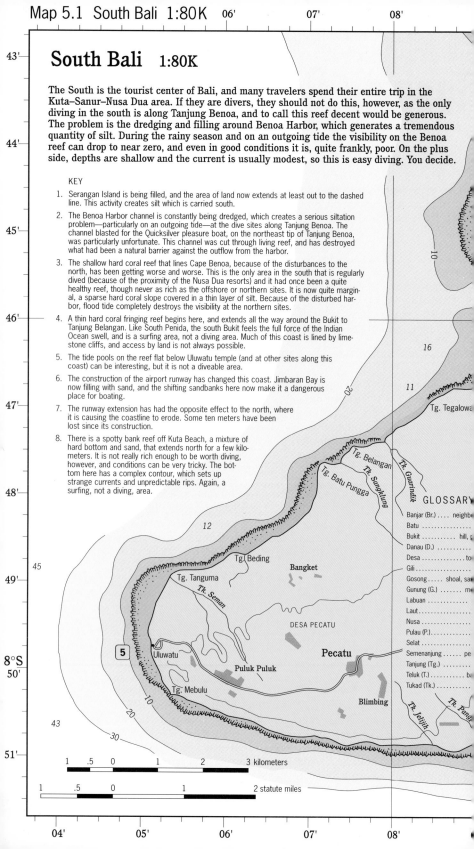

Map 5.1 South Bali 1:80K

South Bali 1:80K

The South is the tourist center of Bali, and many travelers spend their entire trip in the Kuta–Sanur–Nusa Dua area. If they are divers, they should not do this, however, as the only diving in the south is along Tanjung Benoa, and to call this reef decent would be generous. The problem is the dredging and filling around Benoa Harbor, which generates a tremendous quantity of silt. During the rainy season and on an outgoing tide the visibility on the Benoa reef can drop to near zero, and even in good conditions it is, quite frankly, poor. On the plus side, depths are shallow and the current is usually modest, so this is easy diving. You decide.

KEY

1. Serangan Island is being filled, and the area of land now extends at least out to the dashed line. This activity creates silt which is carried south.

2. The Benoa Harbor channel is constantly being dredged, which creates a serious siltation problem—particularly on an outgoing tide—at the dive sites along Tanjung Benoa. The channel blasted for the Quicksilver pleasure boat, on the northeast tip of Tanjung Benoa, was particularly unfortunate. This channel was cut through living reef, and has destroyed what had been a natural barrier against the outflow from the harbor.

3. The shallow hard coral reef that lines Cape Benoa, because of the disturbances to the north, has been getting worse and worse. This is the only area in the south that is regularly dived (because of the proximity of the Nusa Dua resorts) and it had once been a quite healthy reef, though never as rich as the offshore or northern sites. It is now quite marginal, a sparse hard coral slope covered in a thin layer of silt. Because of the disturbed harbor, flood tide completely destroys the visibility at the northern sites.

4. A thin hard coral fringing reef begins here, and extends all the way around the Bukit to Tanjung Belangan. Like South Penida, the south Bukit feels the full force of the Indian Ocean swell, and is a surfing area, not a diving area. Much of this coast is lined by limestone cliffs, and access by land is not always possible.

5. The tide pools on the reef flat below Uluwatu temple (and at other sites along this coast) can be interesting, but it is not a diveable area.

6. The construction of the airport runway has changed this coast. Jimbaran Bay is now filling with sand, and the shifting sandbanks here now make it a dangerous place for boating.

7. The runway extension has had the opposite effect to the north, where it is causing the coastline to erode. Some ten meters have been lost since its construction.

8. There is a spotty bank reef off Kuta Beach, a mixture of hard bottom and sand, that extends north for a few kilometers. It is not really rich enough to be worth diving, however, and conditions can be very tricky. The bottom here has a complex contour, which sets up strange currents and unpredictable rips. Again, a surfing, not a diving, area.

GLOSSARY

Banjar (Br.) .... neighbo
Batu ....
Bukit .... hill,
Danau (D.) ....
Desa .... to
Gili ....
Gosong ..... shoal, sa
Gunung (G.) ...... m
Labuan ....
Laut ....
Nusa ....
Pulau (P.)............
Selat ....
Semenanjung ...... pe
Tanjung (Tg.) ....
Teluk (T.) .... ba
Tukad (Tk.) ....

Tg. Tegalowa

Tg. Belangan
Tk. Sangklung
Tk. Guarindih
Tg. Batu Pungga

Tg. Beding
Bangket

Tg. Tanguma
Tk. Seman

DESA PECATU

Uluwatu
Puluk Puluk
Pecatu

Tg. Mebulu
Blimbing

Tk. Jelitih
Tk. Pang

1 .5 0   1   2   3 kilometers

1   .5 0   1   2 statute miles

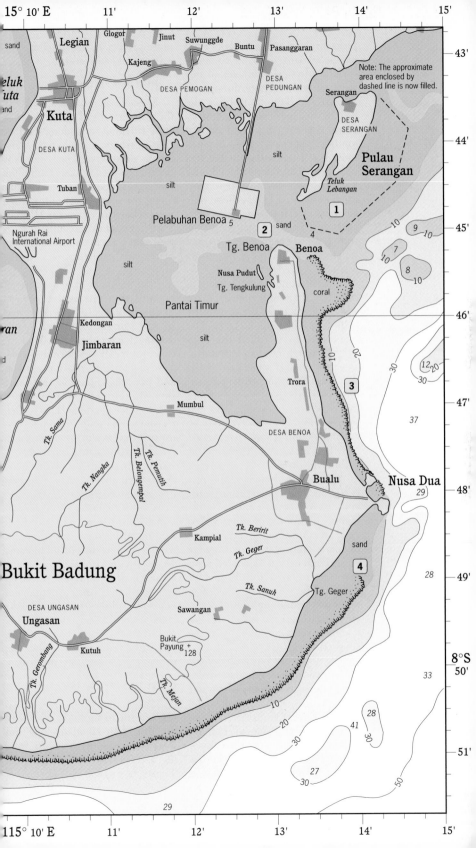

picks up again, and extends for eight kilometers along the Sanur coastline.

The physical character of this reef is roughly the same throughout its length. Beginning from the beach, the reef forms a shallow lagoon, in places just a meter deep at low tide, that extends seaward for almost half a kilometer to the reef edge. The extreme width of this lagoon has led some people to term the Sanur–Nusa Dua reef complex a barrier reef. It is, however, a classic Indo-Pacific fringing reef. This wide lagoon of calm water is perfect for surface water sports, but divers work the reef edge.

If you look out from the beach at Sanur or Tanjung Benoa, the place where the waves are breaking is the beginning of the fore-reef area. The highest point is called the algal ridge, a tough crest of calcareous algae and a few durable hard corals that takes the brunt of the punishment delivered by the waves. From the algal ridge seaward, the reef slopes down at a moderate angle, becoming sand at about twenty meters. This area, roughly fifty meters wide, is the diveable part of the reef.

Throughout its length, this reef is characterized by a classic "spur-and-groove" structure. In this formation, the coral grows in rounded ridges or spurs that extend perpendicularly outward from the algal crest. Each spur is separated from the next by a sandy channel or groove. The spur-and-groove formation is a common feature of the reefs that fringe exposed islands, but it can be seen in Bali only on the southern reefs.

The incessant pounding of the waves against the algal ridge creates this pattern, as the outgoing water sweeps downslope through the grooves. On the more exposed section of the reef, along Tanjung Benoa, the spurs are about seven meters across and rounded; further north at Sanur, where the reef is more protected, the spurs are flat-topped, and narrower.

BUILT BY A PROTOZOAN

Most of Bali is volcanic rock, and the reefs clinging to its margin, such as at Tulamben and along the East Coast, are in a geological sense merely decorative. The reefs of the South, however, actually built Bukit Badung. The dramatic white cliffs lining the south coast of the Bukit are reef limestone from the Miocene Epoch (about twenty million years ago) that have been forced up—in places, two hundred meters—by the movements of crustal plates.

The aragonitic skeletons secreted by coral polyps are the most visible and famous structures created by reef animals, and many people assume that weathered and broken-up coral is what creates the white sand that lines the beach near reefs, and eventually, the old reef limestone that forms the very substance of places like the Bukit. This is often true, but not always. In some areas, the primary producers of limestone are calcareous algae—such as *Halimeda,* with its chains of carbonate disks—or molluscs, and coral makes only a minor contribution.

In South Bali, the primary carbonate producers are tiny, shell-bearing protozoans called foraminafera. The shells, technically "tests"—a sand dollar, for example, is the test of a sea urchin—make up eighty to ninety percent of the sand at Sanur, and almost as much of the sand along Tanjung Benoa. Look closely at this sand—each round, pinhead-sized grain was once the skeleton of a single living protozoan.

I'LL TAKE CARL HIAASEN

My first dive off Tanjung Benoa was at a site in about the middle of this thin, four-kilometer-long spit that extends almost due north from the eastern tip of Bukit Badung. There are a number of sites along

WALLY SIAGIAN Inimicus didactylus

this five-kilometer stretch, but they are almost indistinguishable from each other. The dive is on the relatively narrow shoulder of coral that forms the fore-reef area, and the sloping spurs of coral hit a sand bottom at fifteen to twenty-five meters. The coral cover in this area here has been assessed at about fifty percent, which is actually quite good.

Conditions at these sites rarely produce surprises. There might be a bit of current along the reef edge, but nothing to cause problems. Visibility is decent—eight or ten meters.

The scientists who studied the Tanjung Benoa and Sanur reefs in September 1992 measured water clarity with a Secchi disk. Their readings averaged fifteen meters at Tanjung Benoa, which seems like pretty good visibility. But a stark black and white Secchi disk is designed to be easy to see, and here—and elsewhere in this book where visibility figures are given—we apply a more conservative and functional standard.

If you approach a dive at Benoa with the right level of expectation, you can actually enjoy yourself. Think of it as an airport novel, or a made-for-TV movie. These might not deliver the same rewards as Nabokov or Malick, but then they don't make the same demands either. The simple charms of a dive on a coral reef are all here. The clownfish nestled in their anemones, the bright colors of a juvenile angelfish, the loopy-eyed triggerfish spinning off in a rage at your intrusion, the alien appearance of a mantis shrimp, and the impossibly intricate structure of the corals themselves.

The relative lack of drama—no big fish, no wild currents, no extreme depths—encourages you to look closely at interesting things that are often overlooked on more "exciting" dives.

A RIVER OF MUD

As my plane left Bali on my return to the United States, I craned my neck to get a view of Serangan Island from the air. I have found no map recent enough to show the true

The devilfish has one of my favorite generic names: "Inimicus." Contact with its dorsal spines—raised in the photograph above—would be very unfortunate, indeed, as only the stonefish is more venomous than this one.

Despite the fierce name and reputation, behaviorally this fish is a pussycat (unless you are a small fish or crustacean, of course) and to get stung you would basically have to stick your hand on the spines.

Inimicus usually lies buried, or partially buried, in the sand, waiting for passing prey. Like a stonefish, it never really swims. The first two rays of the pectoral fins have evolved into little claws, which the fish uses to crawl around on the bottom.

The Saddest Eyes in the World

SOME YEARS AGO, WHILE WALLY AND I WERE running an errand, we noticed an old woman selling satay at the corner of a side street. Being hungry, we stopped, and Wally reached out of his window and traded a couple thousand rupiah for two bundles of her product. The satay was crispy and delicious, and over the next few days we went out of our

Both by KAL MULLER   Tanjung Benoa

Boats returning from as far afield as Irian Jaya unload their turtles at Benoa, where they are kept in bamboo pens until sold. Around major Balinese holidays, the pens are full and the market is bustling.

way to stop at this same corner. On about the third day, we had Wally's son Mat along. As we were all gobbling down the satay, Mat said, rather too nonchalantly, "You know this is turtle, right?"

Although Mat has been known to tell the truth, it must be said that he doesn't make a habit of it, and we were furious. "No way, Mat!" "Quit talking bull!" "Knock it off!" In any case, he had succeeded in making the satay a lot less tasty, and even though neither of us believed him, we felt guilty enough that

we quit visiting the old woman. Upon reflection, we are both sure Mat was right. (We never went back to ask the woman directly, however, for the same reason one of the bullets used by a firing squad is a blank).

THE WORLD ON ITS BACK

South Bali is probably the biggest market in the world for green sea turtles. This seems very strange in a place where the universe rests on the back of the world turtle Bedawang Nala, but sea turtles have been an important ceremonial food in South Bali for at least a century, chiefly in *ebat,* the spicy setting of pounded meat and vegetables that accompanies temple feasts. A big ceremony-sized green turtle might fetch $100, but the smaller animals, which don't live long in the pens, are butchered and sold as soup and saté.

Chelonia mydas is the only one of the world's eight species of sea turtles not protected by Indonesian law. Despite a formal catch limit of five thousand, estimates of the number of turtles sold and eaten in Bali range from fifteen to thirty thousand a year. And many hundreds of thousands of their eggs are eaten each year throughout the archipelago. The average turtle caught is getting smaller, and since sea turtles don't reach breeding age until they are thirty, scientists worry that the population has already crashed—they just haven't seen the results yet.

Eating a green turtle seems deplorable, especially when you are looking at one of the forlorn specimens sitting helplessly in a cage at Benoa, greasy water washing over its sad, sixty-year-old eyes. The sea turtle is one of those "big, charismatic vertebrates" beloved of conservation organizations, and sympathy for the victim comes easy.

But resist the urge to self-righteous rage, particularly as you dig into your filet of orange roughy, or bluefin tuna sashimi, or the huge lobster you just ordered at that Kuta seafood restaurant (itself probably sixty years old). Taking the weight off the turtle's back will require time, cultural sensitivity, and compromise.

outline of this low island, which lies just north of Tanjung Benoa. A program of reclamation has been ongoing at Serangan for the past several years. From the brief glimpse I got from the airplane, this now looks to have more than doubled the original area of this island, and the eastern shoreline has, by my estimation, reached to almost the original edge of the fringing reef.

While this filling is going on at Serangan, a bit further south the channel leading to the Benoa harbor is continually being dredged. The bay behind Tanjung Benoa is so shallow that at low tide you could basically walk from Benoa to Jimbaran, and the depths in the channel leading to the harbor must be constantly maintained. Even so, the passage for a large boat is a tricky zigzag marked by signal lights.

And the mangrove lining this bay has been cut for shrimp ponds and development, disturbing the natural filtering capacity of this coast. Thus runoff produced from the expanding Jimbaran–Kuta–Sanur area now finds it easier to reach the bay. Some of the cut mangrove was replanted, but these trees are extremely slow-growing. I have watched the replanted plots visible from the bypass for more than a decade now, and they are still more bushes than trees.

The ongoing dredging and filling, combined with the past destruction of the mangroves in the harbor area, is the real problem with the Tanjung Benoa reef. The scientists studying the reef in 1992 noted a "conspicuous increase" in seagrass growth in the area closest to the harbor opening, which they attributed to an increase in silt and nutrient-rich effluent from the bay. But their overall conclusion was that this reef was in basically sound health.

After diving Benoa in 1998, I'm not so sanguine. During the rainy season and on an outgoing tide, the

northern stretch of the Tanjung Benoa reef is pretty much undiveable. Even from the boat you can see the brown water spilling out of the Benoa channel. Underwater, visibility drops to just a few meters, and a thin layer of brown silt, like a foul snowfall, has settled on the living surface of the reef.

The operators compensate for

KAL MULLER   Tanjung Benoa

this by diving the southern sites at these times, and during the dry season—the southeast monsoon—conditions improve. But how long before things degrade further? Perhaps we should change our recommendation, and suggest Tanjung Benoa as your first choice among Bali's reefs. Ten years from now Tulamben will still be alive and healthy, but Benoa might not.

Wally inspects a fisherman's catch from the Badung Strait. The tourist centers of the south have created a ready market for fresh fish.

I Made Budi 1979
UNTITLED, INK ON PAPER

In the collection of David Pickell

Contents

PERIPLUS TRAVEL MAPS

Asia's Number One Selling Maps!

This map program was launched in 199_
with the goal of producing accurate an_
up-to-date maps of every major city an_
country in the Asia Pacific region. Abo__
12 new titles are published eac_
year, along with numerou_
revised editions. Titles i_
BOLDFACE are already availabl_
Titles in *ITALICS* are scheduled f__
publication in 2000.

INDIVIDUAL COUNTRY TITLES

Australia	ISBN 962-593-641-6
Cambodia	ISBN 0-945971-87-7
China	ISBN 962-593-107-4
India	ISBN 962-593-047-7
Indonesia	ISBN 962-593-042-6
Japan	ISBN 962-593-108-2
Korea	ISBN 962-593-111-2
Laos	ISBN 962-593-069-8
Malaysia	ISBN 962-593-777-3
Myanmar (Burma)	ISBN 962-593-070-1
Nepal	ISBN 962-593-062-0
New Zealand	ISBN 962-593-092-2
Philippines	ISBN 962-593-113-9
Singapore	ISBN 0-945971-41-9
Thailand	ISBN 962-593-572-X
Vietnam	ISBN 962-593-648-3

AUSTRALIA REGIONAL MAPS

Brisbane	ISBN 962-593-049-3
Cairns	ISBN 962-593-048-5
Darwin	ISBN 962-593-089-2
Melbourne	ISBN 962-593-050-7
Perth	ISBN 962-593-088-4
Sydney	ISBN 962-593-640-8

CHINA REGIONAL MAPS

Beijing	ISBN 962-593-031-0
Hong Kong	ISBN 962-593-571-1
Shanghai	ISBN 962-593-032-9
Taipei	ISBN 962-593-132-5
Taiwan	ISBN 962-593-090-6

INDONESIA REGIONAL MAPS

Bali	ISBN 0-945971-49-4
Bandung	ISBN 0-945971-43-5
Batam	ISBN 962-593-144-9
Bintan	ISBN 962-593-139-2
Jakarta	ISBN 0-945971-62-1
Java	ISBN 962-593-040-X
Lake Toba	ISBN 0-945971-71-0
Lombok	ISBN 962-593-639-4
Medan	ISBN 0-945971-70-2
Sulawesi	ISBN 962-593-162-7
Sumatra	ISBN 0-945971-67-2
Surabaya	ISBN 0-945971-48-6
Tana Toraja	ISBN 0-945971-44-3
Ujung Pandang	ISBN 962-593-138-4
Yogyakarta	ISBN 0-945971-42-7

JAPAN REGIONAL MAPS

Kyoto	ISBN 962-593-143-0
Osaka	ISBN 962-593-110-4
Tokyo	ISBN 962-593-109-0

MALAYSIA REGIONAL MAPS

Johor Bahru	ISBN 0-945971-98-2
Kuala Lumpur	ISBN 0-945971-75-3
Malacca	ISBN 0-945971-77-X
Penang	ISBN 0-945971-76-1
Sabah	ISBN 0-945971-78-8
Sarawak	ISBN 962-593-780-3
West Malaysia	ISBN 962-593-129-5

THAILAND REGIONAL MAPS

Bangkok	ISBN 962-593-574-6
Chiang Mai	ISBN 962-593-573-8
Ko Samui	ISBN 962-593-576-2
Phuket	ISBN 962-593-575-4

OTHER REGIONAL MAPS

Auckland	ISBN 962-593-130-9
Kathmandu	ISBN 962-593-063-9
Manila	ISBN 962-593-124-4
Seoul	ISBN 962-593-127-9

*Periplus Travel Maps are available at bookshops around the world. If you cannot find them wher_
live, please write to us for the name of a distributor closest to you:*

Berkeley Books Pte Ltd

*5 Little Road, #08-01, Singapore 536983. Tel: (65) 280 1330 Fax: (65) 280 629_*

Bali in Brief

To make someone jealous, tell them you're going to Bali. The word itself will conjure up an intoxicating vision of a tropical paradise. This is nice at a party, but the real history of Bali and Indonesia—great Indic empires, anti-colonial struggle, and newly minted democracy—is far more interesting.

THE TINY VOLCANIC ISLAND of Bali is one of the most physically beautiful and culturally rich places in the world. The balmy climate, lush, green ricefields and lavish productions of the Hindu-Balinese cultural calendar never fail to charm visitors. Although writers continue to flatter Bali with adjectives, none has surpassed Indian prime minister Pandit Nehru, who called the island "the morning of the world."

Bali-Hinduism

Indonesia is the largest Islamic country in the world, but the 2.5 million Balinese are overwhelmingly Hindu. Agama Hindu Dharma as practiced in Bali is a philosophy, religion and cultural organizing principle that has resulted from Buddhist and Hindu doctrines and practices arriving from India—partly through Java—between the 8th and 15th centuries. It is a uniquely Balinese meld.

Balinese cultural life cycles according to the Pawukon, a complex 210-day ritual calendar. Holiday celebrations—New Year, temple anniversaries, Galungan—and rites of passage—tooth filings, weddings, cremations—are scheduled according to the Pawukon. These ceremonial events, marked by bright costumes, lavish offerings of food, and dance performances, leave visitors with some of their fondest memories of Bali.

Cultural riches

Bali has been famous for her art since the arrival of the first European tourists in the early 20th century. The island's artists turn out painted Hindu icons like Garuda, whimsical animals, and unfinished abstract and surrealistic figures. Most of Bali's painters work in watercolor, producing intricate group scenes.

Balinese dance ranges from stately processionals to wild leaping and posturing. In general it is more lively than the very refined Javanese court dances, which are considered ancestors to Balinese dance. Some of the most popular forms—such as the monkey dance or *kecak*—are hybrids of old court dances and western-influenced sensibilities.

Dance is accompanied by the *gamelan*, an all-percussion orchestra of metallophones, gongs and cymbal-like instruments. Rhythm is everything in *gamelan* music, and the musicians' overlapping runs on their bright-sounding instruments create an unforgettable sound.

Early Bali

Before about the 9th century, when writing and other Indian influences made their way to Bali, little is known of the island's history. Stone altars and sarcophagi, dating back to several centuries B.C. have been found on the island, and these suggest a Bronze Age culture of herders and farmers who practiced a form of ancestor worship.

From the 9th century onward, Bali had regular contact with Java, at the time being influenced by Indian cultural practices. During the 14th and 15th centuries, East Java was dominated by the Majapahit empire, of which Bali became a colony in 1365.

This event and date—though by no means certain, as its source, the *Negarakertagama*, is something of a panegyric—marks the point when the Hindu caste system, court culture, performing arts, and other Javanese influences came to Bali.

For the next several centuries Bali was ruled by a single court, but factions developed, and by the time the Dutch arrived in the 19th century, Bali was made up of nine realms: Badung, Gianyar, Bangli, Klungkung, Karangasem, Buleleng, Mengwi, Tabanan, and Jembrana.

The Dutch come late

Although they had been in the archipelago since the turn of the 17th century, the Dutch avoided Bali at first. The Balinese had a reputation of being quite fierce, and the fractious internal politics of the little island were considered too great an obstacle to Dutch ule there. Besides, the only important trade item the Balinese offered were slaves.

The Dutch finally subjugated Buleleng (now Singaraja) on the north coast and established a colonial center here in 1849. Then, some 50 years later, a Dutch ship ran aground on the reef off Sanur. The disappearance of the cargo to freelance salvage operators served as a pretext for an armed invasion of the south. The Badung court expired in 1906 in a *puputan,* a ritual mass suicide.

an island nation

The Republic of Indonesia is the world's fourth largest country, with 210 million people. The vast majority (88%) is Muslim. More than 400 languages are spoken, but Bahasa Indonesia, a variant of Malay, is the national language.

The nation is a republic, headed by a president, with a 500-member legislature and a 700-member People's Consultative Assembly. There are currently some 30 provinces and special territories. The capital is Jakarta (pop. 9.3 million). The archipelago comprises 2 million square km of land distributed over 17,508 islands.

Indonesia's gross national product comes from oil, textiles, lumber, mining, agriculture and manufacturing, and the country's largest trading partner is Japan. Much of the population still makes a living through agriculture, chiefly rice farming.

famous early empires

The Buddhist Sriwijaya empire, based in southeastern Sumatra, controlled parts of western Indonesia from the 7th to the 13th centuries. The Hindu Majapahit kingdom, based in eastern Java, controlled even more from the

13th to the 16th centuries. Beginning in the mid-13th century, local rulers began converting to Islam.

In the early 17th century the Dutch East India Company (VOC) founded trading settlements and quickly controlled the Indies spice trade. The VOC went bankrupt in 1799, and a Dutch colonial government was established.

Anti-colonial struggle

Anti-colonial uprisings began in the early 20th century, when nationalism movements were founded by various Muslim, communist and student groups. Soekarno, a Dutch-educated nationalist,

was jailed by the Dutch in 1930.

Early in 1942, the Dutch Indies were overrun by the Japanese army. Treatment by the occupiers was harsh. When Japan saw her fortunes waning, Indonesian nationalists were encouraged to organize. On August 17, 1945, Soekarno proclaimed Indonesia's independence.

The Dutch sought a return to colonial rule after the war. Four years of fighting ensued between nationalists and the Dutch, and full independence was achieved in 1949.

During the 1950s and early 1960s, President Soekarno's

government moved steadily to the left, alienating western governments. In 1963, Indonesia took control of Irian Jaya and began a period of confrontation with Malaysia. On September 30, 1965, the army put down an attempted coup attributed to the communist party.

In the so-called "year of living dangerously" that followed, several hundred thousand people were killed as suspected communists, many of them in Bali.

General Suharto formally became president in 1968. His administration encouraged Western and Japanese investment, and the nation enjoyed three decades of steady economic growth.

Suharto falls

In May 1998, facing charges of corruption and nepotism, and with the rupiah collapsing, Suharto stepped down, leaving his unpopular vice president, Bacharuddin Jusuf Habibie, in charge.

Following the nation's first democratic election in more than three decades, a new assembly in October 1999 selected Abdurrahman Wahid ("Gus Dur") to be Indonesia's president, and Megawati Soekarnoputri, Soekarno's daughter, as vice president.

Travel Advisory

Some 1.3 million tourists visit Bali each year, and this beautiful island is by far the easiest part of Indonesia in which to travel. At least some English is spoken at hotels and restaurants, and transportation, food, and other tourist necessities are everywhere available.

General

TOURIST INFORMATION

The Indonesian Tourist Promotion Board maintains offices overseas that can provide information and literature about Indonesia, including the *Indonesian Travel Planner* (published yearly), calendars of events, and a variety of tourist maps. Contacts:
Australia Level 10, 5 Elizabeth Street, Sydney NSW 2000, Australia. ☎(61-2) 233-3630, Fax: (61-2) 233-3629, 357-3478.
Germany Wiesenhuttenstrasse 17, D.6000 Frankfurt am Main 1, Germany. ☎(49-169) 233677, Fax: (49-169) 230840.
Japan Sankaido Building, 2nd Floor, 1-9-13 Akasaka, Minatoku, Tokyo 107. ☎(81-3) 3585-3588; Fax: (81-3) 3582-1397.
Singapore 10 Collyer Quay #15–07, Ocean Building, Singapore 0104. ☎(65) 534-2837, 534-1795; Fax: (65) 533-4287.
Taiwan 66 Sung Chiang Road, 5th Floor, Taipei, Taiwan. ☎(886-2) 537-7620. Fax: (886-2) 537-7621.
United Kingdom 3–4 Hanover Street, London W1R 9HH. ☎(44-171) 493-0334; Fax: (44-171) 493-1747.
United States 3457 Wilshire Boulevard, Los Angeles, CA 90010-2203. ☎(213) 387-2078, Fax: (213) 380-4876.

VISAS

Nationals of the following countries are granted visa-free entry for 60 days upon arrival: Argentina, Australia, Austria, Belgium, Brazil, Brunei, Canada, Chile, Denmark, Egypt, Finland, France, Germany, Greece, Hungary, Iceland, Ireland, Italy, Japan, Kuwait, Liechtenstein, Luxembourg, Malaysia, Maldives, Malta, Mexico, Monaco, Morocco, Netherlands, New Zealand, Norway, Philippines, Saudi Arabia, Singapore, South Korea, Spain, Sweden, Switzerland, Taiwan, Thailand, Turkey, United Arab Emirates, United Kingdom, United States, Venezuela.

A visa is required in advance for all other nationals or arrivals at minor ports. Upon arrival you will be given a white embarkation and disembarkation card, which you must keep and present when leaving. Visa-free entry to Indonesia cannot be extended and cannot be converted to any other kind of visa.

Check your passport before leaving for Indonesia. You must have at least one empty page and the passport must be valid for at least six months after the date of arrival. For visa-free entry, you must also have proof of onward journey, either a return or through ticket. Employment is strictly forbidden on tourist visas.

CUSTOMS

Narcotics, firearms and ammunition are prohibited. The standard duty-free allowance is: 2 liters of alcoholic beverages, 200 cigarettes, 50 cigars or 100 grams of tobacco.

There is no restriction on import and export of foreign currencies in cash or travelers checks, but there is an export limit of 50,000 rupiah.

All narcotics are illegal in Indonesia. The use, sale or purchase of narcotics result in long prison terms, huge fines and death, in some cases Westerners are currently serving sentences as long as 30 years for possession of marijuana in Indonesia.

CONSULATES

Although Bali is the center of Indonesia's tourist industry the diplomatic corps are for the most part stationed in the capital, Jakarta, and all foreign embassy offices are there. Bali has some consular branches and in an emergency they can be helpful. All are in the south (☎0361):
Australia Jl Mochammad Yamin 4, Renon, Denpasar ☎235092/3, ☎234139 ext 3311 (emergencies); Fax 231990.
E-mail: ausconbali@denpasar.wasantara.net.id
France Jl Bypass Ngurah Rai Sanur. ☎/fax: 285485.

Germany Jl Pantai Karang 17, Sanur. ☎288535; Fax: 288826.

Netherlands Jl Raya Kuta 599, Kuta. ☎751517, 753174 (emergencies); Fax: 752777.

United States Jl Hayam Wuuk 188, Renon, Denpasar. ☎233605, 234139 ext. 3575 (emergencies); Fax: 222426.

Embassies

All are in Jakarta (☎021):

Australia Jl. H.R. Rasuna Said, Kav. C/15-16, ☎522-7111.

Austria Jl. P. Diponegoro No. 44, ☎338090.

Belgium Jl. Jend. Sudirman, Kav. 22-23, ☎5712180.

Brunei Darussalam Jl. Jend. Sudirman, Kav. 22-23, ☎571-2180.

Canada Wisma Metropolitan , 15th Floor, Jl. Jend. Sudirman, Kav. 29, ☎525-0709.

China Jl. Jend. Sudirman, Kav. 69, ☎714596.

Denmark Bina Mulia Bldg., 4th Floor, Jl. H.R. Rasuna Said, Kav. 10, ☎5204350.

Finland Bina Mulia Bldg., 10th Floor, Jl. H.R. Rasuna Said, Kav. 10, ☎516980.

France Jl. M.H. Thamrin No. 20, ☎3142807.

Germany Jl. Raden Saleh 54-56, ☎384-9547.

Greece Jl. Kebon Sirih No. 16, ☎360623.

India Jl. H.R. Rasuna Said No. S-1, ☎5204150.

Italy Jl. Diponegoro 45, ☎337445.

Japan Jl. M.H. Thamrin No. 24, ☎324308

Malaysia Jl. H.R. Rasuna Said Kav. X/6/1-3, ☎522-4947.

Myanmar Jl. H. Agus Salim No. 109, ☎3140440.

Mexico Wisma Nusantara, 4th Floor, Jl. M.H. Thamrin No. 59, ☎337479.

Netherlands Jl. H.R. Rasuna Said, Kav. S-3, ☎511515.

New Zealand Jl. Diponegoro No. 41, ☎330680.

Norway Bina Mulia Bldg. I, 4th Floor, Jl. H.R. Rasuna Said, Kav. 10, ☎5251990.

Pakistan Jl. Teuku Umar No. 50, Tel: 3144009.

Papua New Guinea Panin Bank Centre 6th Floor, Jl. Jend. Sudirman No. 1, ☎725-1218.

Philippines Jl. Imam Bonjol No. 6-8, ☎3149329.

Singapore Jl. H.R. Rasuna Said, Block X Kav. 2, No. 4, ☎520-1489.

South Korea Jl. Gatot Subroto, Kav. 57-58, ☎520-1915.

Spain Jl. Agus Salim No. 61, ☎331414.

Sweden Bina Mulia Bldg. I, Jl. H.R. Rasuna Said, Kav. 10, ☎520-1551.

Switzerland Jl. H.R. Rasuna Said B-1, Kav. 10/32, ☎516061.

Thailand Jl. Imam Bonjol No.74, ☎3904055.

United Kingdom Jl. M.H. Thamrin No.75, ☎330904.

United States Jl. Medan Merdeka Selatan No. 5, ☎360360.

Vietnam Jl. Teuku Umar No. 25, ☎3100357.

Lost passport

Always keep a photocopy of your passport, visa and driver's license separate from the originals (and it is a good idea to leave a copy with a friend at home) to prove your identity in case of theft or loss. When theft occurs, report to your consulate. Verification of your identity and citizenship takes two or three weeks and involves going to the local immigration office.

WHAT TO PACK

When packing, keep in mind that you will be in the tropics, but that evening sea breezes can be cool, as can boat rides. Bring wash and wear, light cotton clothes that absorb perspiration. (Synthetic fabrics are really uncomfortable in the tropics.) A medium-weight sweater or wind breaker is also a must, as is a light rain jacket with a hood. If you visit a government office, men should wear long trousers, proper shoes, and a shirt with collar. Women should wear a neat dress, covering knees and shoulders, and shoes.

A sarong purchased upon arrival in Indonesia is one of the most versatile items you could hope for. It serves as a wrap to get to the bath, a beach towel, pajamas, bed sheet, towel, etc. Earplugs (the moldable silicone ones are best) are useful, as are tiny padlocks for luggage zippers, and a small flashlight.

Bring along some pre-packaged alcohol towelettes (swabs). These are handy for disinfecting your hands before eating, or after a trip to the *kamar kecil* (lavatory). The big stores in Bali are quite well stocked, but things like contact lens solutions, dental floss, tampons, sunscreen, and insect repellent are still better to buy at home and pack. Passport photos may come in handy for applications and permits, or even as gifts.

On your travels you will meet people who are kind and helpful, yet you may feel too embarrassed to give money. In this kind of situation a small gift is appropriate. Chocolates, biscuits, pens, stationery from your hotel, even your T-shirt with foreign designs are appreciated.

CLIMATE

Bali is tropical, and daily highs average 31°C (88°F) and nightly lows, 22°C (72°F). It is much cooler in the highlands, and along the coast, where most divers will find themselves, sea breezes moderate the temperatures and the climate is quite pleasant. On the coast, air conditioning is not really necessary.

Bali experiences two yearly seasons of monsoon winds. The wet, northwest monsoon normally runs from October to April, with peak rainfall in December and January. During this time it rains for several hours each day, although it always stops for a time, and the sun may come out. During the dry, southeast monsoon, May to September, rainfall is less frequent. January is the wettest month, receiving an average of 400 mm of rain; September is the driest, receiving an average 10 mm of rain. The northwest and north of Bali are in the rain shadow of the island's central mountains, and are drier than south central Bali, where most of the rain falls.

TIME ZONE

Bali is in Central Indonesia Time, GMT +8, the same time zone as Shanghai, Hong Kong, Manila, Singapore, and Perth.

ELECTRICITY

Bali's electrical grid is 220~240 VAC at 50 hertz. The plugs are European style, with two round-section pins. There is little excess capacity, and particularly in the remote areas, hotels and restaurants make do with very little power. Voltage stabilizers are a good idea for computers and other sensitive equipment.

OFFICE HOURS

Many government offices have converted to a five-day work week and are officially open Monday to Friday, 8 am to 4 pm, but if you want to get anything done, be there by 11 am. In the larger cities most private businesses are open 9 am to 5 pm. Shops from 9 am to 9 pm. In smaller towns shops close for a siesta at 1 pm and reopen at 6 pm.

SECURITY

Indonesia is a relatively safe place to travel and violent crime is almost unheard of, but petty crime is on the upswing. Pay close attention to your belongings, especially in big cities. Use a small backpack or moneybelt for valuables. Be especially wary in crowds; this is where pickpockets lurk. They usually work in groups and are very clever at slitting bags and extracting valuables without your noticing anything.

Be sure that the door and windows of your hotel room are locked at night, including those in the bathroom, as thieves are adept at sneaking in while you are asleep. Big hotels have safety boxes for valuables. If your hotel does not have such a facility, it is better to carry all the documents along with you.

KEEP YOUR COOL

At government offices like immigration or police, talking loudly and forcefully doesn't make things easier. Patience and politeness are virtues that open many doors in Indonesia. Good manners and dress are also to your advantage.

Money

Standard currency in Indonesia is the rupiah. Notes come in denominations of 50,000; 20,000; 10,000; 5,000; 1,000; 500; and 100. Coins from Rp1,000 to Rp50. At many shops, any change smaller than Rp50 is handled by a small, wrapped candy.

At the time of this printing, the rupiah was trading at about Rp7,000 to US$1, but over the past year the currency's value has fluctuated widely. Many tourist services are priced in US dollars, and are likely to remain stable.

CHANGING MONEY

Although most dive operators and diving-associated hotels price their services and rooms in dollars, rupiah will be needed for taxis, eating out, and shopping. Bali is an easy place to change money. Moneychangers (which are in all of the tourist areas) almost always beat the bank's formal exchange rate, and hotel desks are always much worse.

The South—Kuta, Nusa Dua, Sanur—is by far the best place to change money. Exchange rates get worse as you get further away. In the northwest and along the north coast it can be difficult to change money, so take care of this beforehand in the south. The rates at the airport bank counters are only 5%-10% from being competitive, so it is worth changing at least some money on your way in.

Banks and moneychangers accept a range of currencies, including US dollars, Australian dollars and (usually) Japanese yen, Deutsche marks, Singapore dollars, English pounds, and French and Swiss francs. The bills must be in good condition.

Moneychangers

When changing money, shop around. The changers post signboards out front with that day's rates, and they can vary considerably. Be very alert when you are changing, and keep your amounts even so you don't get confused. Cheating is far from uncommon. Use your own calculator, or do the math yourself on their calculator, and write down the total. Be polite, but watch like a hawk, and always count your money. Also, when changing large amounts, you should get large denomination bills (Rp50,000 or Rp20,000) so your wad is manageable.

Moneychangers often use a sliding scale for bills of different denominations, with the best rate awarded to crisp, new style U.S. $100 bills. Old style $100s come next, then $50s, $20s, and smaller notes. The difference is substantial, and if you are bringing cash from the United States, get new $100s. For other currencies the difference is less dramatic, but always bring the newest and largest denomination notes you can get.

Banks

Banks are the safest way to change money, but are a lot less convenient. State banks are open from 8am–3pm, Monday to Friday. Private banks open also on Saturday until 11am. Bank lines in town can be long; best to arrive promptly at opening time.

Travelers checks

Banks and moneychangers will take travelers checks, although the rate is always lower than for currency, usually about 5%. The checks should be from a familiar company.

CREDIT CARDS

Visa, Mastercard, and American Express credit cards are accepted by most upscale tourist service operators. You can get cash advances at most banks, but there will be a commission. Even though you receive dollars from the bank, the advance formally takes place in rupiah, and the exchange rate according to which you will be billed back home will surprise you (and it won't be a nice surprise).

TAX AND TIPPING

Most larger hotels and restaurants charge 21% tax and service on top of your bill. Tipping is not a custom here, but it is appreciated for special services. The polite way to give money in Indonesia is to fold the notes and hand them over with the right hand only.

Communications

Bali is one of the best-connected places in Indonesia. On most parts of the island, telephone lines are good, if not excellent, and mail and express services are reliable.

TELEPHONE

The country code for Indonesia is 62, and Bali has six area codes. Following the organization of this book, from Northwest to South, the relevant codes are:

Gilimanuk (0365)
Banyuwedang (0362)
Pemuteran (0362)
Lovina (0362)
Tulamben (0363)
Jemeluk (0363)
Candidasa (0363)
Padangbai (0363)
Sanur (0361)
Kuta (0361)
Nusa Dua (0361)

The zero preceding these codes is only used for a call from within the country. When calling from overseas, it should be dropped (e.g. 62-361+number for calling South Bali from overseas).

Local calling

Telecommunications within Indonesia are provided by a government monopoly satellite network, Telkom.

The most convenient public phones take a magnetic debit (*kartu telpon*) card, which can be purchased at hotels, post offices and many other outlets. Card phones are becoming more and more common, eliminating the need for small change.

Some Useful Numbers

Local directory assistance	108
Long distance directory assistance	106
International directory assistance	102
Operator assisted local calls	100
Operator assisted long distance calls	101
Ambulance	118
Fire department	113
Police	110

Long distance

There are two long distance services in Indonesia, Indosat (access code 001) and Satelindo (access code 008). To dial your own international calls, find an International Direct Dial (IDD) phone, otherwise you must go through the operator, which is far more expensive.

If your hotel has no IDD link you have to go to the main telephone office (*kantor telpon*), which is often crowded and inconvenient, or use a silver card phone (*kartu telpon*) and pay an uninflated rate, or use a private telephone service called a *wartel* (an abbreviation of *warung telekommunikasi,* literally "telecommunications shop").

Wartels are all over Bali and the most convenient way to call international. They are often run by well-trained, efficient staff and offer fast IDD services, and their rates are not much higher than the official rate, although few offer the night and Sunday discounts available at the main telephone office.

International calls via MCI, Sprint, ATT, and the like can be made from IDD phones using the access code for your calling card company. Recently, special telephones have been installed in Indonesia's airports with pre-programmed buttons to connect you via these companies to various countries.

Faxes

Faxes can be sent and received at *wartel* offices and most main post offices.

INTERNET

The telephone lines in Bali are rarely good enough to allow for a really fast internet hookup, but for e-mailing and general communications, they can be satisfactory. (Our modem usually got a baud rate of 10K–12K on a decent line).

If you are traveling with a laptop, you can hook up in your hotel room. Some of the *wartels* will let you hook up and make a long-distance connection to your ISP back home, for the same price as a call. This sounds awkward, but if you just use your time online to download and upload messages, it can be relatively inexpensive and a reliable way to keep in touch.

Internet cafés are popping up in the tourist areas of the South, as well as Ubud and Lovina. These can be a fun way to contact home (grab a beer or a coffee or a fruit juice and start typing). Prices vary, but are usually around Rp10,000 for the first 15 min, then taper off.

THE POST

Indonesia's postal service is reliable, if not terribly fast. *Kilat* express service is only slightly more expensive and much faster. *Kilat khusus* (domestic special delivery) will get there overnight. International express mail gets postcards and letters to North America or Europe in about a week.

Kantor pos (post offices) are in every little village, generally open M–Th 8 am–2 pm, F until 11, Sat until 1 pm. Main post offices in bigger cities are open daily (except Sunday) 8 am–8 pm.

Hotels normally sell stamps and will post letters for you, or you can use private postal agents to avoid hassles. Look for the orange *Agen Kantor Pos* (postal agency) signs.

Courier Services

Some big international courier outfits operate in Indonesia, along with some domestic ones. DHL Worldwide Express and LTH Worldwide Courier Service are probably the most reliable.

Health

A trip to Bali does not represent a major risk to your health. Accidental cuts and scrapes, and stomach upset from unfamiliar food are the most likely problems. Malaria and dengue fever are not a major problem here (unlike parts of Eastern Indonesia) but you do face a small risk, particularly in the rural parts of the Northwest.

Check with your physician for recommended vaccinations before leaving home. Frequently considered vaccines are: diphtheria, pertussis and tetanus (DPT); measles, mumps and rubella (MMR); and oral polio vaccine. Gamma globulin every four months for hepatitis A is recommended. For longer stays many doctors recommend vaccination to protect against hepatitis B requiring a series of shots over the course of 7 months. Vaccinations for smallpox and cholera are no longer required, except for visitors coming from infected areas.

Find out the generic names for whatever prescription medications you are likely to need as most are available in Indonesia but not under the same brand names as they are known at home. Get copies of doctors' prescriptions for the medications you bring into Bali to avoid questions at customs. Those who wear spectacles should bring along prescriptions.

FIRST AID KIT

A basic first aid kit should consist of aspirin and multivitamins, a decongestant, an antihistamine, disinfectant (such as Betadine), antibiotic powder, fungicide, an antibiotic eyewash, Kaopectate or Lomotil, and sunscreen. Also good antiseptic soap (e.g. Asepso or Betadine). Avoid oral antibiotics unless you know how to use them. For injuries, make up a little kit containing Band-aids and ectoplast strips, a roll of sterile gauze and treated gauze for burns, surgical tape, and an elastic bandage for sprains. Also very important are cotton swabs, tweezers, scissors, needles, and safety pins. Keep your pills and liquid medicines in small unbreakable plastic bottles, clearly labeled with indelible pen.

HYGIENE

Hygiene cannot be taken for granted in a tropical place like Bali. To *mandi* (bathe) two or three times a day is a great way to stay cool and fresh. But be sure to dry yourself off well, and you may wish to use a disinfectant soap and/or apply a medicated body powder (e.g. Purol) to avoid the nastiness of prickly heat and skin fungus, especially during the rainy season.

THE WATER

In general, Indonesian tap water is not potable and must be boiled before drinking. Actually, Bali's water, particularly at the better hotels and restaurants, is not particularly unsafe, but it is best to avoid drinking water out of any tap. Bottled water of many brands is available everywhere. Some sources advise even brushing your teeth with bottled water, but this is probably unnecessary. Use your judgment. Obviously there is a big difference between a nasty old tap encountered during a road trip pit stop and the sink of your bathroom at a nice hotel. Ice in Bali is made in government regulated factories and if handled properly should be safe. But if you are particularly sensitive, or have not traveled to the tropics before, you might want to avoid it.

COMMON AILMENTS

The most common health problems encountered in Bali are minor and easily treated.

Exposure

Many visitors insist on instant tans, so overexposure to the heat and sun are frequent health problems. Be especially careful on long boat rides where the roof gives a good view. The cooling wind created by the boat's motion disguises the fact that you are frying like an egg. Wear a hat, loose-fitting, light-colored, long-sleeved cotton clothes, pants, and use a strong sunscreen. Bring your sunscreen along, as what is available in Bali is somewhat limited and expensive. Tan slowly—don't spoil your trip. Drink plenty of fluids and take salt.

Cuts and scrapes

Your skin will come into contact with more dirt and bacteria than it did back home, so wash your face and hands more often. Cuts should be taken seriously and cleaned with an antiseptic (e.g. Betadine, Dettol) available from any pharmacy (*apotik*). Once clean, antibiotic powder or

ointment, both available locally, should be applied. Cover the cut during the day to keep it clean, but leave it uncovered at night and whenever you are resting so that it can dry. Repeat this ritual after every bath. Areas of redness around the cut indicate infection and a doctor should be consulted. At the first sign of swelling it is advisable to take broad spectrum antibiotics to prevent a nasty infection.

Not every mosquito bite leads to malaria, but in the tropics a scratched bite or small abrasion can quickly turn into a festering ulcer. You must pay special attention to these things. Apply Tiger Balm—a widely available camphorated salve—or some imitation thereof to relieve the itching. For light burns, use Aristamide or Bioplacenteron.

Stomach complaints

Most cases of stomach complaints are attributable to your system not being used to the strange foods and stray bacteria. Diarrhea is a likely traveling companion. In addition to the unfamiliar micro-fauna, diarrhea is often the result of attempting to accomplish too much in one day. Taking it easy can be an effective prevention. Ask around before leaving about the latest and greatest of the many remedies available, and bring some along. Imodium is locally available as are activated carbon tablets (Norit) that will absorb the toxins giving you grief.

When it hits, "Bali Belly" is usually self-limiting to two or three days. Relax and drink lots of fluids, perhaps accompanied by rehydration salts (e.g. Oralit and Pharolit). Also helpful is water from the young coconut (*air kelapa muda*) and weak, unsweet-

ened tea. The former is an especially pure anti-toxin. Get it straight from the coconut without sugar, ice or food color or added. When you are ready, bananas, papayas, plain rice, crackers or dry biscuits, and *bubur* (rice porridge) are a good way to start. Avoid fried, spicy or heavy foods and dairy products for a while. After three days without relief, see a doctor.

Not all bouts of diarrhea mean dysentery. If you contract the latter, which is much more serious, you must seek medical help. Do this if your stools are mixed with blood and pus, are black, or you are experiencing severe stomach cramps and fever.

To prevent stomach problems, try to eat only thoroughly cooked foods, don't buy already peeled fruit, and stay away from unpasteurized dairy products. For constipation, eat a lot of fruit.

TROPICAL DISEASES

Malaria, dengue fever, and encephalitis are not major problems in Bali, but outbreaks occur on occasion. In some parts of Eastern Indonesia, malaria accounts for a sizeable percentage of total mortality, and is nothing to be irresponsible about. The risk in Bali is considered highest in the rainy season, and in areas of far West Bali, including Gilimanuk and Pemuteran.

Malaria

If you will be spending considerable time in far West Bali during the rainy season, or plan any trekking activites, a course of malaria prophylaxis might be wise. If you are staying in the South, it is probably unnecessary.

Malaria is caused by a protozoan, *Plasmodium,* which affects the blood and liver. The vector for this parasite is the *Anopheles* mosquito, which bites late at night. After contracting malaria, it takes a minimum of six days—or up to several years—before symptoms appear.

There are several forms of malaria, two of which are found in Indonesia: *Plasmodium vivax*, which is unpleasant, but is rarely fatal to healthy adults, and *P. falciparum,* so-called cerebral malaria, which can be fatal. *P. falciparum* is a zoonosis, a disease that, in evolutionary terms, shifted quite recently from domestic poultry to humans, which is why the fever is so intense. (Birds have a higher normal body temperature than humans.)

Recommendations for malaria prophylaxis have changed of late, and the traditional form of protection—chloroquine phosphate—is almost useless against *falciparum* malaria. The stronger drugs now recommended have serious side-effects, and should not be taken casually. Follow your doctor's advice.

Dengue and encephalitis

Another mosquito-born disease is dengue fever, spread by *Aedes* sp., which bites in the morning and early afternoon, especially during the rainy season. Dengue fever symptoms are headache, pain behind the eyes, high fever, muscle and joint pains, and rash, appearing between the third and fifth days of illness. Within days, the fever subsides and recovery seldom has complications. The more serious variant, dengue hemorrhagic fever (DHF), which can be fatal, may be the reaction of a secondary infection with remaining immunities following a primary attack. There is no prophylaxis against dengue, and the most effective prevention is not getting bitten.

Cases of Japanese encephalitis, a viral infection affecting the brain, have occured recently and are added cause to take protective measures against mosquito bites.

Prevention

If you don't get bit by a mosquito, you don't get any of these diseases.

1) Use a good quality mosquito repellent, and be very generous with it, particularly around your ankles. Wear light-colored, long-sleeved shirts or blouses and long pants. Effective insect repellent is hard to find in Bali, so bring some from home. The strongest contain the chemical DEET (diethyl toluamide), which is quite effective, but in concentrations greater than about 10%, can irritate skin. Use caution with high-strength DEET repellents, and application to clothing may be the most effective.

2) While eating, relaxing in one spot, or sleeping, burn mosquito coils. These are those green, slightly brittle coils of incense doped with pyrethrin (called *obat nyamuk bakar* in Indonesia). They last 6–8 hours and are quite effective, and you will get used to the smell. If you are bothered by mosquitoes at a restaurant, just ask and someone will bring a coil for under your table.

AIDS AND HEPATITIS B

Safe sex is a good idea even in Bali. Documentation, awareness and education of AIDS is just beginning in Indonesia. Another area of concern is the hepatitis B virus which affects liver function and is only sometimes curable and can be fatal. The prevalence of hepatitis B in Indonesia is the basis for international concern over the ominous possibilities for the spread of HIV.

Medical Treatment

There are two good, large hospitals in Denpasar, and a number of smaller hospitals and clinics around the island. In the south, there are private clinics specializing in tourists. Any decent hotel will have a relationship with a doctor and be able to get you to a clinic or hospital if necessary.

DOCTORS AND CLINICS

Doctors and health care are quite inexpensive by western standards, but the quality may not be as high. (At least they're familiar with the symptoms and treatment of tropical diseases, however, which is something that may not be true of your family doctor back home.) Three clinics in Denpasar specialize in treating foreigners. **Surya Husadha Klinik** Jl Pulau Serangan 1-3, Denpasar (next to the hospital, see below). ☎(0361) 233786/7. **Gatotkaca Klinik** Jl Gatotkaca, Denpasar. ☎(0361) 223555. **Manuaba Klinik** Jl Cokroaminoto, Denpasar. ☎(0361) 426393.

PHARMACIES

Called *apotik*, pharmacies in Bali are common, and stock many useful medications, including anti-bacterial ointment, fungicide, and oral rehydration salts. Tiger Balm, excellent for itching bites and muscle pain, is a must.

HOSPITAL

The best hospital in Bali is the Sanglah provincial public hospital (*rumah sakit umum propinsi*) in Denpasar. It is open 24 hrs, and has English-speaking doctors on staff. Sanglah also has a hyperbaric medicine department and a recompression chamber (see below). If you check into Sanglah or any hospital in Indonesia, always ask for the best room (VIP), which is still inexpensive by western standards. Cheaper rooms and wards tend to get less attention from the medical staff.

Sanglah General Hospital (RSUP Sanglah Denpasar) Diponegoro Street, Denpasar 80114. ☎ (0361) 227911 through 15 (general), 223190 (ICCU), 232603 (VIP), and 224556 (director). Fax: 224206 (director), 226363 (emergency unit).

EVACUATION SERVICES

Emergency care even at Sanglah can be inadequate, and your best bet in the event of a life-threatening emergency or accident is to get on the first plane to Jakarta or Singapore. Contact your embassy or consulate by phone for assistance (see below). Medivac airlifts are very expensive ($26,000) and most embassies will recommend that you buy insurance to cover the cost of this when traveling extensively in Indonesia.

Check your health insurance before coming to make sure you are covered. Travel insurance should include coverage of medical evacuation to Singapore and a 24-hour worldwide phone number, as well as extras like coverage for lost luggage and trip cancellations.

Two good insurers are AEA International, a Singapore-based outfit that offers world-wide medical evacuation insurance, and the non-profit Divers Alert Network (DAN) which offers low-cost secondary insurance for divers.

AEA International The Americas: ☎ (206) 340-6000, Fax: (206) 340-6006; Asia:

☎ (65) 338 2311, Fax: (65) 338 7611; Europe: ☎ (33-1) 53-05-05-55, Fax: (33-1) 53-05-05-56; Australia: ☎ 61 (2) 9372--2468, Fax: 61 (2) 9372-2494.
E-mail: info@aeaintl.com
Web: www.aeaintl.com

This is a seasoned outfit that has been providing emergency services in the region for more than a decade. They combined with International SOS Assistance early in 1998. AEA offers individual and corporate insurance packages, with world-wide coverage.

AEA maintains 24-hour alarm centers throughout the world, including one in Bali: ☎ (0361) 227271, contact: Frederika Nault, and one in Jakarta: ☎ (021) 750-6001, contact: Jim Williams.

Divers Alert Network (DAN) Peter B. Bennett Center, 8 West Colony Place, Durham NC 27705 USA. Membership services: ☎ (800) 446-2671. Web: www.dan.ycg.org

This well-known U.S.-based non-profit has been providing medical advice in the case of diving injuries, researching diving medicine, and promoting diving safety for a long time. They are often the first organization called by local emergency personnel in the case of a diving accident.

The organization publishes the bimonthly *Alert Diver*, which is distributed to members. DAN offers yearly membership for US$29, and three different insurance packages for an additional US$25 to US$35 a year. We highly recommend DAN membership and insurance.

The organization maintains a medical information line for questions about diving health and problems (☎ [919] 684-2948; 9 am–5 pm U.S. Eastern Time) and a 24-hour-a-day hotline for dive emergen-

cies: ☎ (919) 684-8111.

DAN also maintains a Southeast Asia branch in Australia:

DAN Southeast Asia–Pacific 49a Karnak Road, P.O. Box 384, Ashburton, Vic. 3147, Australia. ☎ (61-3) 9886-9166, Fax: (61-3) 9886-9155; Emergencies: ☎ (61-3) 9828-2958.

DCS EMERGENCIES

There are two hyperbaric chambers in the area, one at Sanglah hospital in Denpasar, Bali, and the other in Surabaya, East Java. Most decompression sickness problems in Bali end up at the Sanglah unit.

Sanglah General Hospital Sanglah Denpasar, Diponegoro Street, Denpasar 80114. ☎ (0361) 227911 through -15 ext. 232 for the hyperbaric medicine department. The chief doctor for the chamber is Dr. Antonius Natasamudra (home: ☎ [0361] 420842), and Dr. Etty Herawati (home: ☎ [0361] 223570) works the chamber as well. Both speak English and are very competent. The standard hours for the hyperbaric medicine unit are 8am–1:30pm M-Th, 8am–11am F, and 8am–12:30pm Sat.

The chamber is kept in good service and the doctors and nurses are familiar with its operation. They use the United States Navy tables for their treatment regime, and the prices are quite reasonable. The table below lists prices for treatment during normal business hours (treatment time in parentheses). After hours the price doubles.

Kindwall (135 min)	$20
Table 5 (135 min)	$40
Table 6 (245 min)	$80
Table 6A (319 min)	$110

The chamber was built by

A-1 Welding and Fabrication of Houston, Texas and is a model PVHO-1. It has capacity for 5 patients and a nurse, and a working pressure of up to 80 psi (5.4 atmospheres). It began operation in July 1996.

We checked the logs for the chamber, and found that it gets quite a bit of use, averaging almost 500 visits a year, mostly for beauty treatments (chamber time is good way to get oxygen to your skin), but also for "washing out" treatments for dive guides and for DCS emergencies. Below are the serious (Type I and Type II) DCS treatments conducted, and the results.

1996 (half year) 9 cases (1 paralyzed, 1 dead)

1997 24 cases (all recovered)

1998 21 cases (4 paralyzed, 2 dead)

1999 (half year) 13 cases (1 dead)

All of the cases of death and paralysis were traditional divers, most of them working on hookah rigs. Many of these men, once afflicted, had to make a long, slow trip from Komodo and points even further east before getting treatment.

Lakelsla Direktorat Kesehatan TNI-AL, Lembaga Kesehatan, Keangakatan Lautan, Jl. Gadung No. 1, Surabaya, Java. ☎ (031) 45750 and 41731. This chamber, operated by the Indonesian Navy, is run by Dr. Suharsono, who was trained in Australia and speaks English very well. The chamber has a volume of 75 cubic meters, with a capacity for five patients at a maximum working pressure of 6 atmospheres. The unit was built in 1981 by Aqualogistics International, St. Helena, UK. Other instrumentation includes spirometry, audiometry, EKG, and chromatography.

Transportation

The best way to arrive in Bali is at the Ngurah Rai International Airport which, despite its often being referred to as "Denpasar" is actually on the isthmus connecting the Bukit Badung peninsula to Bali, much nearer to Kuta Beach than to Bali's capital city. Daily Garuda flights from Jakarta, Yogyakarta, and many other Indonesian cities connect to Ngurah Rai, and a growing number of international flights—including those from Australia, Hong Kong, Japan, the Netherlands, Singapore and the United States—land here as well.

Flights from the Soekarno-Hatta International Airport in Jakarta are frequent, and if you land in Jakarta before 5pm you can usually get a connection to Bali, although in peak season these 90-min flights are almost always full.

International airlines

Many international airlines have offices in the Grand Bali Beach Hotel in Sanur, ☎ (0361) 288511. Opening hours are M–F 8:30am to 4:30pm, and Sat 8:30am to 1pm. Their direct lines (all 0361) are:

Air France ☎ 288511
Ansett Australia ☎ 289636
Cathay Pacific ☎ 286001
Continental Micronesia ☎ 287774
Japan Airlines (and **Japan Asia Airways**) ☎ 287577
Lufthansa ☎ 287069
Malaysia Airlines ☎ 285071
Northwest Airlines ☎ 287841
Qantas ☎ 288331
Singapore Airlines ☎ 288511
Thai Airways International ☎ 288141

Several others keep offices in the Wisti Sabha Building at the Ngurah Rai Airport:

Air New Zealand ☎ 756170 and 751011 ext. 1116
China Airlines ☎ 754856 and 757298
EVA Air ☎ 298935
KLM-Royal Dutch Airlines ☎ 756127
Korean Air ☎ 289402
Royal Brunei ☎ 757292

Indonesian airlines

Indonesian airlines have gone through a shake-up lately, and service has been shrinking. The state airline Garuda is still the most reliable, and flies internationally to the United States, Australia, and Asia.

Garuda Main office at Jl. Melati 61, Denpasar. ☎ (0361) 225245, Fax: 226298; for bookings and confirmations, ☎ 227824/5; the Garuda desk at the airport, ☎ 751026. The main office is open M-F 7:30am to 4:45pm, Sat 9am to 1pm. Garuda also keeps desks and sales offices at several of the larger hotels.

Merpati Jl. Melati 51, Denpasar. ☎ (0361) 261238, Fax. 231962; at the airport, ☎ 751011 ext. 3107.

Arrival overland

If you are coming from Jakarta, you can get to Bali by train, which is romantic, but very slow, and a nightmare with scuba gear. A night bus is a better option (24 hrs, Jakarta–Denpasar, about $30.) From Ubung Terminal outside Denpasar, where you are dropped off, a minibus to the tourist triangle of Kuta–Sanur–Nusa Dua runs $3–$5. All in all, best to arrive by plane.

LOCAL TRANSPORTATION

Airport taxis

One-way fares from Ngurah Rai airport to the tourist centers are fixed. You pay a cashier inside, and receive a coupon which you surrender to your driver. (Of course, there will be plenty of touts and free-lancers offering you their services. These are never a better deal.) Fares range from $2 to nearby Kuta Beach to $10 to Ubud, far inland.

Minibuses

All hotels have minibuses for hire with a driver or English-speaking driver/guide. Rates run $3–$5/hr, with a 2-hr minimum. Day rates run $30–$40, more for an air-conditioned vehicle.

Bemos

Public minibuses in Bali are called *"bemos,"* a compression of *becak* (bicycle-like pedicabs) and *mobil*. This is the way the Balinese travel and the cheapest way to get around the island. Fares are very inexpensive and you could probably get all the way across the island for less than $2, but you will need to know some Indonesian or be very good at charades to make sense of the routes and drop-off points.

For a diving visitor to Bali, *bemos* are most useful for short day trips around the area or to hop locally around town. Get one of your diving guides or someone at the hotel to explain the ins and outs of the local routes.

Vehicle rental

In almost all cases, it is best to leave the driving in Bali to someone who knows how to negotiate the roads and traffic. The roads are narrow, twisting, and full of hazards: unmarked construction sites, chickens, dogs, children, Vespas as wide as cars due to huge baskets of produce, and tough, unflinching truck drivers, to name just a few. You can rent a small (150cc) mo-

torcycle for $7/day if you have an international motorcycle driver's license, but you better know how to ride.

Renting a car—particularly since you will be carrying diving gear—is perhaps a more practical solution. These run $15/day for little Suzuki jeeps; more for larger, more comfortable Toyota Kijangs. Rent through an agency (even Avis has outlets) or from numerous local rental companies. Ask at your hotel or comb the streets where there's an agent on nearly every block. Be sure your rental includes insurance for loss and damage.

Accommodations

A hierarchy of lodgings and official terminology has been set by the government. A "hotel" is an up-market establishment catering to businessmen, middle- to upper-class travelers and tourists. A star-rating (one to five stars) is applied according to the range of facilities. Smaller places with no stars and basic facilities are not referred to as hotels but as *losmen* (from the French *logement*), *wisma* (guesthouse), or *penginapan* (accommodation) and cater to the masses and budget tourists. Prices and quality vary enormously. In Bali you can get very comfortable and clean rooms with a fan for less than $6 a night, and fancy air-conditioned rooms for $100 or more. The sweet spot in the range is probably around $30 night.

Food and drink

You can get all types of cuisines in Bali, and can pay as much or as little as your budget allows. At the fancier places in the Kuta–Nusa

Dua–Sanur area, you can get excellent, high-end Thai food, Chinese food, European food, and even quite good sushi. The South is also the best place for seafood, and there are some very good beachside restaurants near the airport. If you are ordering fish, we recommend rabbitfish or grouper. Also excellent, and relatively inexpensive, are the mangrove crabs in chili sauce. Lobster is available also, but this is becoming scarce, and very expensive. A spiny lobster costs at least double in Bali what a good Maine lobster costs in the United States.

There is a kind of standard menu at most mid-priced tourist restaurants and cafés that includes Indonesian standards like *gado-gado*, chicken soup, satay, and fried rice, varieties of the Australian jaffle (a kind of sealed sandwich), and a few "Italian" dishes, including pizza and pastas, the latter usually with a heavy, meaty sauce. This routine is okay to begin with, but can get tiring very quickly. Put some effort into experimenting with different places to eat.

In general, the restaurants that feature a single cuisine are the best, and probably your safest bet is a Padang joint. Padang—a region in Sumatra—has produced Indonesia's most widespread cuisine, for good reason. It is spicy and tasty, and has great variety. The classic serving method is for many small plates, each with a different morsel, to be placed on the diners' table. The dishes that are eaten are billed, the others are returned to the case. Today many places serve you from a kind of steam table, but the result is the same: lots of variety of vegetables and meats, with rich, spicy gravies.

Traditional Balinese cuisine is a little harder to come by. Most restaurants will offer such delicacies as *babi guling* (roast young pig) and *bebek betutu* (slow-cooked duck) but only with a day's notice. For *babi guling,* your best bet is to try a night market, or one of the small restaurants that specializes in this dish.

BEER, WINE, AND SPIRITS

The beers available in Bali are Bintang, Anker, Carlsberg, and Bali Hai, this being, in our opinion, their order of palatability as well. Bintang is quite good, and you will do yourself a favor if you stick with this brand exclusively. Anker will do in a pinch, but Carlsberg is nasty, and Bali Hai is simply a bad joke. There is a domestic wine available in Bali as well, but if you like wine at all you'd best avoid this pinkish "rosé," which manages to be both too sweet and too tannic.

Traditional refreshments include *tuak, arak,* and *brem.* You can find *tuak,* a pleasant, frothy toddy from palm sap, at roadside stands, markets, and in the little back alleys of Kuta. *Tuak* is usually called "palm wine," but it is much more like beer. It continues fermenting all day long, so it is milder in the morning than in the evening. Most Balinese prefer *tuak* from the *enau* palm, as does Wally, but my own preference is *tuak* from the *lontar* palm, which is more common in north Bali. Coconut palm *tuak* is considered by everyone to be an inferior species.

Arak is Bali's traditional high proof spirit (it is distilled from *tuak*), and it is a rough customer: clear, oily and fierce, with a strong nose of turpentine. *Arak*'s alcoholic content is high enough for it to be a fire hazard, and yet it is served in a water glass. Be cautious with this one. If you

have a taste for rum, not fine aged Caribbean rum, but something cheap, sharp, and raw, like African or Indian rum, you might like *arak.* If so, probably the best on the island is distilled just inland of Padangbai, which is as good a place as any to get it.

Brem is a "wine" brewed from sweet, sticky rice. It is not strong, but is very sweet, and not everyone can take it. Tourists like to mix *brem* and *arak,* which is easier to get down than either on its own.

FRUITS

Tropical fruits in Bali are delicious. The undisputed king is the *duren* or durian, a large, thick-husked fruit full of a creamy flesh that is very rich, very strong-smelling, and certainly unlike anything else in the world. If you get a chance, you must try durian. Other unusual fruits include *salak,* a palm fruit which looks like a large garlic covered with brown snakeskin and has crisp segments that taste like a cross between an apple and a walnut, and *manggis* (mangosteen), which has juicy white segments hiding under a thick purple-brown cover that melt in your mouth. The season varies for these juicy delights, and can be frustratingly short. Bananas, apples, tangerines, papaya, pineapples, pomelos (*jeruk Bali*), starfruit (*blimbing*), guava (*buah biji*), and watermelon are found year round.

Photography

Indonesians generally enjoy being photographed. However, if you are in doubt or the situation seems awkward, it is polite to ask. Some religious activities, eating, and bathing are inappropriate subjects.

Beware of the strong shad-

ows from the equatorial sun. Late afternoon and early morning provide the most pleasing light and the richest colors. The only way to deal with the heavy shadows in midday is to use a fill flash.

The heat and humidity of the tropics is hard on equipment. Be particularly careful when moving cameras from an air-conditioned room to the muggy outdoors, as moisture can condense on the inside and outside of the camera. Wait until it evaporates; don't be tempted to wipe it off. Also, watch the location of your camera bag and film. Temperatures in hot cars or on boats can be searing.

Some 35mm Fuji and Kodak film is widely available in Indonesia, including color print film from ASA 100 to 400 and Ektachrome and Fujichrome 100 ASA daylight transparency film. In larger towns you can also buy Fuji Neopan 100 ASA black-and-white negative film and Fuji Velvia. Kodachrome is unavailable here. Print and E-6 slide processing is generally quite inexpensive, but the quality can vary widely. Important shots should be processed at home.

PHOTOGRAPHIC SUPPLIES

The biggest range of photographic equipment and supplies can be found in Denpasar at **Tati Photo**, Jl. Sumatra 72, ☎ (0361) 226912, and **Prima Photo**, Jl. Gajah Mada 14, ☎ 222505.

The best E-6 processing we have found in Bali is at Bali Fotografi in Kuta. They offer color and black and white print developing and processing, film sales, and camera cleaning and repair. **Bali Fotografi** Jl Raya Kuta 57X, P.O. Box 2088, Kuta 80361. ☎ (0361) 751329 and ☎/fax: 755827.

Diving AND ACCOMMODATIONS

Bali has at least thirty dive operators, some excellent, some okay, and some frightening. Those we list below have a good reputation on the island (and it is a lot fewer than thirty). Still, there is considerable variation even among these operators, and if possible you should always meet with them first.

Dive operators

Most dive operators on the island keep their main offices in the South, in the tourist triangle—Kuta, Nusa Dua, and Sanur. Some of these maintain branches, with tanks and compressors, in the Northwest or Lovina or at Candidasa on the East Coast, and there are local operators clustered around the good sites, such as Tulamben. The bigger outfits maintain desks at the major hotels, or at least keep brochures at the desk.

Bali is not very big, and you could dive any site in this book on a day trip starting from a hotel or *losmen* anywhere in the South. We don't recommend this, however, as you will spend half of your vacation cooped up in the back of a Kijang or minibus, as your driver fights his way through an unending stream of traffic.

The South is convenient for diving Tanjung Benoa and Nusa Penida, and the East Coast sites are not too far away. But Tulamben, and particularly the Northwest, are too remote. We recommend you stay near where you are diving, which means the Pemuteran area or perhaps Lovina for the Northwest, Tulamben for that area, and Candidasa or Padangbai for the East Coast.

If this is your first trip to Bali for diving, you should plan to stay at Tulamben for at least a while. This is the most popular purely diving area, and from here you can run across to Menjangan on a day trip without too much trouble (it is a pleasant drive along the relatively empty north coast road; there is nothing pleasant about the drive from the south) or, going the other way, run down to Padangbai to dive the East Coast or Nusa Penida.

If you are a serious diver, and you have the time, we would recommend staying a few days at Pemuteran or Banyuwedang, diving Menjangan, then a few days at Tulamben, diving that area, then a few days at Candidasa or Padangbai, diving the East Coast, then a few days in the South, diving Nusa Penida (or stay on and dive Penida from Candidasa or Padangbai). This gives you a taste of the island's different diving areas, and also its different towns and environments, with the minimum amount of driving.

It also allows you to work with guides who are specialists in the various areas. You have a better chance of being shown something interesting by a guide who has been diving a single area on a daily basis. It is our experience that the guides and outfits based in the Northwest—or based in Tulamben, or based on the East Coast—know their area better than the South-based operators who run clients to these areas on day trips.

Any of the bigger dive operators will book you a package that includes any combination of the sites in this book, putting you up at various hotels as required. These days, you can even do most of this ahead of time through the web and e-mail.

This is not necessarily a bad idea, but it is just as possible to do your booking when you arrive. If at all possible, we think you should have a look at the operation and meet the guides before committing. Unless you've already found an operator you like, we'd be more inclined to use the internet resources as a way to gather information. During the high season, it may be useful to book ahead, but even then, we would book only the first part of a planned trip, leaving the rest open.

Remember that Bali—and all of Indonesia—is a very flexible place, which is one of its great charms. Try not to lock yourself in (either contractually or mentally) to some kind of fixed program. Make sure you have the freedom to follow the weather and other serendipities. You don't necessarily want to arrive on the island with bookings for Menjangan, then get all the way out there only to learn about a run on molas at Gili Mimpang.

The diving boom on Bali is not yet over, although it seems

to be entering the stage where the biggest growth is coming from new expatriate-run businesses and international franchises. This, in our estimation, is neither for better or for worse. (It does seem to yield better production values in the brochures, although I'm afraid some of the expatriate businesses are getting sloppy with their photographs—for the record, folks, the millet-seed butterflyfish is a Hawai'ian species, and you won't find the Caribbean species *Chromis cyanea* or *C. multilineata* in Bali.)

COURSES

Like everywhere else in the world, and for the same business and marketing reasons, most of the operators in Bali are or have become PADI franchises, some of them having earned stars and golden palms and other merit badges. The bigger operators offer basic and advanced certification and other resort courses, averaging $300 to $400 for open water certification.

Bali is not a bad place at all to learn to dive, and Tulamben is probably the best area for this. If you decide to do this, we recommend that you make your decision on who to take a course from based on the knowledge, attitude, and experience of the person who will be teaching you, period.

Decide for yourself, but if it were us, we would not care a gnat's whisker for how many decorations a resort is entitled to display on its stationary, or which letters of the alphabet. We would care a lot about who was going to do the teaching. There are expatriate PADI instructors on the island with a handful of dives and the tact and human relations skills of a badger. There are Indonesian POSSI instructors on the island with

years of experience, excellent language skills, and a real gift for teaching. And vice-versa. You should play an active role in evaluating a potential instructor.

DIVE GUIDES

This is good advice for choosing a dive guide as well. Even among the safe ones (and we hope we have weeded the following list to at least this level), there are good guides, and, well, not so good guides.

We have attempted in this book to give you the tools to be independently informed about diving and dive sites in Bali, and hope we have succeeded at least to the extent that you can have a knowledgable discussion with a guide about diving one of the sites. Open the book to one of the maps, and sit down with a potential guide and ask where and how he or she plans to dive the site. This discussion should provide a good basis for deciding whether or not you want this person to be the one taking you diving.

Guides, particularly Indonesian guides, are sometimes thought of as a commodity item in this business. The pay scale is low, and some operators seem more concerned about their compressors, say, than the people who will actually be leading their clients underwater.

We think this is a mistake, and believe that a good guide is an operator's most important asset. In this section we list the members of each operator's dive team, as much to make a point to the operators as to offer information to our readers.

PRICES

The cost of diving in Bali is pretty standard among operators, and is almost always priced in dollars. A basic

day's package, including two full tanks, weights, transportation, and a guide, runs $40 to $60 for a shore dive (e.g. Pemuteran, Tulamben), $65 to $90 for a dive that requires a boat ride (e.g. Menjangan, Tepekong), and $80 to $120 for a dive that requires a long boat ride (e.g. the far side of Nusa Penida, Gili Selang).

Land transportation adds to the cost as well. The cost from South-based operators for diving at Menjangan is $20–$30 more than the Pemuteran operators, a difference that could cover most of the cost of a nice room at Pemuteran. The same can also be true of Tulamben, which is another reason we recommend you stay locally if you are diving these areas.

The following are price ranges for a day of diving at the different areas:

Menjangan	$65–$75
from the south	$80–$115
Pemuteran	$40–$55
from the south	$85–$100
Gilimanuk	$45
Lovina	$50–$60
from the south	$75–$85
Tulamben	$50–$60
from the south	$60–$80
Jemeluk	$55–$75
from the south	$60–$80
Tanjung Sari	$50–$70
Tepekong	$65–$95
Mimpang	$65–$90
Biaha	$65–$95
Gili Selang	$95–$120
Nusa Penida	
near side	$80–$110
Nusa Penida	
far side	$95–$120
Tanjung Benoa	$45–$80
Sanur	$45–$80

The range between the cheapest and most expensive operators can seem considerable, but in many cases you get what you pay for, for example, a fast, comfortable boat to Nusa Penida, or an experienced, well-trained guide, or brand new rental gear, or some other tangible benefit.

Price should not be the main issue. The quality of the operator, and even the personal chemistry between you and your guide, is far more important. Bear in mind also that although many things are inexpensive in Indonesia, diving gear, cylinders, compressors and parts, fuel, and outboard engines are not among them.

Most operators offer 2-day to 5-day packages, which are more economical, with a cost per dive of $30–$40. Serious divers should take time to plan a dive series with the operator, taking into consideration time, budget and weather.

EQUIPMENT

Dedicated divers always like to bring their own equipment, which is a good idea in Bali as well. But take note of the water temperatures mentioned in the text. We recommend a full-length, 3mm neoprene suit, and something thicker wouldn't hurt (or bring a hood). Leave the Lycra and other pajamas at home.

We also recommend that you bring an inflatable signal device, and keep it clipped to your BC at all times. These long, safety orange tubes—unavoidably nicknamed "giant condoms"—can make the difference between a quick pick up, or drifting for two hours. The good ones are made of thick material, and very long. Buy a good one and bring it.

It is not strictly necessary to bring your own gear. The operators listed here keep good rental equipment. Some price their dives with equipment included, offering a discount of typically $10 if you bring your own. Others rent gear, usually $20 for everything; $10–$15 for a BC and regulator; $5 for a wetsuit; $3–$5 for

a mask, snorkel, and fins set; and $3–$5 for a flashlight.

ABOUT THE LISTINGS

Below we have gathered information on those of Bali's many operators that we know have good reputations. We have not personally dived with all of them, and the quality of the instruction, facilities and dive guides varies. Use this information as a guide, and do some investigating of your own.

The area listings follow the organization of this book, working their way around the island from the Northwest to the South.

Bali, the land of 10,000 temples, has more than that number of hotel rooms and it would be impossible for us to list all the available lodgings here. There are enough hotels and *losmen* to fill two volumes the size of this book. We list only those places associated with dive operations. All the up-market places charge 21% government tax and service on top of the listed prices.

The Northwest

This is the furthest area from the airport and the resorts of the South. Although most of Bali's operators offer Menjangan packages, unless you want to spend half of your day on the road, you are better off staying at one of the resorts in the area. The cluster of resorts in Pemuteran offer the most variety, but the new up-market resort at nearby Banyuwedang Bay is also a good option. There is a single operator at Gilimanuk, which specializes in that site.

We have also included information here on Lovina, which is not covered in the main text of the book. There is diving at the little resort

beach of Lovina, which lies on the North Coast about 25 km west of Singaraja, but it is not exceptional. Before the development of the Pemuteran resorts about seven years ago, Lovina offered the closest lodging to Menjangan. Even today, it is the only place in this area offering really cheap (less than $20) accommodations. If you are on a very tight budget, diving Menjangan out of Lovina might still be the best option.

LABUHAN LALANG

The little port of Labuhan Lalang inside Teluk Terima is where all dive outings to Menjangan Island begin. It can be a slightly dreary place, but there is a nice view out over the water. There is not much here, just a small store, a couple of open air restaurants, and the park service kiosk and office. The oldest of the restaurant/cafés sit next to each other, Pak Asam's "Mulia Merah" on the western side (it has been there for 20 years) and Ibu Dewa's "Wild West" on the east (at least 10 years). The owners are good-humored, and either establishment is a nice place to sit and have a bit of food, a coffee, or post-dive beer. On Ibu Dewa's side you can watch the tame deer, and on Pak Asam's side a little macaque will happily pick nits from your hair or reach into your shoulderbag and pull out receipts, money, jewelry, sunglasses, and other trinkets and gnaw on them.

The public restrooms at Lalang used to be a horrendous little strip of doorless cells with rotten floors, but a new facility has been built behind them (leaving the scenic old ones there, naturally). You can use this for Rp1000, and it even has showers and facilities to soak equipment. Use this facility quickly, however, as even just six months after it was built the concrete was already flaking. (There is plenty of room behind it to build another one, though.)

You need a permit to dive Menjangan, which is in West Bali National Park. You stop at the kiosk and fill out your particulars for a day-use park permit. You also have to pay for parking, and for the boat. All of this is taken care of if you come on a package, otherwise the total comes to something like $15.

The boats at Labuan Lalang are run by a local cartel, with a fixed price and a limit of five divers. Unless you are staying at Banyuwedang or Pemuteran, you have to take one of these boats to dive Menjangan. The wooden boats are not expensive, and they are comfortable enough. One continuing problem at Labuan Lalang, however, is theft by the skippers. We cannot recommend you leave anything valuable on the boat while you are diving. Keep such things locked in your car on land.

PEMUTERAN (0362)

The first tourist-oriented resort went up here eight years ago, and the first dive operation followed. It is a quiet, pretty, isolated setting. There are now a handful of resorts, all quite close to each other. Most offer hiking trips to the nearby park as well.

Dive resorts

Archipelago Dive Sarana (P.T. Arkipelago Selam) est. 1997, PADI. Taman Sari Bungalows Resort, Desa Pemuteran, Gerokgak, Singaraja 81155. ☎(0362) 92623, Fax: (0362) 93264. *Main office:* Sol Elite Paradiso Hotel, Shopping Parade No. 4, Jl Kartika Plaza, Kuta 80361.

☎(0361) 761414 ext. 7810; Fax:(0361) 756944. E-mail: tamanri@indosat.net.id; Web: baliwww.com/arkipelago. Owner: Peter Ross.

This outfit offers a Baliwide program. The dive center at Pemuteran is right on the beach, in front of the Taman Sari, with which they are partnered. Their staff is friendly and competent, and their gear is new.

Two dives $35 Pemuteran (shore); $55 Pemuteran (boat); $65 Menjangan. Also $50 Lovina; $55 Tulamben.

Dive team Peter Ross (U.K.), PADI Instr. (1996), in Bali since 1996; Paul M. Turley (British), PADI OWSI (1996), in Bali since 1997, also speaks Indon.; Wayan Cerita (Indo.), PADI AOW (1998), also speaks Eng.; Made Radiasa (Indo.), NAUI Rescue (1996), also speaks Eng. and Jap.

Courses PADI OW to DM.

Boats Modified traditional wooden fishing boats, 4m, 15hp, cap. 5 divers.

Equipment Bauer Mariner and Lenharst & Wagner W190 compressors, 60 tanks, 40 regulators (US Divers), 45 BCs (SeaQuest), and 10 reg/BC sets (Oceanic). US Divers, SeaQuest, Tusa, and Oceanic gear for sale.

Taman Sari Bali Cottages Desa Pemuteran, Gerokgak, Singaraja 81155. ☎/Fax: (0362) 93264. Sales office: ☎/Fax: (0361) 286879. E-mail: tamanri@indosat.net.id Web: baliwww.com/tamansari Mgr: Gusti Agung Prana. The successor to the Pondok Sari (built by the same partners) with similar features. More upscale, but still very tasteful. 29 units, 8 w/fan, 21 w/AC. $35 w/fan, $50–$80 AC, $105–$140 suite.

Reef Seen Aquatics Dive Center (est. 1993, PADI).

Desa Pemuteran, Gerokgak, Singaraja 81155, Bali. ☎/Fax: (0362) 92339. E-mail: reef seen@denpasar.wasantara.net .id. Owner and contact: Chris Brown.

Chris Brown pioneered the Pemuteran sites, and his operation is close to the Pondok Sari and other resorts. He now specializes in horseback-riding retreats (perhaps even more so than diving), and has accumulated quite a stable of livestock. If your interests are both horses and diving, his is a perfect operation. Reef Seen clients get a discount at the nearby Taman Selwi.

Two dives $55–$70, depending on location.

Dive team Chris Brown (Aus.), PADI Instr. (1989), also speaks Indo.; Gede Kartika (Indo.), PADI DM (1995), also speaks Eng.; Putu Budiyasa (Indo.), PADI Rescue (1996), also speaks Eng.

Boats Wooden monohull w/glass panels in hull (for survey work), 8m, 25hp, cap. 8 divers. Radio, GPS available. Two traditional style wooden outriggers, modified for diving, 6.6m and 5.8m, 15hp, cap. 6 divers each.

Equipment Poseidon 7cfm compressor, 26 tanks, 10 sets reg/BC (ScubaPro/Seaquest) @ $20/day.

Taman Selwi Wahana Desa Pemuteran, Gerokgak, Singaraja 81155. ☎/Fax: (0362) 93449. E-mail: taslina@dps. mega.net.id Mgrs: Mrs. Ana Ganefiati, Mrs. Ediana Vourloumis. 11 bungalows with AC and hot water. $65, $40 for Reef Seen clients.

YOS Diving Centre and Marine Sports (est. 1989, ADS, CMAS, PADI, POSSI). At the Pondok Sari, Desa Pemuteran, Gerokgak, Singaraja. ☎(0362) 92337, Contact: Mr. Suryono. Main office: Jl Pratama 106X, Tanjung

Benoa, Nusa Dua. ☎(0361) 773774, 775440, 752005; Fax: (0361) 752985. E-mail: yosbali@indosat.net.id Owner: Yos W. K. Amerta.

This is a branch of the well-regarded Tanjung Benoa–based operator, associated with the Pondok Sari bungalows. See below under Tanjung Benoa for full details.

Two DIVES $40–$60, depending on location.

Pondok Sari Desa Pemuteran, Gerokgak, Singaraja. ☎/Fax: 92337. This is the original resort in the area. The bungalows are clean and comfortable, and the setting is very peaceful. The tasteful room furnishings and the open-air bathrooms with Japanese touches—smooth river pebbles, dripping bamboo—are very nice. Room rates are good for the quality. The restaurant offers decent western and Indonesian cuisine, plus cold beer. 20 units in 10 bungalows. $32S, $36D w/fan; $39S, $43D w/AC. Breakfast and tax included.

Other accommodations

Matahari Beach Resort Pemuteran, Singaraja. ☎92312, Fax: 92313. New, exclusive, 5-star resort. Built in Balinese style with German management, spacious bungalows, each with two rooms with marble terraces, living room, AC, and outdoor baths. Full facilities include tennis, watersports, mountain biking, and a dive center. 32 units. $160–$350.

BANYUWEDANG BAY (0362)

The first bay east of Teluk Terima is quiet, and lined with mangrove. It is just outside the park boundary. A hot spring here produces salty, sulfurous water that is thought to be healing. The only resort here is the new Mimpi Menjangan, part of a chain that in-

cludes resorts in Tulamben, Jimbaran, and soon the Gili Islands of Lombok.

Dive resort

Mimpi Resort and Dive Center Menjangan (est. 1999, PADI) Banyuwedang 81155, Buleleng. ☎(082) 8362729, Fax: (082) 8362728. E-mail: menjangan@mimpi.com Web: www.mimpi.com Owner: Wirya Santosa.

This was a brand new operation in 1999. The equipment is in good shape, and the staff is competent. They were in the process of hiring more guides when we visited. This operator is very close to two excellent sites just outside this bay, and significantly closer than the Pemuteran sites to Menjangan Island.

Two DIVES $65 Banyuwedang point; $75 Menjangan; $85 Pemuteran *takas*.

DIVE TEAM Sachiko Matsuda (Jap.), PAC, also Eng., in Bali since 1999; Putra Kumbara (Indo.), PAC, also Eng., in Bali since 1998.

COURSES PADI OW to DM BOATS *Mimpi I*, 200 hp, 20 divers; *Mimpi II*, two 40 hp, 5 divers.

Equipment Bauer Mariner compressor, 50 tanks, 18 sets reg/BC (Mares, ScubaPro, Tusa), camera. Masks, fins, snorkels, BCs (Mares) for sale.

Mimpi Resort Menjangan (est. 1999). Contacts as above. Sales and head office: Mimpi Resorts, Kawasan Bukit Permai Jimbaran, Denpasar 80361. ☎(0361) 701070, Fax: (0361) 701074. E-mail: sales@mimpi.com Web: www.mimpi.com Mgr.: Margit Arnold. This is a very upscale resort, tucked at the inside of Banyuwedang Bay. The restaurant, on the water, faces an artificial beach with its own coconut palms. The rooms are very luxurious, and if you can afford it, it is a real

treat after a day of diving to soak in your own private hot tub, fed by the salubrious water of a natural spring. 30 rms, 24 bungalows. $90–$375. Courtyard w/hot tub, $225.

GILIMANUK (0365)

This scruffy little port is not much of a tourist center, so if you come here do so to dive Gilimanuk bay only. One operator has set up a small resort on the bay. If you are serious about a long series of dives here, staying at this resort might be the best idea. If you would just like to try it out, you could also come on a day trip from one of the Pemuteran resorts or the Banyuwedang resort (which are much, much nicer places to stay), or even go yourself with a guide and some tanks, and negotiate with Pak Haji and his crew (as we did) to take you out on the bay.

Dive resort

Secret Bay Dive Center and Resort (est. 1999) Gilimanuk, Jembrana. ☎(0365) 61037, Fax: (0365) 61320. E-mail: divedive@indo.net.id Mgr: Takamasa Tonozuka.

The resort, set up by Dive and Dive's (see below under Sanur), is a refurbished *losmen* just in back of the ferry terminal. It is well designed for divers, particularly underwater photographers, with camera cleaning tables, wash basins, and charging facilities. It faces the quiet bay.

Diving runs $20 per shore dive, $25 per night dive, and another $5 per dive if you want a guide. The lodge is plain and the AC rooms in particular seem overpriced (although cost of diving is reasonable). 10 rms. 5 rms w/fan, $17S, $12 twin share; 5 rms w/AC $45 twin share. (Prices include local breakfast and dinner).

LOVINA (0362)

Lovina is the generic name for a cluster of villages spread along Bali's north coast. They are, from east to west: Tukad Munggah, Anturan, Kalibuk-buk (Lovina), and Temukus. The beach is shiny black sand and the surf is calm. If you want to dive at Menjangan and if you don't stay in Pe-muteran or Banyuwedang, then Lovina, about an hour's drive away, is the next closest place to stay. Operators here can arrange diving in both Lovina and Menjangan as well as local snorkeling, dolphin viewing, and fishing.

The reef off Lovina is a rea-sonably good spot for begin-ning divers, with shallow depths and sometimes excel-lent visibility. The reef has a good variety of corals and fish. We wouldn't make a special trip to dive here, but if you would like an easy warm-up dive before trying Menjangan, and you enjoy the atmosphere at the North Coast's only real tourist town (like Candidasa five years ago, or Kuta twenty years ago, as they say) you might want to stay here and try this site.

Dive operator

Spice Dive (est. 1989, PADI) On the south side of the main coastal road, Lovina Beach. P.O. Box 157, Singaraja, Bali. ☎(0362) 41305 and 41509, Fax: (0362) 41171. E-mail: spicedive@singaraja.wasan tara.net.id Web: www.damai. com/spicedive Owner: Imanuel Jarakanta.

A small, well-run operation that has been in business for a long time. The staff and guides are experienced and good humored, and a lot of fun to be around. A youthful place, appropriate to Lovina. Equipment in very good shape. Good sense of the en-vironment. Relationship with Celuk Agung Hotel (below).

Dive staff Imanuel Jarakanta (Indo.), PADI OWSI (1993), also Eng., in Bali since 1984; Max (Swiss), PADI OWSI, French and Eng., Ger., and Ital.; and nu-merous guides, all PADI DM: Ajir (1993), Mohammad (1993), Gundul (1994), Iwan (1994), Jojo (1996), and Tony (1996).

Boats The *Spice Dive* 12m, 315hp, GPS, sounder, SSB, cap. 8 divers; *Karisma* 7m outboard, 40hp.

Equipment Two Bauer compressors and air bank, 98 tanks, reg/BCs (US Divers/ SeaQuest). Mask, snorkel, fins, BCs, etc. for sale.

Hotel Celuk Agung Antu-ran–Lovina, Buleleng. P.O. Box 191, 81101. ☎(0362) 41039, Fax: (0362) 41379. E-mail: celukabc@singaraja. wasantara.net.id. Spice Dive has a relationship with this hotel. Comfortable place near the beach with a pool. Fair prices. $25–$65S, $30–$70D, tax and bkfst included. There are many other options for ac-commodation in Lovina.

Tulamben Area

Most divers travel to Tulam-ben on a package tour from Kuta, Sanur, Nusa Dua, or Candidasa, but independent-minded divers can make their way by rented car or, if not carrying gear, motorcycle. It's about 4 hrs from Kuta or Nusa Dua, 30 min. less from Sanur. The traffic through Candidasa will likely be heavy, but the last hour of the trip—from Candidasa onward—is very scenic. From Tulamben to Menjangan takes another 3 hrs.

Operators in Tulamben of-fer tanks, weights, and equip-ment rental, along with guides for independent divers who arrive on their own, and we highly recommend staying in Tulamben if you want to dive here or in Jemeluk.

By the way, when driving up from the South, you'd be crazy not to stop and have lunch at the Warung Tali-wang. This is a little roadside stall that pops up just as you climb a hill after passing Gi-anyar. (To be more precise, 8°32'20"S, 115°20'06"E.) We always call this place "Su-per Chicken" for reasons that are not important, except that it is certainly the best chicken on the island, if not the plan-et. (The style of cooking and sauce is from a village in Sum-bawa Besar.) The specialty is young chickens (pullets, where I come from) that are split and grilled over coconut charcoal, elegantly flattened by tucking in the wings. The livers and gizzards are made into satay, and the birds are served with vegetables, rice, limes, and a beautiful spicy sauce. With an iced lime juice, you cannot do better. Some-thing like Rp20,000 for two. Skip this at your peril.

TULAMBEN (0363)

This is the center of Bali's dive community, and you should head straight here if you have not been diving in Bali before. All but one of the operators are in a row, lining the cobbled beach of Tulam-ben Bay. The exception is a tiny resort past the hill behind the drop-off.

From the bayside resorts, diving the wreck, the shallow reef, the river, or the wall re-quires nothing more than walking down to the site (your gear will be brought by porters). If you want to dive Batu Kelebit, or the other sites around the point, you have to take one of the village *jukung*s, about Rp40,000 per trip. Your operator should take care of this for you.

Dive resorts

Dive Paradise Tulamben
(est. 1986, PADI, CMAS) Tulamben, Kubu, Karangasem. P.O. Box 111, Amlapura. Tel: (0363) 22913 and 41052, Fax: (0363) 41981. Owner: Dewa Nyoman Candra, Contact: Emiko Shibuya.

The Paradise, associated with the resort of the same name, is the orginal Tulamben operator, and still a good one. Emiko, who has been in Bali for 12 years, keeps her compressor, tanks and equipment in fine order, and you can usually get fresh Fuji Velvia at the counter (but don't expect it to be cheap). It may no longer be the only operation in town, but for many divers who have been coming over the years, the Paradise remains a sentimental favorite. The prices are also a bargain.

Two DIVES $50 wreck or drop-off ($30 single dive, $35 night dive); $55 Jemeluk; $60 Tanjung Sari; $65 Tepekong; $75 Menjangan (min. 4); $85 Nusa Penida (min. 4). Note: these prices include equipment. Deduct $10 if you have your own.

DIVE TEAM Emiko Shibuya (Jap.), CMAS OWSI (1996), also Eng. and Jap., in Bali since 1986; Wayan Sujana (Indo.), PADI DM (1996), also Eng.

COURSES PADI, CMAS (in Japanese)

EQUIPMENT Bauer Mariner compressors (2), 61 tanks, 20 sets reg/BC (10 US Diver, 10 Mares). Also rents flashlights, mask/fins.

Paradise Palm Beach Bungalows
(est. 1986). Same contact as above. Pleasant, thatched bungalows, each with two beds and attached toilet, with fans or AC. Simple accommodations, geared toward divers. Like the diving, a very good value. Beach restaurant, souvenir shop and dive center attached. Meals at the beachside restaurant are inexpensive, but dull. Management has recently made a grievous error by signing an exclusive contract with Carlsberg beer. Wait help are charming and good-humored. Reserve in high season. 29 units. $8 w/fan and cold water; $20 w/fan and hot water; $35 w/AC and hot water.

Ena Dive Center and Water Sports
(est. 1993, PADI) Runs the small Saya Resort. Main office: Jl Tirta Ening No. 1, Sanur, Denpasar. P.O. Box 3798 DPS. ☎ (0361) 288829 and 281751, Fax: (0361) 287945. E-mail: enadive@denpasar.wasantara. net.id Web: enadive.wasan tara.net.id *and* www.indo. com/diving/ena Owner: I Ketut Ena Partha.

One of Bali's pioneer operators, specializing in Japanese clients, and based in Sanur (see below). Runs the Saya Resort, located southeast of the drop-off. Not as convenient for the wreck, but good access to the sites past the wall. Operator maintains a compressor and four sets of diving equipment on site.

Saya Resort
(1993) Tulamben, Karangasem. Book through Ena main office above. Catering to Japanese travelers. Isolated and quiet. Four modest rooms with private balconies, AC, minibars, 24-hr room service, restaurant. $30S, $35D, $45T. Add $5 during high season for Japanese travelers, Dec. 20–Jan. 5.

Mimpi Resort and Dive Center Tulamben
(est. 1995, PADI) Desa Tulamben, Kubu, Karangasem. ☎ (0363) 21642, Fax: (0363) 21642. E-mail: tulamben@mimpi.com Web: www.mimpi.com Owner: Wirya Santosa.

This is a good outfit that has built a strong reputation for itself over the past few years. Quality equipment and staff. Well managed operation and facilities. Very comfortable accommodations.

Two DIVES $60 wreck or drop-off ($35 single dive); $75 Jemeluk; $85 Mimpang; $95 Selang, Tepekong; $100 Menjangan or Nusa Penida. Note: Includes equipment. Deduct $5 if you bring yours.

DIVE TEAM Sascha Dambach (Ger.), PADI Instr., also Eng. and Lithuanian, in Bali since 1998; Wakako Matsotuta (Jap.), NAUI Instr., also Eng., in Bali since 1999; Lisa Grosby (Can.), PADI DM, also Ital. and Indo., in Bali since 1999; Doris Hug (Swiss), PADI Instr., Eng. and Ger.

COURSES PADI OW to DM

EQUIPMENT Bauer Mariner compressor, 60 tanks, 12 sets reg/BC (ScubaPro/Mares). Also rents prescription masks, ScubaPro scooter, and Sea & Sea camera. Masks, fins, and snorkels (Mares) for sale.

Mimpi Resort Tulamben
(est. 1995). Contacts as above. Sales and head office: Mimpi Resorts, Kawasan Bukit Permai Jimbaran, Denpasar 80361. ☎ (0361) 701070, Fax: (0361) 701074. E-mail: sales@mimpi.com Web: www.mimpi.com Mgr.: Margit Arnold. This is definitely the high end of the Tulamben accommodations, and like the other Mimpi resorts, very tasteful and comfortable. Has a pool, though it is always freezing cold. The restaurant, on a deck facing the water, has the best food in the area, but this isn't saying much. Compared to the others, the Mimpi has a more refined, suit-and-tie feel. Stay here if you can afford it. 29 units. $75–$150.

Tauch Terminal Bali (est. 1995, PADI) Tulamben, Kubu 80235, Karangasem. Office: Jl Br Basangkasa 111, Kuta. ☎(0361) 730200, Fax: (0361) 730201. E-mail: tauchtermi@denpasar.wasan tara.net.id Web: www.dive bali.com, www.tauchbali.com Owner: Ms. I. Fityriati Contact: Axel Schwan.

A competent operator specializing in Austrian, Dutch, and German clients.

TWO DIVES $60–$95. Offers local diving, and diving from Kuta. Numerous packages combining different sites. Prices include equipment. $10 discount if you bring your own.

DIVE TEAM Axel Schwan (Ger.), PADI M.Instr. (1992), also Eng. and Indo., in Bali since 1995; P. Mosev (Austria), PADI OWSI (1997), also Eng. and Indo., in Bali since 1997; S. Moffat (U.K.), PADI OWSI (1997), also Ger., in Bali since 1999; Y. Godecke (Ger.), PADI OWSI (1996), also Eng., in Bali since 1999; Made Mertayasa (Indo.), PADI DM (1998), also Eng. and Jap.; Wayan Suada (Indo.), PADI DM (1997), also Eng. and Jap.; Made Rejataka (Indo.), PADI Resc. (1998), also Eng.; Nengah Geria (Indo.), PADI Resc. (1998), also Eng.; Ketut Suata (Indo.), PADI Resc. (1998), also Eng.

COURSES PADI OW to DM; IDC center in Dutch.

EQUIPMENT 2 Max Air compressors, 90 tanks, 40 sets reg/BC (Spiro/Dacor). Rents computers. SeaQuest BCs, Suunto comp. for sale.

Tauch Terminal hotel (est. 1995) See contacts above for booking. Decent, basic lodging. Has training pool, classroom. 21 rms. $20 w/fan, $40 w/AC.

Tulamben Dive Center P.O. Box 31, Amlapura 80811.

☎(0363) 22907/8. Next to the Paradise on the main road. Small, but well-run. Has a compressor, tanks and rental gear. Same low prices as the Paradise. This operator is associated with the *losmen* Tulamben Beach Pondok Wisata, better known as "Sunrise" for its beachside restaurant. Accommodations here are probably too modest for most divers, although if you are skint, this is the place to be (Wally and I have stayed here many a time). About $5/night, no amenities at all. The restaurant is lively, and their fresh chicken soup is the best post-dive restorative in town. Great staff, and there is always cold Bintang.

JEMELUK (0363)

There are a few small *losmen* near Jemeluk Bay and further south along the coastal road. Some of these offer snorkeling, and have offered diving, but we cannot recommend any of them at this time. To dive Jemeluk or Lipah, you are still best off coming in with your operator by car with tanks and equipment from Tulamben, and hiring a *jukung* from Jemeluk Bay to take you out. If you make this trip, note the open pavilion where the road hits the coast and turns (still Amed). There is an old man here who brews some very fine *tuak*. If you think this mildly intoxicating beverage is bad for you, just take a look at his face—he is a very accomplished drinkard (in Amos Tutuolo's sense), and he has the skin of a baby. Often a woman sells satay *banteng*, a perfect accompaniment to the *tuak lontar*.

East Coast

It is not too inconvenient to dive the East Coast sites from

the South, nor in fact is it difficult to dive them from Tulamben (and the drive is more pleasant). But if you are serious about this area, it is best to stay here. These sites are very dependent on conditions, and it's nice to be able to look out at the actual water you are going to be diving in the mornings and evenings, to get a feel for what you are up against.

The places to stay are either Candidasa or Padangbai. Candidasa has by far the bigger range of accommodation, but Padangbai is the better port for working this area.

CANDIDASA (0363)

This town is quiet and relatively uncrowded compared to Kuta and Sanur to the south, but a veritable New York City compared to Tulamben. There are at least 50 hotels, *losmen,* and homestays, and plenty of restaurants. Because the fringing reef here was "mined" for construction material, Candidasa's beautiful beach is now a piece of history. Ugly groins have been built in an attempt to stop the erosion, but it seems unclear if they are helping. There are at least three dive operators in the Candidasa area, and the Padangbai operator will pick up clients in Candidasa.

Dive operator

Spice Dive (est. 1996, PADI, CMAS), Balina Beach, Buitan, Manggis, Karangasem. P.O. Box 157, Singaraja, Bali. ☎(0363) 41725, Fax: (0363) 41171. E-mail: spicedive@ singaraja.wasantara.net.id Web: www. damai. com/ spicedive/ Owner: Imanuel Jarakanta. Contact: Andi or Michelle.

A newer offshoot of the respected Lovina operator. A good, reliable operation, with personable staff and well-kept tanks and equipment. Relationship with the Balina Beach Resort (below).

"Balina Beach" is the name given to Buitan, south of Candidasa (toward Padangbai). It is a quiet and attractive little strip, with a handful of places to stay and a few small restaurants. The beach is rocky black sand.

DIVE TEAM Wayan Ratih (Indo.), PADI DM, also Eng.; Gobang (Indo.), PADI DM, also Eng.;Gembel (Indo.), PADI DM, also Eng.

BOATS Wood outrigger, 11m, 25hp (2); aluminum monohull, 5m, 25hp.

EQUIPMENT Bauer compressor, 30 tanks, reg/BCs (US Divers/ Cressi-Sub).

Balina Beach Resort (est. 1985). Balina Beach, Buitan, Manggis, Karangasem. ☎(0363) 41002, Fax: (0363) 41001. E-mail: balina@denpasar.wasantara.net.id

One of the more upmarket hotels along this strip, with nice cottages, gardens, and a pool. Faces the beach. A bit overpriced at $70–$90D, but nice if you can afford it, and a package will bring the price down. There are cheaper places along this strip as well.

This is a quiet, and somewhat odd little town. The local Balinese community seems very tight, and still curious about the ways of foreigners, as if this isn't a tourist town at all. Yet this is the terminus of the Bali–Lombok ferry, and a constant stream of backpacking tourists passes through here (most of them are on their way to Lombok's Gili Islands to eat mushrooms and look for romance).

The beach is quiet and relaxing, and the little beachfront restaurants are a great place to sit of an afternoon and watch the fishermen pull

in their *jukung*s and the kids fly their kites. On the other hand, the cheaper *losmen* are full of bedbugs, and the village policeman has a rather harrassed look about him. Personally, we kind of like the chemistry overall.

Dive operator

Geko Dive (P.T. Baliniki Geko) est. 1997, PADI. Jl Silayukti, Padangbai, Manggis, Karangasem. ☎(0363) 41516, Fax: (0363) 41790. E-mail: gekodive@indosat.net.id Web: www.gekodive.com. Owners: Robert Jarvis and David Ruland.

We'd be tempted to say that this outfit knows more about the East Coast and Nusa Penida sites than any other operator on the island, and they are constantly exploring. Nobody in this operation has lost their wonder for the underwater world, or for Bali. They have started a plastics program to help clean up the area, and when the rupiah crashed, established a medical fund to cover health care costs for the Padangbai community. Their boats are fast and slick, their captain is skilled, and even their prices are good.

Their operation is right across the street from the DEPOT DHARMA, the first of the little restaurants along the Padangbai beach (and the original one).

TWO DIVES $35 Tanjung Sari; $45 Mimpang, Tepekong; $50 Biaha; $60 Nusa Penida; $65 Selang. Also: $45 Tulamben, $45 Jemeluk, $175 Menjangan (2 days, hotel incl.). Add $10 if you need equipment. Several packages available, mixing East Coast, Nusa Penida, and Tulamben. $130 3 days; $250 6 days. Prices include pickup in the Candidasa or Padangbai area. (Candidasa is about 20 min from Padangbai).

DIVE TEAM Sue Jarvis (U.K.), PADI MSDT, also Indo., in Bali since 1993; Robert Jarvis (U.K.), PADI DM, in Bali since 1993; David Ruland (Ger.), PADI OWSI, also Eng. and Indo., in Bali since 1995; Coral Karang (Indo.), PADI DM, also Eng., in Bali since 1989.

BOATS *S. Metta Paramitha I*, fiberglass speedboat, 85hp (2), 20knots, depth finder, VHF radio, mobile phone, cap 10 divers; *S. Metta Paramitha II,* fiberglass speedboat, 115hp (2), 20+ knots, depth finder, VHF radio, mobile phone, cap. 8 divers.

EQUIPMENT Bauer compressor, 50 tanks, 20 reg/BCs (Sherwood, Spiro, SeaQuest), 40 3mm wet suits, masks (including w/corrected lenses).

Geko has contract room rates at two hotels and a *losmen* in the area, and they pass the savings on directly to their clients (requires a three-day stay). The KEMBAR INN *losmen,* simple and inexpensive, is 100m from the operator in Padangbai. NIRWANA COTTAGES (☎41136, Fax: 41543), about 1km on the Padangbai side of Candidasa, has 12 very nice cottages on the beachfront, a swimming pool, and a good restaurant (list price $45–$60, check w/Geko for contract rate). The DASA WANA (☎41444, Fax: 242993), in Candidasa, has six new AC bungalows, a pool, and a restaurant. Between these three, there should be something to suit your tastes and budget.

Nusa Penida

There are no operators on Nusa Penida itself, and the best way to dive it is from Padangbai or the South: Sanur or Tanjung Benoa. The time across the Badung Strait depends on the boat and the location, but can be as short as 35 min with a strong vessel (e.g twin 85 hp outboards or better). There is one operator, specializing in diving Ental Point off Lembongan, that offers a diving package where clients stay on Nusa Lembongan, but otherwise, staying on this island, which has no telephones, is for surfers only.

The South

Most of Bali's tourist services, and dive operators are no exception, are clustered in the South, in Kuta, Sanur, and Tanjung Benoa/Nusa Dua. Again, we would use a South-based operator only for diving the South or Nusa Penida, or perhaps for a single day on the East Coast. Because of travel time, for diving the Northwest, or for serious diving in Tulamben or the East Coast, it is better to stay in those areas.

KUTA (0361)

A town has grown up around the beach here that has become the tourist center of Bali. Robert and Louise Koke, surfers from southern California, first built their Kuta Beach Hotel here in 1936. It wasn't until the late '60s and early '70s, when a generation of hippies and other western drop-outs "discovered" Bali, that Kuta exploded.

Today, the town, which now extends north up to Legian, bustles with activity, its streets and tiny gangs (alleyways) lined with shops, restaurants, discos, and *losmen*. It is even an international fashion center with a distinct, colorful style falling somewhere between neon sporting wear and a Grateful Dead T-shirt. Although it has long been fashionable to ma-

lign Kuta, the place has an irrepressible, youthful charm.

Dive operators

Archipelago Diving (P.T. Arkipelago Selam) est. 1997, PADI. At the Sol Elite Paradiso Hotel, Jl. Kartika Plaza, Kuta 80361 Bali. ☎(0361) 761414 ext. 7153, Fax: (0361) 756944. E-mail: tamanri@indosat.net.id Web: baliwww.com/arkipelago Owner: Peter Ross.

This outfit, which maintains a branch in Pemuteran (see above) also offers a Bali-wide program. Their staff is friendly and competent, and their gear is new. Associated with two hotels, the Kuta Paradiso ($140–$950) in Kuta, and the Raddin Hotel ($140–$650) in Sanur.

Two DIVES $60 Tanjung Benoa or Sanur; $65 Tanjung Sari; $75 Tepekong or Mimpang; $70 Jemeluk; $70 Tulamben; $75 Lovina; $100 Pemuteran; $90 Menjangan.

Pro Dive Bali (est. 1994, PADI). Kuta Center Shop 14–15, Jl Kartika Plaza, Kuta. ☎(0361) 753951, Fax: (0361) 753952. E-mail: prodivebali@ bali-paradise.com Web: www. bali-paradise.com/prodivebali Owners: Putu Arnama, Richard Johnstone, Troy Lowrie. Contact: Troy Lowrie.

This is the Bali franchise of Pro Dive, the world's largest dive operation. Well run, with an experienced team. They offer diving at all of the basic sites. Departures are regularly scheduled. More than half of their clients are Australian.

Two DIVES $60 Tanjung Benoa or Sanur (1 dive, unscheduled); $105 Nusa Penida or Lembongan (M,W); $80 Tepekong (unscheduled); $80 Jemeluk (unscheduled); $80 Tulamben (Tu,Th, Sat); $115 Menjangan (Tu, Th, Sat).

DIVE TEAM Troy Lowrie (Aus.), PADI MSDT (1990), also Indo., in Bali since 1994; Richard Johnstone (Aus.), PADI IDC staff (1994), also Indo., in Bali since 1994; Putu Arnama (Indo.), PADI MSDT (1996), also Eng., Jap., working since 1990; Komang Mertana (Indo.), PADI OWSI (1998), also Eng., working since 1994; Asril Duvardi (Indo.), PADI DM (1998), also Eng., Dutch, working since 1994; Ketut Suarta (Indo.), PADI As.Instr. (1996), also Eng., Jap., working since 1994; Ketut Merta (Indo.), PADI As. Instr. (1996), also Eng., Jap., working since 1994.

COURSES PADI OW to DM
BOATS *Pro Diver,* Aus.-built aluminum, 10 m, 115 hp (2), GPS, depth finder, cap. 12 divers.

EQUIPMENT Bauer K-14 and Capitano compressors, 100 tanks, 40 sets reg/BC (Sherwood). Sherwood, Tusa, Pro Dive, US Divers, SeaQuest gear for sale.

SANUR (0361)

Sanur was Bali's first resort town and is, in a sense, the gray eminence of the tourist triangle. Compared to Kuta, it is quiet and dignified (or just dull, depending on your point of view and, inescapably, your age) and compares to Nusa Dua as old wealth does to new. The town is very quiet at night and the beach here, protected by the reef flat, is very calm. People who intend to spend a long time on Bali often stay in Sanur.

Dive Operators

Dive & Dive's (P.T. Mahkota Baliwisata Bahari) est. 1993, PADI. Jl. Bypass Ngurah Rai 27, Sanur, Denpasar. ☎(0361) 288652, Fax: (0361) 288892. E-mail: divedive@indo.net.id Owner: Takamasa Tonozuka

Contact: Mr. Gusti, Mr. Tri

This well regarded outfit specializes in photographers and Japanese clients. Dive shop with gear for sale and rent, small cafe, nice diver ambiance. They can arrange multi-day dive tour packages and trips around Bali, and have set up a center at Gilimanuk for macrophotography specialists (see above). They offer one of the fullest ranges of sites.

Two DIVES $55 Tanjung Benoa or Sanur; $95–$110 Nusa Penida near side or Lembongan; $100–$120 Nusa Penida far side; $60–$75 Tanjung Sari; $75–$80 Tepekong or Mimpang; $100 Selang; $65 Lipah; $70 Jemeluk; $65 Tulamben; $75 Lovina; $95 Menjangan.

DIVE TEAM Takamasa Tonozuka (Jap.), PADI M.Instr., also Eng., Indo.; Akira Ogawa (Jap.), PADI Instr. (1993), also Eng.; Kazuko Ishibashi (Jap.), PADI Instr. (1993), also Eng.; Eva Dahlquist (Swed.), PADI Instr. (1998), also Eng., Fr.; I Wayan Sujana (Indo.), PADI DM (1993), also Eng., Jap.; I Ketut Suradnya (Indo.), PADI DM (1993), also Eng., Jap.; I Ketut Wiryana (Indo.), PADI DM (1993), also Eng., Jap.; I Wayan Parsa (Indo.), PADI DM (1993), also Eng., Jap.; I Made Sukiasa (Indo.), PADI DM (1993), also Eng., Jap.

COURSES PADI OW to DM, Eng. and Jap.

EQUIPMENT Bauer Mariner, Bauer Capitano, Coltri Sub MCH 13/ET Compact compressors, 108 tanks, 20 sets reg/BC (US Divers/SeaQuest). Regs, suits, BCs, computers, masks, etc. by SeaQuest, US Divers, Technisub, Wenoka, and Suunto for sale.

Ena Dive Center and Water Sports (est. 1993, PADI) Jl Tirta Ening No. 1, Sanur, Denpasar. P.O. Box 3798 DPS. ☎(0361) 288829 and 281751, Fax: (0361) 287945. E-mail: enadive@denpasar. wasantara.net.id Web: enadive. wasantara.net.id *and* www. indo.com/diving/ena Owner: I Ketut Ena Partha.

One of Bali's pioneer operators, specializing in Japanese, European, and Southeast Asian clients. Also offers Jet-ski, parasailing and other water sports. Runs the small Saya Resort, located southeast of the drop-off at Tulamben (see above).

Two DIVES $40 Tanjung Benoa or Sanur (1 dive); $80–$95 Nusa Penida; $60 Tanjung Sari; $65 Tepekong; $60 Jemeluk; $60 Tulamben; $60 Lovina; $80 Menjangan.

DIVE TEAM Koji Yamagatha (Jap.), PADI MSDT, also Eng., in Bali since 1998; Ryan Dowling (U.K.), PADI M Instr., in Bali since 1996; I Ketut Sudirtha (Indo.), PADI Instr., also Eng., Jap., working since 1993; I Ketut Ena Partha (Indo.), PADI DM, also Eng., working since 1983; I Ketut Sadia (Indo.), PADI DM, also Eng., working since 1993; I Ketut Somadhyana (Indo.), PADI DM, also Eng., Jap., working since 1993; Gusti MD Subawa (Indo.), PADI DM, also Eng., Jap., working since 1997; Nyoman Suteja (Indo.), PADI DM, also Eng., Jap., working since 1998; Nyoman Sutikta (Indo.), PADI DM, also Eng., working since 1999.

COURSES PADI OW to DM, Eng. and Jap.

BOATS *Ena I* trad. wood, 25hp, 5 divers; *Ena II* and *Ena II,* trad. wood, 85hp (2), 20 divers; *Ena IV,* speedboat, 85hp (2), 20 divers.

EQUIPMENT Bauer Capitano, Mariner, and Poseidon compressors, 28 regs (US Divers, Sherwood), 34 BCs (US Divers, Technisub, SeaQuest), small range of gear for sale.

TANJUNG BENOA (0361)

Tanjung Benoa is a recently established resort just north of Nusa Dua. The beach hotels here are small and cozy, although there are some newly opened larger hotels. The nice, white-sand beach here is popular for water sports: parasailing, windsurfing, waterskiing and, of course, snorkeling and diving. All the accommodations are intermediate or budget.

Nusa Dua offers luxury, and isolation from touts, peddlers, stray dogs, cold-water showers and other indignities. It's also quite antiseptic. Preferred by the international jet set. There are no cheap lodgings here. Dive operators keep desks at most big hotels here.

Dive operators

Bali Hai Diving Adventures ☎(0361) 724062, and Fax: (0361) 720334. After hours, (081) 2380-2036 or (0361) 286544. E-mail: diverse@ indosat.net.id. Contact: Michael Cortenbach.

This outfit is a specialist for Lembongan Island, especially Tanjung Ent21 ("Blue Corner"). They offer several packages, which include staying on the island itself, at the Waka Nusa (about $150 a night) or the Mushroom Beach Bungalows ($10–$15). The operator claims the site always has molas around the time of the autumn equinox.

Wally Siagian Puri Kampial, Blok A-15, Kampial, Nusa Dua. ☎(0361) 775998. E-mail: walldive@denpasar. wasantara.net.id

My co-author is an independent dive guide on Bali, earning a modest living by crafting custom tours for individuals or small groups, particularly photographers, scientists, or other divers with a special interest in marine life. He is certainly the most knowledgeable diver on the island, and working with him would be a good choice if you are looking for some special animals or want to dive an unusual location. He has his own compressor and gear, and can get vehicles and boats as needed. His rates are reasonable. Contact him through E-mail.

YOS Diving Centre and Marine Sports (est. 1989, ADS, CMAS, PADI, POSSI). Jl Pratama 106X, Tanjung Benoa, Nusa Dua. ☎(0361) 773774, 775440, 752005; Fax: (0361) 752985. E-mail: yosbali@indosat.net.id Owner: Yos W. K. Amerta, Contact: Frans W. K. Amerta.

This professional, family-run business has established a good reputation for itself. The owner, who worked as an architect in Berlin for 14 years, is currently chair of The Indonesian Marine Tourism Association. English-, German-, Indonesian-, and Japanese-speaking staff. YOS diving runs fast boats from the main Tanjung Benoa center to Nusa Penida, and takes divers by land to any of the other sites. The outfit maintains counters at the Nusa Dua hotels, and a full dive center at the Pondok Sari in Pemuteran (see above). Also offers fishing, parasailing, Jet skis, and other marine sports (contact for fishing and marine sports: Adhek Amerta).

Two DIVES $40–$90, depending on location.

DIVE TEAM Adiputera (Indo.), PADI OWSI (1998), also Eng., Jap., working in Bali since 1989; Sidartha (Indo.), PADI OWSI (1998), also Eng., Jap., working in

Bali since 1989; Frans Amerta (Indo.), CMAS Instr. (1987), also Eng., Ger., working in Bali since 1988; Yos Amerta (Indo.), CMAS Instr. (1987), also Eng., Ger., working in Bali since 1988; Gede Cahyanta (Indo.), PADI DM (1999), also Eng., Jap., working since 1992; Mustarif (Indo.), CMAS Divecon (1980), also Ger. and Jap., working in Bali since 1988; Wayan Sukadana (Indo.), CMAS Divecon (1980), also Eng., Jap., working in Bali since 1988; Martinus (Indo.), PADI DM (1999), also Eng. and Jap., working since 1989.

COURSES ADS, CMAS, PADI, and POSSI certification in Eng., Ger., Jap.

BOATS Longboat, 7.5m, 40hp (2), cap. 4–6; *Mahimahi*, *Lumba-lumba*, and *Wahoo*, all 9m fiberglass powerboats, 115hp (2), radio, cell phone, head, cap. 6–8; *Mola mola*, 11m, 115hp (2), radio, cell phone, head, 12.

EQUIPMENT Bauer Mariner and Capitano compressors, 100 tanks, 50 regs (US Divers, Scubapro, Sherwood), 50 BCs (SeaQuest, Scubapro, Mares), 15 computers. No sales.

Live-aboards

A new live-aboard boat was experimenting with a Bali program at the time we were completing our research.
Sea Contacts Dive Voyages (est. 1999) Jl. Mertasari no. 64A, Sidakarya Batan Kendal, Suwung, Denpasar, Bali. ☎(0361) 725430, Fax: (0361) 725431. E-mail:smithdiv@ dps.mega.net.id Contact: Larry Smith.

The runs are in the *Sea Contacts 1*, a well-equipped 35-meter ship with capacity for 12 divers. This 360 hp vessel has Bauer K-14 and

Mariner compressors onboard, individual AC in each of six cabins (w/attached bathrooms), full GPS and other instrumentation, and two American divemasters.

Equipment sales

Although a number of operators offer equipment for sale, their selection is limited and prices usually expensive. There are now two retail dive equipment outlets.

Divemasters Bali (est. 1999) Jl Bypass Ngurah Rai No. 61X, Sanur, Denpasar 80228. Tel: (0361) 289028. Main office: Aquasport, Jl. Bangka Raya 39A, Pela, Jakarta 12720. Tel: (021) 719-9045, Fax: (021) 719-8974. E-mail: divers@aquasport.com.id Owner: Vimal Lekhraj. Contact: Sri.

A brand new operation at the time we went to press, although the parent organization, in Jakarta, is well known as the best retailer in Indonesia. This is a very welcome development for the Bali dive community. The Aquasport store in Jakarta is well laid out, and has prices and selection that are in line with a good U.S. retailer.

For sale at the Bali store: US Divers, SeaQuest, Technisub, Deepsea, Wenoka, Suunto, Sea & Sea, Underwater Kinetics, Ikelite, and Trident. Bauer and Coltri Sub compressors. PADI diver education materials. Also will be a PADI IDC center.

P.T. Jayausaha Binabersama Pertokoan Citra Bali, Jl Bypass Ngurah Rai, Jimbaran. ☎Fax: (0361) 702688. This exclusive Mares dealer has been around for a couple years. Good equipment, but breathtakingly expensive.

Further Reading

A short bibliography of generally available resources for field identification of animals and reef ecology.

Abbott, R. Tucker and S. Peter Dance, 1991. *Compendium of Seashells*. London: Charles Letts and Co. Hardbound, 416 pages. Covers 4,200 species of shells, worldwide. Cleaned specimens are illustrated, limiting its usefulness for divers.

Allen, Gerald R., and Roger Steene, 1994. *Indo-Pacific Coral Reef Field Guide*. Singapore: Tropical Reef Research. Sofcover, 384 pages. This book, by an expert scientist and photographer team, is a very handy resource covering the basic algae, plants, invertebrates, and fishes that you will see on an Indo-Pacific reef. Now widely distributed. Get this one if you don't already have it.

Debelius, Helmut and Rudie Kuiter, 1994. *Southeast Asia Tropical Fish Guide*. Frankfurt: IKAN-Unterwasserarchiv. Hardbound, 320 pages. A useful field guide, with good photographs and brief text entries, in the successful IKAN series. Kuiter's participation has greatly benefited this volume.

Lieske, Ewald and Robert F. Myers, 1994. *Reef Fishes of the World*. Hong Kong: Periplus Editions. Also distributed in the U.K. and United States by Collins. Paper, 400 pages. This is a very nice, compact paperback with watercolor drawings and short descriptions of some 2,000 species, in both the Indo-Pacific and the Caribbean. It is inexpensive and widely available. The drawings are decent, if a bit small, but then modest size is the charm of this book. Every diver should own a copy.

Gosliner, Terrence M., David W. Behrens, and Gary C. Williams, 1996. *Coral Reef Animals of the Indo-Pacific*. Monterey, CA: Sea Challengers. Softcover, 315 pages. A useful field guide to the invertebrates of Indo-Pacific reefs. Moderately extensive, not too many errors. Proabably the best resource available in a weak field.

Last, P.R. and J.D. Stevens, 1994. *Sharks and Rays of Australia*. CSIRO, Australia. Color illustrations by Roger Swainston, line illustrations by G. Davis. Hardbound, 624 pages. A beautiful, thorough, and unfortunately, massive tome. A bit hard to find and expensive, but worth every penny. The very best book on this group of fishes, with Illustrations by the finest artist in the field.

Myers, Robert F., 1991. *Micronesian Reef Fishes. A Practical Guide to the Identification of the Coral Reef Fishes of the Tropical Central and Western Pacific*. Second edition. Guam: Coral Graphics. Hardbound, 304 pages. This book is my fish identification reference of choice. Myers includes line drawings, full meristics, and excellent and detailed field notes for every species. The only drawback of this book for use in Indonesia is its limited coverage (not Myers's fault, it is a Micronesian reference). A new edition is now available, in two versions: an abridged, limp-bound volume, and an unabridged, hardbound volume. Get the full-length version. This is the standard by which all other fish identification books should be judged.

Tomascik et al, eds. 1997. *The Ecology of the Indonesian Seas, Part I and Part II*. Edited by Tomas Tomascik, Anmarie Janice Mah, Anugerah Nontji, and Mohammad Kasim Moosa. Volumes VII and VIII of the Ecology of Indonesia series. Hong Kong: Periplus Editions. Hardcover, 1,392 pages. These excellent volumes cover a wide range of topics concerning Indonesia's reefs, and are probably the most up-to-date compilation of Indo-Pacific reef research available. Available from the same publisher as this guide.

Veron, J.E.N., 1986. *Corals of Australia and the Indo-Pacific*. Honolulu: University of Hawai'i Press. Hardbound, 640 pages. A big, beautiful book, and the best of its kind.

Lourie, Sara A., Amanda C.J. Vincent, and Heather J. Hall, 1999. *Seahorses. An Identification Guide to the World's Species and their Conservation*. London: Project Seahorse. Spiral bound, 320 pages. A thorough, smart, and very pretty little book (too pretty, in fact, the textured stock is a mistake) that has been long-awaited by seahorse fans (like us). Get a copy, now.

Index

Page numbers in boldface indicate the main section on that topic; page numbers in italic indicate photographs

Map index